John Croumbie Brown

Schools of forestry in Germany,

With addenda relative to a desiderated British national school of forestry

John Croumbie Brown

Schools of forestry in Germany,
With addenda relative to a desiderated British national school of forestry

ISBN/EAN: 9783337724306

Printed in Europe, USA, Canada, Australia, Japan

Cover: Foto ©ninafisch / pixelio.de

More available books at **www.hansebooks.com**

INTERNATIONAL FORESTRY EXHIBITION.

WORKS ON FOREST SCIENCE.

By the REV. J. C. BROWN, LL.D.

Edinburgh: OLIVER & BOYD.
London: SIMPKIN, MARSHALL, & CO., and W. RIDER & SON.
Montreal: DAWSON, BROTHERS.

I.—Introduction to the Study of Modern Forest Economy. Price 5s.

In this there are brought under consideration the extensive destruction of forests which has taken place in Europe and elsewhere, with notices of disastrous consequences which have followed—diminished supply of timber and firewood, droughts, floods, landslips, and sand-drifts—and notices of the appliances of Modern Forest Science successfully to counteract these evils by conservation, planting, and improved exploitation, under scientific administration and management.

Extract from Preface.—'At a meeting held on the 28th of March last year (1883), presided over by the Marquis of Lothian, while the assemblage was representative of all interests—scientific, practical, and professional—it was resolved:—"That it is expedient in the interests of forestry, and to promote a movement for the establishment of a National School of Forestry in Scotland, as well as with a view of furthering and stimulating a greater improvement in the scientific management of woods in Scotland and the sister countries which has manifested itself during recent years, that there should be held in Edinburgh, during 1884, and at such season of the year as may be arranged, an International Exhibition of forest products and other objects of interest connected with forestry." It was then moved, seconded, and agreed:—"That this meeting pledges itself to give its hearty co-operation and patronage to the promotion of an International Forestry Exhibition in Edinburgh in 1884; and those present resolve to give their best efforts and endeavours to render the Exhibition a success, and of such importance and general interest as to make it worthy of the name of International."

'It is in accordance with this resolution, and in discharge of obligations which it imposed, that this volume has been prepared.'

II.—The Forests of England; and the Management of them in Bye-gone Times. Price 6s.

Ancient forests, chases, parks, warrens, and woods, are described; details are given of destructive treatment to which they have been subjected, and of legislation and literature relating to them previous to the present century.

EXTRACT FROM PREFACE.—' Contrast with this [the paucity of works in English on Forest Science], the richness of Continental languages in literature on such subjects. I have had sent to me lately *Ofversight of Svenska Skogsliteraturen, Bibliografiska Studieren of Axel Cnattingius,* a list of many books and papers on Forest Science published in Sweden; I have also had sent to me a work by Don José Jordana y Morera, Ingenero de Montes, under the title of *Apuntes Bibliographico Forestale,* a *catalogue raisonné* of 1126 printed books, MSS., &c., in Spanish, on subjects connected with Forest Science.

' I am at present preparing for the press a report on measures adopted in France, Germany, Hungary, and elsewhere, to arrest and utilise driftsand by planting them with grasses and trees; and in *Der Europaeische Flug-sand und Seine Cultur, von Josef Wessely General Domaenen-Inspecktor, und Forst-Academie-Direktor,* published in Vienna in 1873, I find a list of upwards of 100 books and papers on that one department of the subject, of which 30, in Hungarian, Latin, and German, were published in Hungary alone.

' According to the statement of one gentleman, to whom application was made by a representative of the Government at the Cape, for information in regard to what suitable works on Forest Economy could be procured from Germany, the works on *Forst-Wissenchaft,* Forest Science, and *Forst-Wirthchaft,* Forest Economy, in the German language may be reckoned by cartloads. From what I know of the abundance of works in German, on subjects connected with Forestry, I am not surprised that such a report should have been given. And with the works in German may be reckoned the works in French.

' In Hermann Schmidt's *Fach Katalogue,* published in Prague last year (1876), there were given the titles, &c., of German works in *Forst und Jagd-Literatur,* published from 1870 to 1875 inclusive, to the 31st of October of the latter year, amounting in all to 630, exclusive of others given in an appendix, containing a selection of the works published prior to 1870. They are classified thus:—General Forest Economy, 93; Forest Botany, 60; Forest History and Statistics, 50; Forest Legislation and Game Laws, 56; Forest Mathematics, 25; Forest Tables and Measurements, &c., 148; Forest Technology, 6; Forest Zoology, 19; Peat and Bog Treatment, 14; Forest Calendars, 6; Forest and Game Periodicals, 27; Forest Union and Year Books, 13; Game, 91; Forest and Game in Bohemian, 44. In all, 652. Upwards of a hundred new works had been published annually. Amongst the works mentioned is a volume entitled *Die Literatur der letzten sieben Jahre* (1862-1872) *aus dem Gesammtgebiete der Land-und Forst-wirthschaft mit Einschluss der landw. Geweber u. der Jagd, in deutscher, französischer u englisher* Sprache *Herausg. v. d. Buchandl, v.* Gerold and Co., *in Wein,* 1873, a valuable catalogue filling 278 pages in large octavo.

'This volume is published as a small contribution to the literature of Britain, on subjects pertaining to Forest Science.

'It is after due consideration that the form given to the work—that of a compilation of what has been stated in works previously published —has been adopted.

III.—Forestry of Norway. Price 5s.

There are described in successive chapters the general features of the country. Details are given of the geographical distribution of forest trees, followed by discussions of conditions by which this has been determined—heat, moisture, soil, and exposure. The effects of glacial action on the contour of the country are noticed, with accounts of existing glaciers and snow-fields. And information is supplied in regard to forest exploitation and the transport of timber, in regard to the export timber trade, to public instruction in sylviculture, and to forest administration, and to ship-building and shipping.

EXTRACT FROM PREFACE.—'In the spring of 1877, while measures were being taken for the formation of an Arboretum in Edinburgh, I issued a pamplet entitled *The Schools of Forestry in Europe: a Plea for the Creation of a School of Forestry in connection with the Arboretum in Edinburgh.* After it was made known that arrangements were being carried out for the formation of an International Exhibition of forest products, and other objects of interest connected with forestry, in Edinburgh with a view to promoting the movement for the establishment of a National School of Forestry in Scotland, and with a view of furthering and stimulating a greater improvement in the scientific management of woods in Scotland, and the sister countries, which has manifested itself during recent years, the council of the East Lothian Naturalists' Club resolved on having a course of lectures or popular readings on some subject connected with forestry, which might enable the members and others better to profit by visits to the projected Exhibition, and which should be open to the public at a moderate charge. The conducting of these was devolved upon me, who happened to be vice-president of the club. The following treatise was compiled from information then in my possession, or within my reach, and it constituted the basis of these lectures.'

IV.—Finland: its Forests and Forest Management.
Price 6s 6d.

In this volume is supplied information in regard to the lakes and rivers of Finland, known as *The Land of a Thousand Lakes*, and as *The Last-born Daughter of the Sea*; in regard to its physical geography, including notices of the contour of the country, its geological formations and indications of glacial action, its flora, fauna, and climate; and in regard to its forest economy, embracing a discussion of the advantages and disadvantages of *Svedjande*, the *Sartage* of France, and the *Koomaree* of India; and details of the development of Modern Forest Economy in Finland, with notices of its School of Forestry, of its forests and forest trees, of the disposal of its forest products, and of its legislation and literature in forestry are given.

EXTRACT FROM PREFACE.—' I happened to spend the summer of 1879 in St. Petersburg, ministering in the British and American Chapel in that city, while the pastor sought relaxation for a few months at home. I was for years the minister of the congregation worshipping there, and I had subsequently repeatedly spent the summer among them in similar circumstances. I was at the time studying the Forestry of Europe; and I availed myself of opportunities afforded by my journey thither through Norway, Sweden, and Finland, by my stay in Russia, and by my return through Germany and France, to collect information bearing upon the enquiries in which I was engaged. On my return to Scotland I contributed to the *Journal of Forestry* a series of papers which were afterwards reprinted under the title *Glances at the Forests of Northern Europe*. In the preface to this pamphlet I stated that in Denmark may be studied the remains of forests in pre-historic times; in Norway, luxuriant forests managed by each proprietor as seemeth good in his own eyes; in Sweden, sustained systematic endeavours to regulate the management of forests in accordance with the latest deliverances of modern science; in Finland, *Sartage* disappearing before the most advanced forest economy of the day; and in Russia, *Jardinage* in the north, merging into more scientific management in Central Russia, and *Reboisement* in the south. This volume is a study of information which I then collected, together with information which I previously possessed, or have subsequently obtained, in regard to the Forests and Forestry of Finland.'

Translation of Extracts from Letters from DR A. BLOMQVIST, Director of the Finnish National School of Forestry at Evois :—' On my return from Salmos three weeks ago I had the great pleasure to receive your volume on the Forests and Forest Management in Finland. I return you grateful thanks for the gift, and no less for publishing a description of the forestal condition of our country. It is with sentiments of true gratitude I learn that you had previously taken part in a work so important to our country as the preparation of a new edition of the New Testament in Finnish. Your descriptions of our natural scenery are most excellent and interesting. Personally I feel most interest in your accounts of *Koomaree*. I value it much. and not less so your concurrent final conclusion in regard to the effects of the exercise of it in Finland.'

Translation of Statement by M. DE LA GRYE, in the *Revue des Eaux et Fôrets* of January 1884:—'In an address delivered some weeks since at a banquet of exhibitors in the French section at Amsterdam, M. Herisson, Minister of Commerce, expressed an intention to publish a series of small books designed to make known to French merchants foreign lands in a commercial point of view. If the Minister of Commerce wishes to show to our merchants the resources possessed by Finland, he need not go far to seek information which may be useful to them, they will be found in a small volume which has just been published by Mr John Croumbie Brown.

'Mr Brown is one of those English ministers, who, travelling over the world in all directions [some at their own cost], seeking to spread the Word of the Lord in the form of Bibles translated into all languages, know how to utilise the leisure left to them at times while prosecuting this mission. Some occupy themselves with physical science, others with archæology, some with philology, many with commerce; Mr Brown has made a special study of sylviculture. He has already published on this subject many works, from amongst which we may cite these: *Hydrology of South Africa; The Forests of England; The Schools of Forestry in Europe; Réboisement in France; Pine Plantations on Sand Wastes in France.*

'His last book on Finland is the fruit of many journeys made in that country, which he visited for the first time in 1833, but whither he has returned frequently since that time. Mr Brown gives narratives of his voyages on the lakes which abound in Finland, and his excursions in the immense forests, the exploitation of which constitutes the principal industry of the country. The School of Forestry at Evois has furnished to him much precise information in regard to the organisation of the service, and the legislation and the statistics of forests, which, added to what he had procured by his own observation, has enabled him to make a very complete study of this country, poetically designated *The Land of a Thousand Lakes*, and which might also justly be called *The Kingdom of the Forest*, for there this reigns sovereign.'

V.—Forest Lands and Forestry of Northern Russia.
Price 6s 6d.

Details are given of a trip from St. Petersburg to the forests around Petrozavodsk on Lake Onega, in the government of Olonetz; a description of the forests on that government by Mr Judrae, a forest official of high position, and of the forests of Archangel by Mr Hepworth Dixon, of Lapland, of the land of the Samoides and of Nova Zembla; of the exploitation of the forests by *Jardinage*, and of the evils of such exploitation; and of the export timber trade, and disposal of forest products. In connection with discussions of the physical geography of the region information is supplied in regard to the contour and general appearance of the country; its flora, its forests, and the palaeontological botany of the regions beyond, as viewed by Professor Heer and Count Saporta; its fauna, with notices of game, and with copious lists of coleoptera and lepidoptera, by Forst-Meister Gunther, of Petrozavodsk.

EXTRACT FROM PREFACE.—'In the spring of 1877 I published a brochure entitled *The Schools of Forestry in Europe: a Plea for the Creation of a School of Forestry in connection with the Arboretum in Edinburgh*, in which with details of the arrangements made for instruction in Forest Science in Schools of Forestry in Prussia, Saxony, Hanover, Hesse, Darmstadt, Wurtemburg, Bavaria, Austria, Poland, Russia, Finland, Sweden, France. Italy, and in Spain, and details of arrangements existing in Edinburgh for instruction in most of the subjects included amongst preliminary studies, I submitted for consideration the opinion, "that with the acquisition of this Arboretum, and with the existing arrangements for study in the University of Edinburgh, and in the Watt Institution and School of Arts, there are required only facilities for the study of what is known on the Continent as Forest Science to enable these Institutions conjointly, or any one of them, with the help of the other, to take a place amongst the most completely equipped Schools of Forestry in Europe, and to undertake the training of foresters for the discharge of such duties as are now required of them in India, in our Colonies, and at home."

'This year has seen world-wide arrangements for an International Exhibition of forest products and other objects of interest connected with forestry in Edinburgh, "In the interests of forestry, and to promote a movement for the establishment of a School of Forestry in Scotland, as well as with a view of furthering and stimulating a greater improvement in the scientific management of woods in Scotland and the sister countries which has manifested itself during recent years."

'The following is one of a series of volumes published with a view to introduce into English forestal literature detailed information on some of the points on which information is supplied to students at Schools of Forestry on the Continent; and to make better known the breadth of study which is embraced in what is known there as *Forstwissenscaft*, or Forest Science.'

VI.—French Forest Ordinance of 1669; with Historical Sketch of Previous Treatment of Forests in France. Price 4s.

The early history of forests in France is given, with details of devastations of these going on in the first half of the seventeenth century; with a translation of the Ordinance of 1669, which is the basis of modern forest economy; and notices of forest exploitation in *Jardinage*, in *La Methode à Tire et Aire*, and in *La Methode des Compartiments*.

EXTRACT FROM PREFACE.—' "The Celebrated Forest Ordinance of 1669:" Such is the character and designation generally given at the present day to the Ordinance in question. It is known, by reputation at least, in every country on the Continent of Europe; but, so far as is known to me, it has never before been published in English dress. It may possibly be considered antiquated; but, on its first promulgation, it was welcomed, far beyond the bounds of France, as bringing life to the dead; and I know of no modern system of Forest Exploitation, based on modern Forest Science, in which I cannot trace its influence. In the most advanced of these—that for which we are indebted to Hartig and Cotta of Saxony—I see a development of it like to the development of the butterfly from what may be seen in the structure of the chrysalis; and thus am I encouraged to hope that it may prove suggestive of beneficial arrangements, even where it does not detail what it may be deemed desirable to adopt.

' In my translation I have followed an edition issued with Royal approval in 1753, with one verbal alteration to bring it into accordance with certain older approved editions, and with another verbal alteration to bring it into accordance with editions issued in 1699, 1723, 1734, and 1747.'

Translation of notice by M. DE LA GRYE for July 1883 in the *Revue des Eaux et Fôrets:* ' England, which with her immense possessions in India, in Canada, and in the Cape of Good Hope, is beyond all question a State rich in forests, has never up to the present time given to this portion of her domains more than a very moderate share of her attention; but for some years past public opinion is becoming alarmed, in view of the immense devastations which have been committed in them, and the forest question coming forward spontaneously has become the subject of numerous publications: amongst which, after the excellent monthly collection, the *Journal of Forestry and Estate Management*, comes the Translation of the Ordinance of 1669, which has just been published by Mr John Croumbie Brown. This translation of a monument of jurisprudence, well known in France, but which has never before been reproduced in English, has furnished to Mr Brown an opportunity of giving a historical sketch of French Forest Legislation, and an exposition of the different methods of exploitation followed in our country. Drawn from the best sources, and commented on with talent, these documents form an elegant volume, which the author has made the more complete by binding with it a summary of the treatise he has published on the Forests of England.'

VII.—Pine Plantations on Sand Wastes in France. Price 7s.

In this are detailed the appearances presented by the Landes of the Gironde before and after culture, and the Landes of La Sologne; the legislation and literature of France in regard to the planting of the Landes with trees; the characteristics of the sand wastes; the natural history, culture, and exploitation of the maritime pine, and of the Scots fir; and the diseases and injurious influences to which the maritime pine is subject.

EXTRACTS FROM PREFACE.—' The preparation of this volume for the press was undertaken in consequence of a statement in the *Standard and Mail*, a Capetown paper, of the 22d July 1876, to the effect that in the estimates submitted to Parliament £1000 had been put down for the Cape Flats, it was supposed with a view to its being employed in carrying out planting operations as a means of reclaiming the sandy tracts beyond Salt River.

' This volume was originally compiled in view of what seemed to be required at the Cape of Good Hope. It has been revised and printed now, as a contribution towards a renewed enterprise to arrest and utilise sand-wastes which stretch from Table Mountain to the Hottentot Holland Mountains; and additional information is forthcoming if it should be desired.'

VIII.—Reboisement in France; or, Records of the Replanting of the Alps, the Cevennes, and the Pyrenees, with Trees, Herbage, and Bush, with a view to arresting and preventing the destructive consequences of torrents. Price 12s.

In this are given a *résume* of Surell's study of Alpine torrents, of the literature of France relative to Alpine torrents, and of remedial measures which have been proposed for adoption to prevent the disastrous consequences following from them—translations of documents and enactments, showing what legislative and executive measures have been taken by the Government of France in connection with *reboisement* as a remedial application against destructive torrents—and details in regard to the past, present, and prospective aspects of the work.

EXTRACT FROM PREFACE.—'In a treatise on the Hydrology of South Africa I have given details of destructive effects of torrential floods at the Cape of Good Hope and Natal, and referred to the measures adopted in France to prevent the occurrence of similar disastrous floods there. The attention of the Legislative Assembly at the Cape of Good Hope was, last year, called by one of the members of the Assembly to the importance of planting trees on unproductive Crown lands. On learning that this had been done I addressed to the editor of the *Cape Argus* a communication, of which the following is a copy:—

'"I have before me details of destructive effects of torrents which have occurred since I left the Colony in the beginning of 1867. Towards the close of that year there occurred one, the damage occasioned by which to roads and to house property at Port Elizabeth alone was estimated at from £25,000 to £30,000. Within a year thereafter a similar destructive torrent occurred at Natal, in regard to which it was stated that the damage done to public works alone was estimated at £50,000, while the loss to private persons was estimated variously from £50,000 to £100,000. In the following year, 1869, a torrent in the Western Province occasioned the fall of a railway bridge, which issued in loss of life and loss of property, and personal injuries, for one case alone of which the railway proprietors were prosecuted for damages amounting to £5000. In Beaufort West a deluge of rain washed down the dam, and the next year the town was flooded by the waters of the Gamko; and the next year, 1871, Victoria West was visited with a similar disaster. Such are the sums and the damages with which we have to deal in connection with this question, as it affects the case; and these are only the most remarkable torrents of the several years referred to. I have spoken of millions of francs being spent on *reboisement* in France, and some may be ready to cry out, 'Nothing like such an expenditure can be undertaken at the Cape!' Perhaps not; but the losses occasioned by the torrents seem to amount at present to about a million of francs *in the year*. This falls in a great measure on individuals, that would fall on the community; and the community in return would benefit by water retained to fertilize the earth, instead of being lost in the sea, and by firewood and timber being grown where now there is none. These are facts well deserving of consideration in the discussion of the expediency of planting Crown lands with trees."

'Towards the close of last year, 1874, still more disastrous effects were produced by torrential floods. According to the report given by one of the Colonial newspapers, the damages done could not be estimated at much less than £300,000. According to the report given by another, the damage done to public works alone was estimated at £350,000,—*eight millions, seven hundred and fifty thousand francs.* And my attention was called anew to the subject.

'On addressing myself to M. Faré, Director-General of the Administration of Forests in France, there was afforded to me every facility I could desire for extending and verifying the information I had previously collected in regard to the works of *reboisement* to which I have referred. Copies of additional documents were supplied to me, with copies of works sanctioned by the Administration, and arrangements were made for my visiting and inspecting, with every assistance required, the works begun and the works completed; and thus I have been enabled to submit a much more complete report than it would otherwise have been in my power to produce.

'While the compilation I have prepared owes its publication at this time to the occurrence of the inundations of last year at the Cape of Good Hope, the publication has been undertaken in the hope that in other countries besides South Africa the information may be turned to practical account.'

Translation of extract from letter to the author by M. ALEXANDRE SURELL, *Ingenieur des Ponts et Chausses*, chairman of the *Compagnie des Chemins des Fer du Midi et du Canal lateral à la Garonne*, and author of *Etude sur les Torrents des Hautes-Alps, Ouvrage Couronne par l'Academie des Sciences en* 1842 :—' You are rendering an eminent service to society in calling the attention of serious thinkers to the subject of *reboisements* and *gazonnements*. It is a vital question affecting our descendants, specially in southern climates, there are useful truths which have to be diffused there, and you have fulfilled this duty amongst your countrymen.

'In France public opinion, long indifferent, is now sufficiently enlightened on the question, and much has been done.

'I have been able to establish in the course of a recent journey that, throughout a great part of Switzerland, in Styria, in Carinthia, and in the Tyrol, the same phenomena which have issued in the desolation of our French Alps are beginning to produce the same effects. There have been recognised a number of extinct torrents which had originated in the destruction of the forests. If people go on sleeping, and the administration or the communes do nothing to arrest the evil, posterity will have a sad inheritance devolved upon it.

'You have given, with very great clearness, a *résumé* of what I have done in France, be it by my works, or be it by my workings, for the regeneration of our mountains.'

Translation of extract from letter by the late M. Ernest Cézanne, *Ingenieur des Ponts et Chausses, Représentant des Hautes Alpes à l'Assemblée Nationale*, and author of *Une Suite* to the work of M. Surell. 'The post brought to me yesterday your very interesting volume on *Réboisement*. I at once betook myself to the perusal of it; and I am surprised that a foreigner could digest so completely such a collection of our French documents drawn from so many diverse sources. The problem of *réboisement and the regeneration of the mountains* is one of the most interesting which man has to solve, but it requires time and money, and with the authorities and political assemblies, technical knowledge which is as yet but very sparingly possessed. It is by books so substantial as yours, sir, that public opinion can be prepared to face the importance of this great work.'

IX.—Hydrology of South Africa; or Details of the Former Hydrographic Condition of Cape of Good Hope, and of Causes of its Present Aridity, with Suggestions of Appropriate Remedies for this Aridity. Price 10s.

In this the desiccation of South Africa, from pre-Adamic times to the present day, is traced by indications supplied by geological formations, by the physical geography or the general contour of the country, and by arborescent productions in the interior, with results confirmatory of the opinion that the appropriate remedies are irrigation, arboriculture, and an improved forest economy: or the erection of dams to prevent the escape of a portion of the rainfall to the sea—the abandonment or restriction of the burning of the herbage and bush in connection with pastoral and agricultural operations—the conservation and extension of existing forests—and the adoption of measures similar to the *réboisement* and *gazonnement* carried out in France, with a view to prevent the formation of torrents, and the destruction of property occasioned by them.

M. Jules Clavé, of world-wide reputation as a student of Forest Science, wrote in the *Revue des Deux Mondes* of 1st May 1882:—

[*Translated.*] 'Since the first travels of Livingstone, the African continent, hitherto inaccessible, has been attacked on all points at once. By the north, and by the south, by the east, and by the west, hardy explorers have penetrated it, traversed it, and have dragged from it some of its secrets. Travellers have paid tribute and done their work in opening up a path; it is now for science and civilisation to do theirs, in studying the problems which present themselves for investigation; and in drawing in the current of general circulations the peoples and lands, which appear as if destined to stand outside; and in causing to contribute to the increase of social wealth the elements of production previously unknown. Thus are we led to receive with interest works which can throw a new light on the condition of regions which may have been known for a long time, and which make known the conditions of their prosperity. It is under this title that the work of the Rev. J. C. Brown on the *Hydrology of South Africa* appears deserving of notice; but it is so also from other points of view. Mr Brown, after a previous residence in the colony of the Cape, whither he had been sent in 1844 as a missionary and head of a religious congregation, returned thither in 1863 as Professor of Botany in the College of South Africa, and he remained there some years. In both of these positions he had occasion to travel through the colony in all directions, and had opportunities to collect most valuable information in regard to its physical geography. Mr Brown on going out to the Cape knew nothing of the works which had for their object to determine the influence of forests on the climate, on the quantity of rain, and on the river-courses in Europe; he had never heard mention of the work of M. Surell on the torrents of the Alps, or of that of M. Mathieu on forest meteorology, nor of those of M. Domontzey, Costa de Bastelica, and so many others on the subject of *réboisement;* and yet in studying by himself, and without bias, the climatic condition of South Africa, he came to perceive that the disturbances in the regularity of the flow of rivers within the historic period should be attributed in a large measure to the destruction of forests; and he meets in agreement on this point the *savants* whose names have been mentioned. We have thought it might not be without interest to readers of the *Revue* to have in the lines of Mr Brown a collection of phenomena which, in their manifestation at any specified point are not less due to general causes, the effects of which may be to make themselves felt everywhere where there may be existent the same conditions than to aught else.' And there follows a lengthened article in illustration.

X.—Water Supply of South Africa, and Facilities for the Storage of it. Price 18s 6d.

In this volume are detailed meteorological observations on the humidity of the air and the rainfall, on clouds, and winds, and thunder-storms; sources from which is derived the supply of moisture which is at present available for agricultural operations in the Colony of the Cape of Good Hope and regions beyond, embracing the atmosphere, the rainfall, rivers, fountains, subterranean streams and reservoirs, and the sea; and the supply of water and facilities for the storage of it in each of the divisions of the colony

—in Basutoland, in the Orange River Free State, in Griqualand West, in the Transvaal Territory, in Zululand, at Natal, and in the Transkei Territory.

EXTRACT FROM PREFACE.—'Appended to the Report of the Colonial Botanist at the Cape of Good Hope for 1866 was an abstract of a Memoir prepared on the Hydrology of South Africa, which has since been embodied in a volume which has been published on that subject, and an abstract of a Memoir prepared on Irrigation and its application to agricultural operations in South Africa, which embraced a Report on the Water Supply of the Colony ; its sources, its quantity, the modes of irrigation required in different circumstances, the facilities for the adoption of these in different districts, and the difficulties, physical and other, in the way of works of extensive irrigation being carried out there, and the means of accomplishing these which are at command.

'In the following volume is embodied that portion of the Memoir which related to the water supply, and the existing facilities for the storage of this, with reports relative to this which were subsequently received, and similar information in regard to lands beyond the Colony of the Cape of Good Hope, which it has been sought to connect with the Colony by federation, or otherwise ; and the information relative to irrigation has been transferred to a Report on the Rivers of the Colony, and the means of controlling floods, of preventing inundations, of regulating the flow of rivers, and utilising the water by irrigation otherwise.

'In the series of volumes to which this belongs its place is immediately after that on the *Hydrology of South Africa*, which contains details of the former hydrographic condition of the Cape of Good Hope, and of causes of its present aridity, *with suggestions of appropriate remedies for this aridity ;* and it has been prepared to show that, not in a vague and general use of the terms, but in strict accordance with the statement, the severe, protracted, and extensive droughts, and destructive floods and inundations, recorded in the former volume, find their counterpart in constantly alternating droughts and deluges in every district of the Colony,—and that, in every so-called division of it, notwithstanding the deluges, there were protracted sufferings from drought, and, notwithstanding the aridity, there is a supply of water at command, with existing facilities for the storage of the superabundant supply which at present proves productive of more evil than good.'

Statement by Reviewer in *European Mail :*—' Dr Brown is well known at the Cape, for in the exercise of his duties he travelled over the principal part of it, and much, if not indeed the substance, of the bulky volume before us, has been before the Cape public in the form of Reports to the local Government. As these reports have been commented upon over and over again by the local press there is little left for us to say beyond the fact that the author reiterates his opinion that the only panacea for the drought is to erect dams and other irrigation works for the storage of water when the rains come down. There can be no doubt that this is sage and wholesome advice, and the only question is, who is to sustain the expense? Not long ago, somewhere about the time that Dr Brown was prosecuting his labours, it will be remembered that General Wynard said that "Nature had furnished the cups if only science would take the trouble to make them secure." It is but to repeat an oft-told story that with a good supply of water South Africa would be one of the finest of nature's gardens, and would be capable of producing two crops a year, in addition to furnishing fodder for sheep and cattle. The question of the water supply for irrigation and other purposes has been staved off year after year, and nothing has been done. It is not too much to say, however, that the question must make itself felt, as it is one of the chief factors in the ultimate prosperity of South Africa. The author is evidently in love with his subject, and has contributed a mass of facts to Hydrology which will be useful to all countries of an arid character.'

XI.—Forests and Moisture; or Effects of Forests on Humidity of Climate. Price 10s.

In this are given details of phenomena of vegetation on which the meteorological effects of forests affecting the humidity of climate depend—of the effects of forests on the humidity of the atmosphere, and on the humidity of the ground, on marshes, on the moisture of a wide expanse of country, on the local rainfall, and on rivers—and of the correspondence between the distribution of the rainfall and of forests—the measure of correspondence between the distribution of the rainfall and that of forests—the distribution of the rainfall dependent on geographical position, or determined by the contour of a country—the distribution of forests affected by the distribution of the rainfall—and the local effects of forests on the distribution of the rainfall within the forest district.

EXTRACTS FROM PREFACE.—'This volume is one of a series. In the first of the series—a volume entitled—published last year, *Hydrology of South Africa; or, Details of the Former Hydrographic Condition of the Cape of Good Hope and of Causes of its recent Aridity, with Suggestions of appropriate Remedies for this Aridity.*

'This volume, on the effects of forests on the humidity of the atmosphere and the ground, follows supplying illustrations of the reasonableness of the suggestion made in regard to the conservation and extension of forests as a subordinate means of arresting and counteracting the desecration and aridity of the country.'

EXTRACTS FROM LETTERS to the author from the late Hon. George P. Marsh, Minister of the United States at Rome, and author of *The Earth as Modified by Human Action*:—'I am extremely obliged to you for a copy of your *Réboisement in France*, just received by post. I hope the work may have a wide circulation. . . . Few things are more needed in the economy of our time than the judicious administration of the forest, and your very valuable writings cannot fail to excite a powerful influence in the right direction. . . .

'I have received your interesting letter of the 5th inst., with the valuable MSS. which accompanied it. I will make excerpts from the latter, and return it to you soon. I hope the very important facts you mention concerning the effect of plantations on the island of Ascension will be duly verified.

. . . 'I put very little faith in *old* meteorological observations, and, for that matter, not much in *new*. So much depends on local circumstances, on the position of instruments, &c.—on *station*, in short, that it is only on the principle of the tendency of some to balance each other that we can trust to the registers of observers not *known* to be trained to scientific accuracy. Even in observatories of repute, meteorological instruments are seldom properly hung and guarded from disturbing causes. Beyond all, the observations on the absorption of heat and vapour at small distances from the ground show that thermometers are almost always hung too high to be of any value as indicating the temperature of the stratum of the atmosphere in which men live and plants grow, and in most tables, particularly old ones, we have no information as to whether the thermometer was hung five feet or fifty feet from the ground, or whether it was in any way protected from heat radiated from near objects.'

EXTRACT LETTER from the late Professor Henry, of the Smithsonian Institution, Washington :—' The subject of Forest Culture and its influence on rainfall is, just at this time, attracting much attention in the United States. At the last meeting of the American Association for the advancement of science a committee was appointed to memorialise Congress with reference to it. Several of the Western States Governments have enacted laws and offered premiums in regard to it. The United States Agricultural Department has collected statistics bearing on the question, and we have referred your letter to that establishment.

' The only contribution that the Smithsonian Institution has made to the subject is that of a series of rain-fall tables, comprising all the observations that have been made in regard to the rainfall in the United States since the settlement of the country ; a copy of this we have sent to your address.

' It may be proper to state that we have commenced a new epoch, and have, since the publication of the tables in question, distributed several hundred rain gauges in addition to those previously used, and to those which have been provided by the Government in connection with the signal service.'

These notices and remarks are cited as indicative of the importance which is being attached to the subject discussed.

EXTRACT FROM LETTER to the author from Lieut.-Col. J. Campbell Walker, Conservator of Forests, Madras, then Conservator-in-Chief of Forests, New Zealand; author of *Report on State Forests and Forest Management in Germany and Austria* :—' I am in receipt of yours, along with the notices of your works on Forestry, by book post. I think very highly of the scope of the works, and feel sure that they and similar works will supply a want much felt by the Indian forest officers.

' It contains many important data which I should have vainly sought elsewhere, and it will be regarded by all competent judges as a real substantial contribution to a knowledge of the existing surface, and the changes which, from known or unknown causes, that surface is fast undergoing.'

Copies of any of these Works will be sent post-paid to any address within direct Postal communication with Britain, on receipt by Dr JOHN C. BROWN, Haddington, of a Post-Office Order for the price.

SCHOOLS OF FORESTRY

IN

GERMANY,

WITH ADDENDA RELATIVE TO A DESIDERATED
BRITISH NATIONAL SCHOOL OF FORESTRY.

COMPILED BY

JOHN CROUMBIE BROWN, LL.D.,

*Formerly Lecturer on Botany in University and King's College, Aberdeen,
subsequently Colonial Botanist at Cape of Good Hope, and Professor
of Botany in the South African College, Cape Town; Fellow of the
Linnean Society; Fellow of the Royal Geographical Society; and
Honorary Vice-President of the African Institute of Paris.*

EDINBURGH:
OLIVER AND BOYD, TWEEDDALE COURT.
LONDON: SIMPKIN, MARSHALL AND CO.
1887.

KIRKCALDY:
PRINTED BY J. CRAMB.

PREFACE.

IN a *brochure* which I published in 1877, entitled *The Schools of Forestry in Europe: a Plea for the Creation of a School of Forestry in Connection with the Arboretum in Edinburgh;* and in a volume which I published last autumn (1886), entitled, *School of Forest Engineers in Spain, indicative of a Type for a British National School of Forestry*, I expressed and re-affirmed the opinion that, with the acquisition of that Arboretum with existing arrangements for study in the University and in the Watt Institute, there were required only facilities for the study of what is known on the Continent as Forest Science to enable these institutions conjointly, or either of them with the help of the other, to take a place amongst the most completely equipped Schools of Forestry in Europe, and to undertake the training of Foresters for the discharge of such duties as are required of them in India, in our Colonies, and at home.

The following volume shows what is implied in such a statement. No one of the schools described is considered by me of a type which should be followed in a British National School of Forestry; but the details may prove suggestive of much which might be done in the creation of such an institution.

I have ready for the press a companion volume on Forestal Arrangements in Germany, comprising statements of the views entertained in Germany in regard to the position of Schools of Forestry in the educational arrangements of the Empire, and in regard to the appropriate site for such institutions; details of arrangements and operations at Stations for Forestal Experimental Research at the sites of Schools of Forestry; and a report of arrangements for the administration and management of State Forests in Bavaria. But the publication of the volume is deferred till the discussion of the expediency of establishing a British National School of Forestry may be more advanced.

Information in regard to practicable arrangements by which such a British National School of Forestry as is indicated might to be created I have supplied in both of the treatises cited, and in evidence given by me before a Select Committee of the House of Commons appointed to consider whether by the establishment of a Forest School or otherwise our woodlands could be rendered more productive: which evidence in so far as it relates to this matter I have embodied in an Addendum to this volume.

By that Committee, as by one appointed by the previous Parliament, valuable information was collected, and on the 18th June, 1886, they agreed to report to the House of Commons:—'Your Committee have taken some evidence upon the matters referred to them, but have not had sufficient time to conclude their investigation on account of the dissolution of the present Parliament; they have therefore agreed to report the evidence already taken to the House, and to recommend that a Committee on the same subject should be appointed in the next Parliament.'

JOHN C. BROWN.

HADDINGTON, 14th February, 1887.

CONTENTS.

———o———

	PAGE
INTRODUCTION ...	1

Early Literature of Modern Forest Science; and General View of Modern Forest Economy.

CHAPTER I.—*The Royal Saxon Forest Academy in Tharand* ...   12

Transference to Tharand of the School of Forestry commenced by Cotta at Zillbach (p. 12); Subsequent changes till the Celebration of the Jubilee of the Institution on 17th June, 1866 (p. 13); Scheme of Instruction sanctioned by the Minister of Finance in December, 1871 (p. 38); Attendance of Students (p. 44); Description of Locality (p. 45.)

CHAPTER II.—*Royal Prussian Forest Academy at Neustadt-Eberswalde* ...   47

Historical Sketch of the Institution (p. 47); Regulations issued by the Minister of Finance in April, 1875 (p. 49); *Unterrichts Plan* or Programme of Study in Curriculum of two and a half years (p. 54); Summary of Instruction given (p. 55); Annual Attendance of Students (p. 61); Requirements for Employment and Promotion in the Forest Service of Prussia (p. 62); Description of the School and Locality (p. 69).

CHAPTER III.—*Royal Hanoverian Forest Academy in Munden* ...   65

Site (p. 75); Past History (p. 76); Forest Economy and Administration (p. 78). Notice of Arrangements for the Transference of Provision for Instruction in Forest Science to the University (p. 113); and of the importance of the Establishment of Provision for the Prosecution of Forestal Experimental Researches (p. 114).

CONTENTS.

CHAPTER VI.—*Royal Bavarian Central Forest Academy at Aschaffenburg, and Classes for the Study of Forestry in the Royal Ludwig-Maximilian University in Munich* 115

Account of the former condition of the School (p. 115); Account of the same from a Published Programme of what is required of Candidates for Admission to the Forest Service of the State (p. 120); History of the Institution from its origin (p. 129), and Arguments subsequently advanced for the entire transference of the Instruction to the University (p. 139); Present Condition of Arrangements for Instruction on Forestry in Bavaria, (p. 142.)

CHAPTER VII.—*Royal Wurtemburg Forestal and Agricultural Academy at Hohenheim, and Forestal Instruction in the University of Tubingen* ... 145

Arrangements at Hohenheim, (p. 145); Former Arrangements for Forestal Instruction in the University of Tubingen, (p. 154); Transfer of Provision for Instruction in Forestry at Hohenheim to the University, (p. 155.)

CHAPTER VIII.—*Forestal Instruction in the Grand Duchy of Baden in the Polytechnicum in Carlsruhe* ... 160

Educational Appliances, (p. 161); Curriculum of Study, (p. 163); Present Position, (p. 166.)

CHAPTER IX.—*Requirements for Admission into the Forest Service of German States, in which there do not exist Schools of Forestry* 167

Mecklenburg-Schwerin, (p 167); Mecklenburg-Strelitz, Oldenburg, Brunswick, Meinengen, (p. 168); Altenburg, Coburg-Gotha, Anhalt, (p. 169); Schwartzburg-Sondershausen, Schwarzburg, Rudolstadt, Waldeck, Reuss-Greitz, Schaumburg-Lippe, Lippe-Dethold, (p. 170); Alsace-Lorraine, (p. 171.)

CONCLUSION 172

Relation of Schools of Forestry to National System of Education in Germany, (p. 172); Stations for Experimental Research, (p. 175); Expense of Schools of Forestry on the Continent, (p. 176.'

CONTENTS.

ADDENDA

RELATIVE TO A DESIDERATED BRITISH NATIONAL SCHOOL OF FORESTRY.

I.—Suitable Site for a School of Forestry 179

II.—Educational Arrangements deemed suitable for a British National School of Forestry 183

III.—School of Forest Engineers in Spain, cited as indicative of a type for a British National School of Forestry 193

IV.—Treatises on Matters Pertaining to Modern Forest Science and Forest Economy, proffered for publication in the English Language 203

[Offers made to the Colony of the Cape of Good Hope (pp. 204 and 207); Offer made to Citizens of the United States of America (p. 210); Offer made to the Promoters of Edinburgh Forestry Exhibition (p. 223); Offer made to the Council of the Scottish Arboricultural Society (p. 225).]

V.—Proffered Gift of Works on Modern Forestry to Free Public Libraries in any of the British Colonies, and in any of the United States of America ... 229

VI.—Matters Pertaining to Schools of Forestry, on which the Author is ready to supply information to any Government Official, Public Association, or Private Individual, desirous of Establishing a British National School of Forestry 231

SCHOOLS OF FORESTRY IN GERMANY.

―――:o:―――

INTRODUCTION.

THE history of forests and of forestry in Germany is not greatly dissimilar from that of forests and of forestry in France. Of this I have given some details in a volume entitled *French Forest Ordinance of* 1669, *with Historical Sketch of Previous Treatment of Forests in France;* and that forest ordinance marks the commencement of an era in the history of the treatment of forests in the one country and in the other.

Colbert of France, seeing the waste and destruction of forests going on in his day, gave expression to bitter feeling in words which have become famous:—'*France perira faute de Bois*'—France will perish through lack of wood.

And in 1721 Réaumur presented to the Academy of Science a Memoir in which in reference to this fear he says: 'The feeling of uneasiness is general, and it is perhaps only too well founded. The interests of the State demand at the least that the quantity of wood should not be diminished while the consumption is being increased. It is to be wished that the lands still left in wood should be put into the highest possible condition in regard to their value, and above all things, that their produce should not be allowed to fall off.'

And he showed how by a series of experiments it was

possible to ascertain at what age coppice woods could be felled with most advantage—regard being had to securing the greatest supply, and the best material, from the products of the forest.

In reference to the statement by Réaumur, which I have quoted, M. Parade has remarked, 'This is not the place to inquire whether the Government of that day did all that might have been done to attain the end pointed out by Réaumur; but let us tell, to the honour of science, that she was indefatigable in seeking out the proper remedies for the evil, and thus to allay the alarm of the country.'

These could only be found in a more scientific culture of trees; and science showed what were the measures to be successively adopted. These were, in a word, successive thinnings as a means of advancing and improving the growth of the wood, while obtaining an immediate produce; and the prolongation of the term of years allotted for the working of the forests to the exact period necessary to augment the products to the greatest extent in a given time. This had to be determined, and science has accomplished her task.

In 1757 a treatise on Forest Economy was published by Moser, in which he brought before his countrymen the method of management proposed by Réaumur four-and-twenty years before. And from statements made by Pfeil in a work entitled *Die Forsttaxation in ihren ganzen Umfange*, published in Leipzig in 1858, it appears that from the publication of this work by Moser date the earliest trials to determine with precision the future probable increase of wood in standing forests which were made in Germany.

In 1763 some of the works of Duhamel, one of the students of vegetable physiology in France, were translated into German by Schöllenbach, and published. About this time, say from 1760 to 1780, evils which were inherent in the so-called *Regime à tire et aire* (that to which the French Ordinance of 1669 had special reference), were making themselves apparent on all hands. In Prussia, towards the end of the reign of Frederick the Great, there was issued an Ordinance relating to the management of forests, in which it was enjoined ' that the fellings, instead of clearing all away, should be confined to simple thinnings of the trees, having for their object the removal at most of *bad* wood and of *matured* wood in trees upwards of 70 or 80 years of age.'

And this has been considered an indication that it began to be perceived that the artificial restorations, the forced consequence of utter extermination, in the resin yielding woods were difficult of accomplishment when they had to be carried out on ground of great extent, and in circumstances little favourable to success.

Corresponding complaints on other points arose against the employment of the system in question in timber forests of beech, the restoration of which was not secured either by new shoots or by seeds; and a final grievance felt more particularly in the lesser states, in which the forest products constituted often a great part of the public revenue, came to demand a remedy for the great and grievous inequalities in the annual products which were obtained by the continued carrying out of the system.

There was no unwillingness to persevere in the mode of operation sanctioned by the Ordinance of 1669, technically called *à tire et aire*, which was unquestionably useful—namely, the orderly and regular exploitation of the forest; but it was indispensably necessary to modify the application of this, so as to secure the most perfect possible natural restoration of the forest, and to furnish to proprietors annual products pretty equal in amount or value.

The forests which had been subjected to *jardinage*, writes M. Parade, of Nancy, of whose historical sketch of the progress of the art of forest management the following notice may be considered a free translation :—The forests which had been subjected to *jardinage*, in which were felled here and there such trees as promised to supply the material desired for whatever purpose this might be—sale, shipbuilding, house carpentry, or aught else, leaving all others to grow on, if haply they were not crushed by the fall of the felled tree, or broken down in the bringing out of the felled timber—presented standing crops of most unequal density, and without any well-marked gradation of age to which the system *à tire et aire* could be strictly applied without giving rise to many inconveniences, of which the most serious were these:—

1. A great inequality in the successive annual fellings.

2. Considerable loss of increase proceeding not only from great differences in the soil and in the denseness of the patches felled in successive years, but more especially from the circumstance that some portions were cut down too young, while in others many trees, and even entire clumps, were liable to decay before they came within the range of the regular series of fellings.

These were inconveniences to which it does not appear that any attention had been given in France, but which were felt by the foresters of Germany, and to remedy these inconveniences they devised in succession a number of measures, each of them, it may be, insufficient of itself to remedy the evil, but which, combined, resulted in constituting a set of rules, applicable, some to coppice wood and some to timber forests, which have given rise to the publication of numerous treatises on subjects which they embraced, or were connected therewith, which works proved useful not only at the time of publication, but also subsequently, inasmuch as they prepared the ground, and opened up the way for those master minds which have in later times definitely evolved the science of the art.

The rules referred to may be briefly described thus :—

1. In the management of coppice wood, they required the division of these into as many fellings of equal extent as there were years on the rotation to be maintained,

excepting in cases in which a very marked difference in the quality of the soil and the growth of the wood, combined with a necessity existing for obtaining annual products nearly equal in quantity, might require that the extent of the fellings should be made in some respect proportional to the production.

2. In the management of timber forests, these forests, which were no longer the forests *jardinées* of a former day, but which were coming, in whole or in part, under the operation of the system *à tire et aire*, were subjected to the following measures :—

1. A general cropping of the forest.
2. A classification, according to age, of all the standing crops, the oldest of which constituted together the group of exploitable woods, or of what were considered such.
3. The determination of the period of time necessary for the wood not yet matured to attain the predetermined age for felling.
4. The replacement during the successive years of this period of the products obtained from the group of workable woods, and with this in view the preparation of an estimate of the actual solid contents of these woods, and an estimate of their future cubic contents diminishing by progressive arithmetical decrease proportionate to the annual cuttings of the forest.

By these estimates it could be seen at a glance what were the cubic contents of the forest then, and what it was likely to be five years thereafter; ten years thereafter; twenty years thereafter; fifty years thereafter; or at any subsequentary intermediate period.

While the system of management of timber forests which has thus been described was being followed, it was found that the defects of the system were these :—

First of all, the end for the attainment of which the whole system was devised—namely, the establisment of a well-sustained relation of equalisation between the growth and the removal of trees was only imperfectly, and that very imperfectly accomplished. If, for example, woods of a medium age were deficient in the series, the period which must elapse previous to the felling of the younger woods must necessarily be very protracted, and this must to a great extent tend to prevent the possibility of accomplishing the equalisation desired, as the old woods must be made to last to the end of this period, after which there would probably be a super-abundance; or, if on the contrary, the old woods were in excess, and those of a medium age were of corresponding fewer numbers a beginning would be made with an abundance which must ultimately experience a great reduction. A second and more serious defect of the system was the entire absence of any provision for the improvement of the state or condition of the wood, in so far as this might be effected by the gradation of the ages, and the order in which they should succeed one another on the ground; for such as the forest was found in both of these respects at the beginning of the rotation, such must it have been found at the end.

In 1785 there appeared a remarkable work by Varenne de Fenille on the management of coppice woods, in which he thoroughly discussed the whole subject of production, and developed a theory in regard to the simple or absolute maximum of produce obtainable from coppice wood, and the compound maximum of small wood and of timber obtainable from such woods:—a theory which is still quoted in works on forest science and on forest economy, and which is known by his name.

Meanwhile the increasing scarcity of wood, and the importance of securing as large a revenue as possible from the sale of wood raised on Crown forests, combined to secure in Germany a measure of attention to forest economy which led to an important application of science to the regulation of forest operations. The attempts to regulate there what in France is called the system of *jardinage*, in accordance with which, as has been stated, trees are felled then and there, according as they seemed fitted to meet the requirements of the woodcutter, or showed symptoms of having begun to decay, had failed to accomplish what was desired. Subsequently the system of exploitation *à tire et aire*, according to which system of management the foresters divided into sections of approximately equal extent what are cleared in succession in periods of equal duration, so determined that by the time the last is cleared the forest will have been reproduced on the section first felled, had also failed; and evils which were inherent in the system manifested themselves in Germany as they had done elsewhere. These forcing themselves upon the attention of Hartig, a man deservedly held in great respect by students of Forest Science, he set himself to study these evils with a view to the discovery or the devising of some remedy.

About the year 1791 he published a treatise entitled 'Instruction in the Culture of Woods,' in which he gave his views on the clearing of woods, and on the reproduction of these by self-sown seeds. And in 1793 he published his developed system of forest economy.

The work of Hartig was carried forward by Cotta, under whom the modern system of forest economy may be said to have received its completed development, if it be understood that this does not imply that it has been so perfected as to admit of no further improvement, and to have need of none. In this, as in much besides, the highest ever leads to a higher; and improvements have been devised, while others are still desiderated, but such as it is it has become associated with the names of Hartig and Cotta. As in the rising tide the advance made by each successive wave may be noted, and even where no apparent advance is made, but rather an appearance of retrogression presents itself, the results in establishing the hold of the tidal wave on the strips of shore previously captured, may be made subject of record—so has it been in the development of forest science and forest economy; but, compared with what is done by each, the advance of the tide in its continuous flow so far transcends the advance made by each wave or wavelet in succession on the shore, that it is this which chiefly arrests and engages attention, and calls forth remark; and so it is here.

Let all honour be rendered to each and all of successive promoters of forest science in bye-gone days! they laboured, and we have entered on their labours, enjoying by inheritance the fruits of these. But the passing allusions which have been made to some of them have been made solely with a view to make apparent the requirements for educated trained instructors to undertake the administration and management of forests, arising from the advancement of forest science and its embodiment in practical forestry, and the consequent necessity felt, if not also formally declared, for the organisation of Schools of Forestry in which the necessary education, instruction, and training might be obtained, which Schools of Forestry in their turn, in their earlier development, were really schools for foresters, and were made subservient to the still further development of the science and art of forestry. It was with this in view that they were called into being. In a companion volume to this on the Schools of Forest Engineers in Spain, I have had occasion to cite a work by Senior Don Carlos Castel y Clemente, in his ' *Nocticia sobre la Fundacion y Desarrollo de la Escuela Especial de Ingenieros de Montes,*' published in 1877, an amplification of a memoir on the origin and development of the Special School of Forest Engineers in Spain, which he had prepared in accordance with orders received from the higher authorities of the State. In that he says:—

' In the seventeenth century there originated in some of the States of Germany the application of technical science to the treatment of forest masses. The rules, the aphorisms, and the whole of the directions which are comprised in the forestal knowledge of the ancients, are principles indefinite, obscure, uncertain, unconnected, destitute of method or systematized relations. Moser created in 1757 the first body of systematic teaching on the subject; and to the impulse given to this by him, and the weighty energy of Langen, Laspar, Zanthier, and others, are we indebted for the formation of the first plans of scientific treatment of forests begun in 1731 in the forests of the Dukedom of Brunswick. He, in his time, Langen being the first to do so, perceiving the necessity of entrusting the management of the forests to a specially educated and trained body of officials, possessing all necessary knowledge and information, with a view to raising up a body of such men, established the first School of Forestry in Wernigerode in the year 1772. But others consider as the first school that founded by Zanthier in Ilsenberg, which was followed some years later by the establishment of that by Haase in Lauterberg, that which G. Hartig founded in Hungen in 1791, that in Zillbach by H. Cotta in 1795, and various others, all due to the efforts of individuals, and manifesting that essentially practical character which was so requisite to meet the requirements of the time and the conditions in which the distinguished founders were placed, but devoid of means which would allow of there being given to them the influence and development which afterwards became needful.'

While Cotta was preceeded, anticipated if you will, by others in feeling the need of appropriate instruction being given to foresters if there were to be obtained from them, and from their work, all the benefit to their country and to the world which these might be made to yield—who endeavoured to supply the desideratum, and did so according to their means and opportunity—it is the name of Cotta which has become most extensively associated with Schools of Forestry, and not improperly so, seeing that it is from the School of Forestry organised by him there has been developed and produced the advanced Schools of Forestry of the present day.

I have a feeling of great respect for Zanthier, who is said to have been the first systematic teacher of forest science and forest economy who taught on these subjects at Ilsenberg, a town in the county of Stolberg in Upper Saxony, situated not far from the Hartz mountains, and within the precincts of the old Thuringden forest.

But, as stated in the work by Senor Castel, which I have cited: 'The primary organisation of the schools founded in Ilsenberg, Wernigerode, Lauterberg, Hungen, Zillbach, Walterhausen, Rottenhaus, Castel, &c., in the period from 1766 to 1805, was that of several other private centres of instruction, which died out with their founders, or suffered the fate which befell these in the course of their existence. All these made themselves remarkable by the great impulse and development which they gave to the diffusion of forest science, and by their having raised up a numerous and distinguished body of men to assist and direct at a later time the work of bringing into order the forests of the districts in which they were situated. There stands out prominently amongst all these the school founded by Cotta. He, being charged with the reduction to an orderly condition of the Forest of Fishbach, spent some years in the execution of this work, and during these years giving theoretic and practical instruction to the young men who assisted him there: thus was instituted the new centre of forestal instruction at Zillbach. Such reputation was acquired by this establishment of modern times, that in 1795 there was granted to it a subvention from the State, thanks to which he was able considerably to augment the means available then for the prosecution of study.

'In 1810 Cotta was appointed Director of Forest Management in Saxony. He at once perceived and pointed out the lack which existed of a staff of skilled officials, who should execute and assist in the execution of his projects; and with a view to meeting this desideratum the promoted School of Zillbach was transferred to Tharand in 1811, and ceded to the Government on the 12th of May, 1816. Converted into a Government academy, and furnished with all necessary resources, the School of Tharand, devoted to the instruction of the forest engineers of the State, very soon flourished beneficiently, attracting to study there the studious youth of many different countries, and serving as the sharp edge of a wedge for the general diffusion of those truths which, spreading themselves a little later in different countries, proved the occasion of there being opened other schools which take pride in calling themselves daughters of the Saxon Academy.'

CHAPTER I.

THE ROYAL SAXONY FOREST ACADEMY IN THARAND.

THE organisation of a School of Forestry was a natural sequence of the endeavours of Cotta to improve the method of exploitation of forests. We lack the data needful to enable us satisfactorily to differentiate sequences, which were most probably consequences of a common cause. But this much is manifest from the records —to impart to practical foresters the results of his cogitations was at once necessary to the execution of his scheme, and to the acquisition of additional data which were needed for the full development of his views.

As has been intimated, in 1786 Cotta began to give instruction in regard to forests and forest products, and more especially in regard to the proper mensuration of woods and forests, and of forest trees, at Zillbach; and there in 1795 he organised a regular school for the study of such subjects.

This school may be considered as the germ of the first national School of Forestry, or as the seedling which having been transplanted elsewhere, developed into such an institution, and reproduced its kind. This school he may be said to have removed entire to Tharand, a beautiful watering-place, a few miles from Dresden, the capital of Saxony, on his being called to that kingdom as Forstrath and Director of Forstvermessung, or Forest Surveying. Thither followed him, along with his assistants the greater part of his students at the time, and they constituted the body of a new *Forstlehranstalt*, or School of Forestry, which he opened on the 24th of May of that year, 1811.

It has apparently been more or less the case with all the Schools of Forestry in Europe that while they have been designed primarily, and perhaps exclusively, to educate and train foresters for the discharge of their functions as foresters, forest warders, *Forst-meisters*, and inspectors of forests, they have, by the collection of observations made being brought under the consideration of learned men familiar with like phenomena, enjoying a quietude and retirement favourable to study, called to instruct others in regard to these very things, and taking a special interest in such matters, done much to advance the forest science, and to improve the forest economy of the day; and this was pre-eminently the case with the *Forstlehranstalt* and the *Forst Academie* of Tharand, under the direction of Cotta.

From an address delivered by Cotta at the opening of the institute it appears he laid down as a principle that it should supply to the young forester not only an opportunity to study the necessary accessary sciences, but also that which was peculiarly forest science, and the natural history of the game inhabiting the forest; and that this end could only be gained by a judiciously arranged combination of theory and practice. Apparently from the first he associated his students with him in his researches.

The first *Forstlehranstalt* virtually consisted of a number of forest commissioners, who in summer carried on operations in the different forests, under instructions from him as their chief, and in winter re-assembled at his residence, there to conduct, under his direction, the work of the forest bureau, and prepare plans of operations for the summer following. Such a group of educated, zealous, and laborious men supplied a most desirable instrumentality in the hands of such a master as he to be employed by him for such a purpose.

In a report which was made by Cotta to the Royal Privy College of Finance, under date of 12th September, 1815, he gives the following account of the progress and condition of the institute :—

'Scarcely had I gone thither when so many young men took up the study of forestry and of the chase that the number of my auditors, including land surveyors in the service of the State, and selected members of the *jager corps*, or huntsmen, during my first winter must have numbered about a hundred. In the following year, 1812, the collective number was considerably diminished, some of my older students having finished their course of study, some of the others leaving because they did not find here what they had in ample measure at the Zillbach school—a forest within a forest, for practice in forestry and in the chase, and many others leaving because they considered they had learned in the course of a year's attendance all that they needed to learn. Still the collective number of my hearers in the winter of this second year, inclusive of surveyors, was between 70 and 80.

'The war year, 1813, was, as it was to all other educational institutions, exceedingly detremental to the *Forstlehranstalt* at Tharand; as the greater part of the students left the institute, and it was almost only the teachers who continued at their post. In the year 1814 some few students assembled, and bye-and-bye the lecture room gradually filled; but not before the beginning of the current year, 1815, when it was reported everywhere that my *Forstlehranstalt* was being changed into a Royal *Forst Academie*, and that thereby the practical instruction in the Tharand forest, should be entirely and more especially taken into account.'

The change referred to was brought under the consideration of the Privy Finance College in 1814, in consequence of a representation made by Cotta, and was understood to be carried out in accordance with his express desire.

In the so-called Private Institute of Cotta he himself gave instruction in all departments of forest science, forest technology, and forest botany; and Dr John Adam Reum, as second teacher, assisted in giving instruction in mathematics and in forest botany.

By a rescript of the 12th March, 1816, the transformation of the private institute into a national *Forst Academie*, under the conjoint direction of the Privy Finance College and the *Oberhofjagersmeister* — *anglice* Master of the Hounds, was completed.

Cotta, who was at the same time raised to the dignity of Oberforstrath, was nominated Director and forest teacher; as ordinary teachers to share the duty of instruction there were appointed Drs Reum and Krutzsch, both with the rank of professor; and instruction in what related practically to the chase and to forest mensuration, in plandrawing, in the German language, in forest law, and in financial economy, was entrusted to others, in all six persons besides the director and professors. For the purchase of books, specimens, instruments, and implements, 600 thalers was appropriated; for the support of poor but zealous students an annual allowance of 400 thalers was granted. The Academy had no forest of its own, but the forest lands of the Grallenberg Forest Circuit, and more especially the Tharand forest, was made available for practical instruction and demonstrations.

The lectures were begun in the month of June. The number of students who had been entered while it was under the direction of Cotta was 62, of whom 40 remained in the school, the others were employed as assistants in forest surveying and forest conservation.

By proclamation of 13th April, 1816, and by rescript of 10th June, 1816, the arrangements for study were authoritatively prescribed.

The curriculum of study embraced mathematics, pure and mixed, in all departments—arithmetic, geometry, trigonometry, mensuration, levelling, building, hydraulic engineering, in so far as this related to forestry, including dams, waterleadings, drinking places for man and beast, &c.;

Natural Science in all its departments, connected with forestry and the chase— zoology, forest botany, physiology of vegetation, with a more especial reference to the growth of timber, orography, formation of earth and soil, mineralogy, physics, and chemistry, in so far as they might serve to illustrate anything and everything pertaining to forests;

Forstwissenschaft, or Forest Science, inclusive of sylviculture, forest conservation, and profitable exploitation, forest technology, and the administration of forests;

The chase, including the natural history of the game, the use of firearms, training of dogs, &c.; and

Business requirements—correspondence, and bookkeeping, forest laws and game laws, and political economy, in so far as this related to forest products of all kinds.

The course of study was comprehensive and appropriate. In terms of the proclamation, practical instruction was to be the principal object aimed at in the instruction given to the students; every lecture was to have practical demonstrations so connected with it, that what was learned in the class-room should be illustrated and expounded in the forest; and if it should happen that any unusual forest operation, or proceeding in connection with the chase, should occur in the time appropriated to class studies, for that day the class studies should be suspended. The proclamation, moreover, expressly specified that the students should be called whenever the arranging of sites of felling, or of sylvicultural operations were to be fixed, or other important forest work was to be done; and they were to be informed what were the reasons for the work being done, and for that course, and no other, being adopted. The more advanced students were, according to the judgment of the director of the school, to take part in the work, to do other special work prescribed for them, and otherwise to have opportunity of practising all of the manifold operations required in the forest In view of this the *Oberforstmeister*, or chief forester of the Grillenburg Forest Circuit was, by special rescript, ordered not only to allow the students of the forest academy to take part in forest operations, but also to give to the subordinate officials the necessary instructions; that they should not only give notice to the Oberforstrath Cotta of the more important forest operations which were about to be undertaken, but also of all forest work, with specification of time and place, of which he should desire to be informed, that he might make the necessary arrangements for the students obtaining in the best way the practical instruction which these might be made to afford.

Moreover to those scholars in the academy who manifested satisfactory skill and interest in their studies an opportunity was to be given to be present at the revision in the larger forest circuits, that thereby their knowledge of forestry and general information might be expanded, as well as a closer insight into forest operations and forest management might be obtained. And with the same object in view they had once a-year at least to make a forest-excursion under the superintendence of a teacher, according to a pre-arranged plan, that they might be accustomed themselves to keep a journal of operations.

For fourteen years thereafter the *Forst Academie* was simply a School of Forestry, in accordance with a proclamation of 13th April, 1816, and was devoted exclusively to the scientific and practical training of foresters. By the terms of that proclamation, besides the instruction given in theoretical forest science, there was required to be given in it practical instruction in all departments of forestry and the chase, and this, in a course of two years instruction, and six months of special lectures. Real holiday rest was, according to the original prescription, enjoyed only during the weeks of Christmas and Easter; but besides this, in place of the usual spring and harvest holidays, six weeks after Easter and six weeks after Michaelmas were spent in practical work in the forest, or otherwise in forest excursions and in the varied works of the chase. It being afterwards objected that in the latter end of harvest there was a lack of opportunity for the students being exercised in forest work, in 1819 the harvest holidays were curtailed two weeks, and the programme of study was so arranged that this should be resumed regularly on the 1st of November. And in like manner in 1828 the time spent in practical work was shortened, several years experience having shown that this was desirable; and the winter session was thereafter closed with the month of March; the month of April was given to practical work; and the summer session commenced on the 1st of May.

In 1822 there were instituted two distinct *abgangs prufungen*, or exit examinations, at the close of the curriculum—a lower one, for *Revierforsters* or district foresters, and a higher one for those aspiring to higher offices in the forest service. It was optional with the students to which of these they would submit themselves; and subsequently it was left free to the students to choose at what time they would submit themselves for examination.

To the Director of the Forest Academy it was entrusted to see that the teachers discharged their duties, to direct the general course of study in the Academy, to carry out, in concert with the other teachers, the discipline of the school, and so far as possible, personally to conduct the studies in forest science. In the absence of this official any of the teachers might be elected to discharge these functions.

The teachers were appointed by the Royal Privy College of Finance, and were of two grades—the ordinary academic teacher, with the designation professor, and assistant teachers.

The former met once a month under the presidency of the Director, and with the assistance of the *Forstmeister*, or master forester of the Tharand Forest Circuit, for the consideration of all that might relate to the good of the institution; and decisions were adopted in accordance with the majority of votes.

Subsequently a special uniform, indicative of connection with the forest service was appointed for all connected with the Forest Academy.

As means of education there were assigned to the

ROYAL SAXONY FOREST ACADEMY.

Academy all the Forest Circuit of Grettenburg, and more especially the Tharand forest, with at that time in all 9872 acres of forest land, and the pine woods in five *Reviers* or districts, and the partially completed arboretum or forest botanic garden, with allowance for its maintenance, and provision for the purchase of necessary books, collections illustrative of natural history, implements, machinery, and apparatus, a physical and a chemical laboratory, a valuable geological museum, and a museum of woods and seeds. And from time to time additions were made to the buildings.

The attention given to the combination of practical training with scientific instruction was maintained; and the former had more time allotted to it.

I have before me a copy of the time-table or *Lehrstunden* for 1816 and 1817. In this, in accordance with the usage in Germany, is laid down the arrangement of classes meeting at the different hours of the day, but it is interesting now, chiefly as supplying, along with subsequently issued tables, authorative prescriptions indicative of the gradations by which the existing system of study reached its present development. Successive extensions of the course of study continued to be made in the course of the fifteen years following.

In 1821 Professor Kruzsch made a suggestion that the object of this academy should be so extended as to embrace the study of rural economy. And seven years later he submitted to the Royal Privy College of Finance a scheme of instruction by which students could attend together classes in which were studied subjects required by both, and other classes for the subjects peculiar to each. He afterwards showed that such a combination of schools had been carried into practical effect both in the Kingdom of Bavaria and the Grand Duchy of Meiningen, and the measure was carried out by the appointment of Dr Schweitzer to a chair of rural economy, and the establishment of a garden of economic botany, a library of rural economy, and a collection of models of agricultural implements, and other machines pertaining to rural economy. Subsequently, through the advice of the body of instructors, and of the Economical Society of Dresden, arrangements were completed for the erection of a combined Academy of Forestry and School of Rural Economy, and the foundation-stone of the extended buildings was laid by His Royal Highness Prince John, afterwards King of Saxony, accompanied by high officers of State, on the 25th June, 1829. The united colleges were opened on the 10th May, 1830; and the plan of the buildings was successively extended in 1846, in 1852, and in 1862.

About the year 1830 the arrangements of the Academy were extended to provide for the study of rural economy as well as of forestry being pursued in the institution; and on the 10th April, 1830, there was issued a *Lehrplan* or scheme of study, which continued to be followed for some sixteen years from that date.

This combination subsisted for forty years, but not without changes. For sixteen years the two schools were distinct; but in 1846 they were interfused, and constituted a combined School of Forestry and Rural Economy. But in 1870 the combination was terminated, and the Academy became again one for the study of forestry alone, and such it has continued ever since.

In the *Lehrplan* issued in 1830 the object of the School of Forestry was defined to be to train qualified forest economists, and more especially skilful forest masters and district foresters, for the Royal service; and the object of the School of Rural Economy to be to supply to young men devoting themselves to rural economy, or desiring to study rural economy as an auxiliary science, and to obtain sound practical knowledge of this, an opportunity of acquiring sound knowledge of the science required in the attainment of this.

In connection with the Forest Academy, two courses of study were now arranged—one extending over two years, the other one which could be passed through in one year. The latter supplied the instruction deemed necessary for a district forester in the Royal service; the former, the higher instruction required by *forst-meisters;* while a course of three years' study was prescribed for those who aspired to superior positions in the forest service. According to a report of the institution, dated 4th November, 1839, the details were somewhat modified, but the principles were maintained, and the same may be alleged of other modifications which followed.

Several other changes affecting the age, position, &c., of the student, the staff of teachers, the direction of the studies, and the discipline of the school, were introduced. Important among these was the establishment of a Chair of Agricultural Chemistry, with a laboratory and provision for the study of chemistry, theoretical and practical, in all its applications to vegetation; and provision for the study of Veterinary Science, of Botany, Zoology, Entomology, and Natural History. The buildings were extended, and the educational appliances were increased.

In the middle of the century there were organised in Saxony several so called *Real-schulen,* in regard to which additional information will afterwards be given; here let it suffice to state that in these elementary instruction in physical science, as well as other branches of common school instruction, was given, and these *Real-schulen* were made available for increasing the efficiency of the School of Forestry by the provision made in them for the preparatory training of students. The two combined schools were again placed under different directors. Other changes in the internal arrangements were made affecting both the course of study and the discipline of the school. Increased attention was given to practical instruction in forestry; and with the establishment of these changes, was completed the first half-century of the operations of the School of Forestry in Tharand.

Modifications of the powers of the College Court of

discipline were made from time to time. Changes in the staff of teachers occurred through deaths and removals; and improvements, or what were designed to be such, were effected in the arboretum and other educational appliances of the institution; and from 1830 to 1845 the efficiency of the Academy steadily increased. From 1846 to 1857 was a time of civil commotion, and the institution suffered in consequence; but there were also changes made in the Plans of Instruction. According to one issued on 5th February, 1846, it was arranged that, instead of taking the form of two united schools, it should take the form of one combined School of Forestry and Rural Economy, with a curriculum of study embracing two years, after passing through which aspirants for superior appointments in the service were required to spend a third year at the University.

The studies prescribed were these: of *Grundwisenscaften*, or foundation sciences, there were studied in class during the first year of the Course—Simple and applied arithmetic and algebra, for 4 hours a-week in summer; plane geometry and elementary mensuration, for 4 hours a-week in winter; physics, 4 hours in summer; chemistry, 4 hours in winter, with 1 hours *repititorum*;* geognosy, 2 hours in summer; mineralogy, 4 hours in winter; general botany, 4 hours in summer; vegetable physiology, 4 hours in summer; zoology, and special natural history of animals interesting to forestal and rural economy, 3 hours a-week in winter.

In the second year of the Course—Trigonometry and higher mensuration, 4 hours a week in summer; cubic mensuration and forest mathematics, 3 hours in winter; earth, soils, atmosphere, and climatology, 4 hours in summer; forest botany, 2 hours in summer; agricultural botany, 2 hours in summer; *Repititorum* of natural history,

---

* The *Repititorum* is an examination; but in so far as it has come under my attention it seems designed not to test the attainments of the students, but their defects; and this not for the humiliation of the student, but to show the teacher wherein his teaching has been deficient, either in itself or in view of the capabilities and attainments of different students.

and especially of botany, 2 hours in winter; entomology, 3 hours in winter; political economy, 5 hours during two months in winter.

Hauptwissenschaften or Special Sciences of Forestry in the first year of the Course—Foundations of forest science, 3 hours a-week in summer; forest defence, 1 hour in winter; the chase, 2 hours in winter; agriculture, 5 hours in summer; pastoral husbandry, 4 hours in winter.

In the second year of the Course—Sylviculture, 4 hours in summer; forest exploitation, or profitable utilisation, and forest technology, 3 hours in summer; forest taxation, or estimation of produce and probable proceeds, 4 hours in summer; forest history and literature, 2 hours in winter; State forestry, 2 hours in winter; forestal *Repititorum*, 4 hours in summer and 2 in winter; professional rural economy, 5 hours during three months in winter; practical rural economy, 3 hours in summer.

Hilfswissenschaften or Accessary Sciences during the first year of the Course—Bookkeeping and correspondence 2 hours in winter.

In the second year of the Course—Technology of rural economy, 1 hour in summer; veterinary surgery, &c., 3 hours in summer and 3 in winter; rural constructions and building, 2 hours in summer; legislation and jurisdiction relative to forest and rural economy, 2 hours in summer and 3 in winter.

Besides these studies in the class-room, there are given the following practical instructions:—Land Surveying, or practice in mensuration, two afternoons in summer; excursions for field studies in Natural History, 4 afternoons in summer; forest management one day weekly in summer and winter; exercises in shooting in summer, and in the chase in winter; demonstrations of rural economy on Saturdays. Practical instruction in garden and forest agriculture every year in the Botanic Garden in the months of April and October.

Changes or alterations in the plan of instruction thus prescribed could only be made with the permission of the Royal Ministry of Finance. With regard to the students, there was now a distinction drawn between those who entered with a view to attend the whole course of instruction given in the Academy, regular students of the Academy, designated in the corresponding language of the country as *Intanér*, Esoterics; and those who did not enter themselves as full students were called *Extraner*, a designation corresponding to *exoterics:* designations which have given origin to corresponding designations in Schools of Forestry in other lands. And along with this division of the students, there were introduced some changes in the conditions of admission to the Academy. Of every applicant, it was required that he should be at least 17 years of age, and have spent at least a year in practical work, pertaining to forestry or rural economy, and produce evidence of his possessing the preparedness necessary to his understanding the lessons to be given. The certificates required were those of birth and domicile, and of good character from the authorities of the place in which he had last resided, and of the school which he had last attended; and if not independent, a certificate from his father or guardian, attested by the local authorities, that he had their permission to attend the Academy.

Saxon subjects, moreover, who wished to fit themselves for the forest service of the country, and more especially for the charge of a forest circuit, were required, as they had been from the year 1849 onward, to show by submitting to examination, or by certificate from a national school, that they had attained the measure of scientific training required for entrance on the highest class of a gymnasium or *Real-schule* or other educational institution of the same standing; and also to establish by certificate, attested by the *Oberforstmeister* of the district, that they had acquired the required practical preparation by an apprenticeship of at least one year in the forests. Such Saxon subjects, moreover, as desired to fit themselves for the higher departments of the forest service of the state, were required to produce from a national gymnasium a certificate of fitness for entering a University, and besides this, submit, if it should be desired, to an examination in mathematical science; and produce a certificate from the highest forest official in the district that he had for one year (or better for two years) been acquiring the requisite practical knowledge in a Royal Saxon *Forst-revier* or circuit, by personally engaging in the work.

All other students who, though they did not enter the forest service of the State, desired to go through the complete course of the Academy, and to receive on leaving, an exit certificate, were required to prove, by presentation of the necessary certificates from either Saxon or foreign schools, or by submitting to the corresponding examinations, that they possessed the required knowledge. But *extraner* were only required to show generally that they were qualified for attendance with profit on the lectures of the Academy.

With regard to other matters, the commencement of the summer session remained the entrance time for Saxons who desired to devote themselves to forestry, and go through the entire course with a view to subsequently entering the Royal State service of Saxons. Whilst *extraner* and students of rural economy, and with them those foresters who did not intend to enter the Royal State Service, might also enter at the commencement of the winter session. Some few unimportant changes were also made in regard to matters of discipline; but those arrangements which were finally adopted, and are now in force, seem alone deserving of special notice.

In anticipation of a jubilee festival to be held on 17th June, 1866, in commemoration of the opening of the School of Forestry at Tharand, by Cotta, fifty years before; and as part of the preparations for the due celebration of the event, there were prepared a number of documents which were published as a 'Year Book' specially designed for that year—the year of jubilee.

In the frontispiece is given a plate of the Royal Saxon Academy for Forest and Rural Economy at Tharand, and in the first part of the volume is given a historical sketch of the Academy, divided into five marked periods, with an appendix containing a list of all the directors, professors, and other instructors who had served in the Academy; a second appendix contains the names of all the students who had attended the Academy, with their nationalities and time of attendance; and a third appendix supplies additional information tabulated to show the age of the several students at entrance, and several other details, but these relate more to the forest economy of Saxony, as developed by the studies pursued at Tharand, than to the development of the school itself, to which alone attention is being directed here.

These carefully prepared statistics of attendants and attendance during the first fifty years of the existence of the School of Forestry, supply all the information which could be desired in regard to the country, age, attainments, &c., of the student. But it may suffice here to state that, besides students belonging to the kingdom of Saxony, there were students from thirty-three other countries, including, I may say, every country in Europe, five students from America, and one from Britain.

The historical sketch is by Hofrath Dr Schober, Director of the Rural Economy Department of the Academy, and Professor of Rural Economy; and the historical divisions supply detailed information in regard to:

  I. The founding of the Academy and work previously done by Cotta in Zillbach;

 II. The work of the school from 1816, when founded, to 1829, during which period it was exclusively a School of Forestry, but had then an Agricultural School, of School of Rural Economy, established in the same building;

III. This from 1830 to 1845, when the School of Forestry was combined with the School of Rural Economy;
IV. From 1846 to 1851, a period of war and commotion;
V. From 1852 to 1866, from the celebration of the 40th anniversary of Cotta's commencement of his work at Tharand, to the 50th anniversary and jubilee of the opening of the Forest Academy in Tharand as a State institution.

In the second part of this 'Year Book' for 1866 are given, with reference to a map, geognostic and climatic descriptions of the region around Tharand within a distance of three hours' excursion on foot—on the east to Dresden, and on the west to the extreme limit of the Tharand forest towards Freiburg; specifications of the altitudes of all the springs, streams, rivers, hills, and notable places in the district above the Zero of the Elbepegel or float measuring the flow of the Elbe at Dresden, and its level above that of the German Ocean; a list of plants growing wild in the district, nearly 1000 in number, and of arborescent shrubs and trees in the Botanic Garden of the institution upwards of 500 in number; an account of the distribution, physiognomy, and flowering season of the vegetation of the district, with arrangements of excursions in the vicinity and to greater distances, and notices of the new plants likely to be seen within the different hours spent on these different excursions.

In the third part are given several memoirs or reports which may be seen to relate rather to the forest economy of the country than to the history of the Academy, but which are intimately connected with this supplying manifestations of the great development effected in forest science and forest economy in the course of the previous half-century by the teachers and the taught in connection with the school.

The first is a report by Oberforstrath Dr J. F. Judeich, the Director of the Academy, and first teacher of

Forstwissenschaft, embracing—1. Finance ; 2. The normal method of exploitation and its results ; 3. The advanced and perfected method, the *Fachwerkesmethode*, devised by Cotta, and matured by Hartig.

The second is a report by Professor Roch, second teacher of *Forstwissenschaften*. On the development of sylviculture in Saxony, from the establishment of the Academy in Tharand in 1816—in which are reported in succession the earlier neglect of sylviculture and the reasons of this; the culture of the birch, the fir, the larch, and the beech; the earlier methods of renovation of forests; and the methods of culture adopted since 1816 in regard to sowing and in regard to planting.

The third is entitled 'A retrospect of the forestal and chemical physiological researches' undertaken in the laboratory of the Academy as an encouragement to the founding of forestal experimentation by Hofrath Professor Dr. A. Stoeckhardt. In this are decussed—1. Varieties of mountains, and the action of the weather upon them ; 2. Varieties of soil ; 3. Chemico-physiological researches; 4. Forestal technical investigations. The fourth is entitled 'The forest-borer of the newest construction for ascertaining increase of growth'; its importance and practical use for technical forest researches, taxation, administration, and exploration, by Hofrath Professor Pressler, in which are discussed—1. The advantage and necessity of fundamental and special observations of increase of growth ; 2. The instrument in question, and the use of it, which the writer feels himself called on to recommend; and 3. Contributions made to the theory of technical calculations of increase, and observations of increase, with valuable appendices.

An incident connected with the jubilee in anticipation, of which these documents had been prepared, I may not pass without notice. In accordance with the usages of the nation, and the devout religious feelings under which the work had been begun and carried on, the jubilee falling upon a Sabbath, the Sabbath was appropriated to the solemnity. It is a peaceful valley in which the Academy is situated; but there on that holy day, at the very hour at which they had hoped that the students of the past and the present, and the patrons and friends of the institution, would proceed in procession from the Church of God to the Festal Hall, the van of the Prussian army entered the vale!

Throughout the previous century (the eighteenth), French students of forestry were steadily advancing to the discovery and device made by Hartig and Cotta.

But war, civil war, and foreign wars, to which that gave rise, compelled them to abandon their peaceful studies at the very time when a new era of forest economy was about to begin. And now, when after fifty years peace, their fellow-students of forest science in Germany were preparing to hold a jubilee in connection with their peaceful triumphs, they must give place to the requirements of war, and make way for the march of the warrior host!

The details which I have given of the history of the School of Forestry may be uninteresting to the general reader; but I consider them not unimportant as indications of the growth and development of the institution from which the students of such establishments may learn much in addition to what may be learned from the study of a School of Forestry, created perfect in all its parts, as was Minerva, armed *cap à pie*, produced from the head of Jupiter. More recent details have not been given, because for the full appreciation of these, some knowledge of the circumstances which gave rise to the changes would have have been necessary, and information in regard to these might have proved distasteful to some who otherwise may become interested in the subject. But I shall indicate immediately where additional information may be obtained, if it be desired.

Thus far the narration may be considered the history of

the origin and development through childhood and youth to manhood of the first National School of Forestry. The subsequent changes were not unimportant, but like the changes which pass upon man from early manhood to the full maturity of middle life, they are less marked than are some of those occurring in man, and in the earlier development of the school, within the same number of years in early life. In 1870 the School of Agriculture, or Rural Economy, engrafted upon it in 1830, was, after forty years of companionship, separated from it, and it was constituted again a School of Forestry alone. In a letter which I received in the summer of 1883 from the honoured Director of the School, Oberforstrath Dr Judeich, he mentions that in 1870 the agricultural department was removed; and by an order of 14th December, 1871, a new programme, or general plan of instruction, was introduced, in accordance with which the students were required only to spend half a-year in preparatory practice, and two and a-half years in class studies in Tharand. As preliminaries to admission they were required to produce a *Maturitä*, or exit certificate, from a gymnasium or a *Real-schule* of the first class.

In the scheme of instruction referred to by Dr Judeich, which was sanctioned by the Minister of Finance on the 14th December, 1871,* it is declared :—

(1.) That the design of the institution is to supply to foresters a comprehensive instruction in forest science, and the other sciences upon which this is based, or which are otherwise connected with it, so as to qualify them for the efficient discharge of their duties, and to promote the advancement of that science.

(2.) That for the time being the staff of teachers consists of the director, who is also teacher of forest science; a second teacher of forest science, who is also manager of the Tharand forest division; three teachers of physical

---

* Re-issued substantially the same in 1872, and again, with slight modification in 1879.

sciences; two teachers of mathematics, and teacher of rural economy and general economics, and of law and jurisprudence; and a manager of the arboretum, who is also instructor in fruit culture; and, as need may require, an adequate number of assistants.

(3.) The duties of the Director are to exercise—

1. The control of the studies in accordance with the the prescribed plan;

2. The control of the museums and educational apparatus, for which in subordination to him the several teachers are responsible in so far as they are severally concerned.

3. The immediate tenure of the property and inventories.

4. The payment of all accounts due from the funds of the Academy.

5. The calling of conferences of the college of teachers, and to preside and conduct these.

(4.) The ordinary teachers, under the presidency of the the director, constitute the College teachers.

The duties of this college, in the deliberations of which the official agent in what relates to discipline, has a seat and vote, embraces—

1. The examination of applications for admittance to the course of study followed at the Academy, and decision on the same.

2. Deliberation and decision in cases of discipline.

3. Deliberation and confirmation of the special *Lehrplan* or scheme of study for the session.

4. The approval and granting of applications for bursaries.

5. Deliberation and filling up of proposals to the Minister of Finance relative to the filling up of vacant situations of teachers, ordinary or extraordinary, and also of assistants.

6. All matters of importance which the Director declines on any ground to decide by himself, or which may be expressly assigned to the college by the Minister of Finance.

As a rule, meetings are held once a month; but special meetings may be called at any time by the Director.

On proposal by the college, *privat-decanten*, tutors, or lecturers on special subjects, may be appointed by the Minister of Finance.

(5) To the College of Teachers, under the presidency of the Director, is entrusted the examination of certificates submitted by applicants for admission as students, and decision on the same. The trial and decision of cases of discipline, the consideration and decision of the *Lehrplan* or scheme and distribution of studies throughout the day, the session, and the curriculum of study, the sanction and allocation of money grants to students in aid of their education at the Academy, the consideration and decision of proposals to be submitted to the Minister of Finance relative to stipends to teachers and assistants, and in general, the consideration and decision of all matters which the Director may decline to decide on his own responsibility, or which the Minister of Finance may expressely assign to them for consideration.

(6.) The College of Teachers meet monthly, and at such other times as may be necessary, and summoned by the director.

(7.) *Privat docenten*, or tutors, may, by appointment of the Minister of Finance, be entrusted with specified duties.

(8.) The curriculum extends over two and a-half years, and embraces the following studies:—

I.—FUNDAMENTAL SCIENCES.

1. Physical Sciences—including (*a*) Chemistry, Agricultural Chemistry, Practical Chemistry; (*b*) Mineralogy—Geognosy, with a special reference to the study of soils; (*c*) Botany, Structure and Physiology of Plants, and special Forest Botany; (*d*) Zoology, with a special reference to important animals injurious, or the contrary, to forest economy, embracing more particularly forest Entomology; (*e*) Physics and Natural Philosophy; (*f*) Meteorology.

2. Mathematics—(*a*) Cursory revisal of Arithmetic and Geometry, with a special treatment of sections in each which may be of importance to the forester ; (*b*) Analytical Geometry; (*c*) Differential and Integral Calculus ; (*d*) Mensuration, including the drawing of plans.
3. Mechanics and Machinery.
4. Architecture, Hydraulic Engineering, and Road-making.
5. General Economics.

II.—PROFESSIONAL SCIENCES.

1. History and Literature of Forestry. 2. Forest Culture, and Forest Conservation. 3. Forest Mathematics, measurement of standing trees and of felled timber, cubic increase of wood by annual growth, Forest financial reckoning. 4. Forest Economy and Forest Technology. 5. Forest Partition in accordance with the requirements of Scientific Forestry. 6. Forest Management and Administration, with a special reference to these as carried out in Saxony. 7. Forest Police. 8. Game Laws.

III.—ACCESSARY OR COMPLEMENTARY SCIENCES.

1. Science of Finance. 2. Law and Jurisprudence. 3. Rural Economy.
4. Meadow Culture.
5. Fruit Culture.

The lectures are illustrated, when necessary, by practical exercises and demonstrations.

(9.) Amongst provisions for aiding in instruction are :—

1. The *Tharand Forest Revier*, or district, placed under the inspection of the director, and managed under the direction of the second teacher of forest science. 2. A Botanic Garden. 3. A Library. 4. Museums illustrative of Physical Science, Mathematics, and Forest and Rural Economy.
5. A Chemical Laboratory.

(10.) For forest excursions, which can be accomplished in one or in two days, and which are made weekly in summer, facilities are afforded by *Revieren* or forest divisions of the forest of Tharand beyond that connected with the Academy, and by the Dresden *Haide* or heath, and many other State forests and private woods easily reached by railway. And annually, at the close of the summer session, in the month of August, there is undertaken, under the guidance of one of the teachers, an excursion extending over ten days or a fortnight, which is not confined within the limits of Saxony.

(11.) The curriculum is begun annually on the 15th of October.

(12.) The holidays are Easter week, Christmas week, three full weeks in March, between the close of the winter session and the commencement of the summer session, and from the middle of August till the middle of October, the close of the summer and the commencement of the winter session.

(13.) The Academy is open both to the subjects of Saxony and others. Saxons desirous of entering the forest service of the State are required to submit—

1. A certificate of having completed the course of study at a Saxon gymnasium, or a corresponding certificate from some corresponding *Real-schule*.

2. A certificate that he has passed through a preparatory training for six months in some specified *Revier* or circuit of the State forests.

3. An extract register of birth.

4. If under age, a document from his father or guardian giving consent to his studying at the Academy.

Of others there are required only a passport or corresponding document; and if the applicant be under age a notarial certificate from a German Consul that he believes the applicant has the consent of his father or of his guardian to study at the Academy.

In the case of aspirants for employment in the forest service, it is further considered desirable that they should give evidence that they have attained theorectical and practical instruction sufficient to enable them understand the prelections.

(14.) The entrant promises to obey the laws of the Academy, with a copy of which he is supplied. When his name is entered on the roll he receives a ticket certifying the same, for which he pays 5 *Thalers*.

In doubtful cases, the consent of the Minister of Finance is necessary to admission.

(15.) Subjects of Saxony pay 25 *Thalers* each half-year, and others 37 *Thalers* 15 *Groschen* for instruction, irrespective of the number of classes they attend. Students entering when half the session has passed pay only half fees; and students who are not preparing for the forest service of the State pay each session for the use of the chemical laboratory apparatus and re-agents:—

If used 4 hours per week, . 3 *Thalers*.
" 8 " . 5 "
" 16 " . 10 "
" 24 " . 15 "

(16.) Students desirous of employment in the forest service of the State submit to the following examinations:—

1. At the close of the first years' studies a written, and, at the option of the several teachers, also an oral examination on all the subjects which have engaged their study, except the higher mathematics; and any who do not obtain on the average at least the mark 2, or *Satisfactory*, cannot pass into the second division of the curriculum.

2. At the close of the curriculum a written and an oral examination on all the subjects studied in the third, fourth, and fifth sessions of the course, with the exception of the higher mathematics, meadow culture, and rural economy; and no one is passed who does not obtain the average mark 2, or *Satisfactory*, or who receives for the chief forest sciences—forest partitioning, forest culture,

forest economy, and forest mathematics—the mark *Unsatisfactory*.

3. Exceptional cases may be committed to single teachers to examine on specified subjects.

4. At both of the examinations students may voluntarily offer themselves for examinations on the subjects, the examination on which is not obligatory—the higher mathematics, meadow culture, and rural economy.

With students who have not determined to seek employment in the forest service of the State it is optional to submit to examination in any, or all, or none of the subjects of study.

(17.) The marks assigned as the result of examination of these—

Unsatisfactory, . . .	0
Scarcely satisfactory, . .	1
Satisfactory, . . .	2
Good, ...	3
Very good, . . .	4
Distinguished, . . .	5

And there is entered the average yielded by the marks obtained in the whole of the examinations; but this is only granted when examinations on all the prescribed subjects has been undergone.

The conduct marks are these—

1. Reprehensible.
2. Nothing very culpable.
3. Irreproachable.

Students not submitting to examination may obtain certificates of the time they attended, the classes in which they studied, and of their conduct; and if they submit to examination on one or more subjects, certificates of their appearance in these are given.

(18.) Candidates for the State service failing in one or other of the examinations, may present themselves for examination a second time. But with a second failure they lose all title to such employment.

(19.) For promising candidates of limited means there are provided six whole and six half free scholarships—holders of the first paying no fees, holders of the second paying half fees; and a fund has been created from which a certain number, distinguished for their zeal, progress, and good behaviour may obtain an allowance of from 10 to 50 thalers towards their personal expenses. All applications in both cases are submitted to the Minister of Finance.

Deserving students of limited means, who have a long journey to make at the close of each session, may have granted to them, by decision of the teachers, from 60 to 100 thalers for travelling expenses. And there have been founded scholarships obtainable in accordance with prescribed conditions.

(20.) Students are required to conform to the rules of the Academy. Each must be in his place at latest within ten minutes after the hour of lecture. If later, the case is reported to the Director. The provided means of study must be used in accordance with the regulations, and all injuries must be made good. Everything whereby the laws or ordinances of the direction, the amenity of the place, the public safety, order, and peace, may be compromised, respect towards officials, superiors, or teachers, impaired, or private persons injured, must be avoided.

(21.) The punishment to which transgressors are liable are these—

(*a*) Reproof according to sentence, with or without report to the officers of justice, or to the college of teachers, in presence or in absence of the other students, with or without report to parents or friends.

(*b*) Forfeiture of money grants.

(*c*) Imprisonment.

(*d*) Warning, with threatening of expulsion from the Academy.

(*e*) Expulsion.

Two or more of the punishments may be combined; and expulsion is always to be reported to the relatives.

There is issued at the commencement of each session a *Lehrplan*, or scheme of study, specifying how the lecture hours of each day are occupied. The following are translations of copies of those with which I was supplied:—

LEHRPLAN OF THE ROYAL SAXON FOREST ACADEMY AT THARAND,
Summer Session, 1877.

Hours of the day.	MONDAY.		TUESDAY.		WEDNESDAY.	
	Course 1. 2nd Session.	Course 2. 4th Session.	Course 1. 2nd Session.	Course 2. 4th Session.	Course 1. 2nd Session.	Course 2. 4th Session.
7–8	Differential Calculus.	General Economics.	Geognosy.	Forest Protection.		Forest Exploitation.
8–9			Anatomy & Physiology of Plants.	Special Forest Mathematics.		Agricultural Chemistry.
9–10	Geognosy.	Sylviculture.	General Mathematics. Part 2.	Forest Botany.	Exercises in Mensuration.	Forest Botany.
10–11		Forest Exploitation.	Mensuration.	Forest Exploitation.		
11–12		Meadow Culture				
2–3		Roadmaking.	Plan and Architectural Drawing.	Exercises in computing Produce and Products of Forests.		Exercises in Mensuration
3–4	Geognosical and Mineralogical Excursions.	Practical Zoology.				
4–5						
5–6						

LEHRPLAN OF THE ROYAL SAXON FOREST ACADEMY AT THARAND—(Continued.)
SUMMER SESSION, 1877.

Hours of the day.	THURSDAY.		FRIDAY.		SATURDAY.		REMARKS.
	Course 1. 2nd Session.	Course 2. 4th Session.	Course 1. 2nd Session.	Course 2. 4th Session.	Course 1. 2nd Session.	Course 2. 4th Session.	
7—8	Zoology of Vertebrates.	Forest Protection.	Zoology of Vertebrates.				
8—9	Anatomy and Philology of Plants.	Special Forest Mathematics.	Geognosy.	Agricultural Chemistry.	Excursions and Practical Exercises.		
9—10	General Mathematics. Part 2.	Agricultural Chemistry.					
10—11	Practical Study of Physiology of Plants.	Forest Exploitation.		Forest Botany.			The Library is open on Tuesdays and Fridays from 10 to 12 o'clock.
11—12							In Summer, on Tuesdays, as well as Fridays, the Chemical Laboratory is open, and at the disposal of Students for practice.
2—3	Botanical Excursions.		Practice in Chemistry.				
3—4							The Summer Session begins on 9th April, and closes in the middle of August.
4—5							
5—6							The Winter Session begins on the 15th August.

LEHRPLAN OF THE ROYAL SAXON FOREST ACADEMY AT THARAND.
WINTER SESSION, 1877-78.

Hours of the day.	MONDAY.			TUESDAY.		
	Course 1. 1st Session.	Course 2. 3rd Session.	5th Session.	Course 1. 1st Session	Course 2. 3rd Session.	5th Session.
8—9		General Economics			Sylviculture.	Forest Administration.
9—10		Mensuration. Part 2.	Encyclopædia of Rural Economy.	General Zoology.	Special Forest Mathematics.	Meteorology.
10—11	Mineralogy.	Integrate-Calculus		Botany.	Mechanics and Machinery.	
11—12			Laying out of Forests.	Physics.	Entomology.	
2—3		Entomology.		Plan Drawing.		
3—4			Jurisprudence.	Plan Drawing.		Jurisprudence.
4—5	General Mathematics. Part 1.					*Repititorium of Forest Mathematics

*Repititorium, it has been intimated on foot-note (ante p. 22), differs from a revisal or examination in thus:—Revisal does not necessarily imply examination. Examination is generally employed to test the attention given by the student. Repititorium is an examination to test the intelligibility of the lectures by the impressions received by the students.

LEHRPLAN OF THE ROYAL SAXON FOREST ACADEMY AT THARAND—(*Continued.*)

WINTER SESSION, 1877-78.

Hours of the day.	WEDNESDAY.					THURSDAY.			
	Course 1.	Course 2.				Course 1.	Course 2.		
	1st Session.	3rd Session.	5th Session.			1st Session.	3rd Session.	5th Session.	
8–9		History of Literature and Forest Science.				Chemistry.	Sylviculture.	Forest Police.	
9–10	General Zoology.	Special Forest Mathematics.	Forest Police.			Botany.	Special Forest Mathematics.	Meteorology.	
10–11	Botany.	Mechanics and Machinery.	Meteorology.			Zoology.	Practical Chemistry.	Laying out of Forests.	
11–12	Mineralogy.	Mensuration. Part 2.							
2–3		Entomology.	Jurisprudence.			Plan Drawing.			
3–4	General Mathematics. Part 1.							Jurisprudence.	
4–5								Forest Mathematics *Repititorum*.	

LEHRPLAN OF THE ROYAL SAXON FOREST ACADEMY AT THARAND—*(Continued.)*

WINTER HALF-YEAR, 1877-78

Hours of the day.	FRIDAY.				SATURDAY.		
	Course 1.	Course 2.			Course 1.	Course 2.	
	1st Session.	3rd Session.	5th Session.		1st Session.	3rd Session.	5th Session.
8–9	Chemistry.	Sylviculture.			The Chase.	General Economics.	
9–10		History and Literature of Forest Science.	Forest Administration.		Physics.		
10–11	General Mathematics. Part 1.	Practical Chemistry.	Laying out of Forests.			Practical Vegetable Physiology.	
11–12		Integrate-Calculus.					
2–3		Practice of Chemistry.					
3–4						Practical Chemistry.	
4–5							Encyclopædia of Rural Economy.

In the *Lehrplan* there is given also, under each subject of lecture, the name of the lecturer.

In the communication received from Dr Judeich, already referred to, he mentioned that in 1869 there was founded, through the enterprise of Professor Nobbe, an Agricultural and General Physiological Experiment Station.

Of the attendance of students, subsequently to the Jubilee, he gives the following returns :—

Year.	Summer Session.				Winter Session.			
	Students of Forestry.		Students of Rural Economy.	Total.	Students of Forestry.		Students of Rural Economy.	Total.
	Saxons.	Foreigners			Saxons	Foreigners		
1866	55	20	17	92	56	19	13	88
1867	65	24	12	101	64	23	14	101
1868	52	24	11	87	49	25	12	86
1869	29	18	8	55	26	26	6	58

After this, the Rural Economy Department having been withdrawn, there were only students of forestry in atttendance.

Year.	Summer Session.			Winter Session.		
	Saxons.	Foreigners	Total.	Saxons.	Foreigners.	Total.
1870	20	23	43	19	30	49
1871	28	26	54	26	29	55
1872	32	28	60	36	25	61
1873	17	18	35	23	30	53
1874	20	32	52	29	34	63
1875	20	26	46	30	45	75
1876	23	37	60	33	51	84
1877	27	34	61	34	59	93
1878	26	51	77	38	72	110
1879	25	53	78	46	75	121
1880	33	58	91	46	80	126
1881	37	50	87	57	69	126
1882	41	55	96	66	64	130

The occasion of my visit to Tharand was my attendance at a Congress of German foresters, professors of forest science, and administrators of forests, held in the neighbouring capital, Dresden, in the autumn of 1881. I had been made acquainted years before with the history of the Academy. I found Tharand all that I had been led to picture it to myself; and I shall not soon forget the intercourse I enjoyed with the Director and his colleagues, which intercourse was all too short to satisfy the cravings which it gratified. I found Tharand, as I had read it described by another :

'Tharand is beautifully situated at the junction of three valleys, from two of which flow streams which unite and flow through the Planenschegrund into the Elbe. The neighbourhood abounds with pretty romantic walks. From the ruins of the old castle, the remains of a hunting seat of the ancestors of the Royal Family of Saxony, which may be reached in ten minutes from the inn, you look down from a promontory of rock on which it is perched into a deep and picturesque valley on either side.

'The Forest Garden is a nursery forest containing, it is said, 1000 different species of trees and shrubs attached to the Forest School. From this a fine view may be obtained, and there are pretty walks in it. The same may be said of the Heilige Hall, an avenue of beech trees.'

In the history of the Academy at Tharand, published on the occasion of the Jubilee, it is stated in the conclusion of the account given of the fourth period of the history :—

'On the 17th of June, 1851, forty years after the removal of Cotta's private institute from Zillbach to Tharand, the unveiling of the bust of the late Privy-Oberforstrath Cotta in the Botanic Garden was solemnised. On the same day the bust of him by A. Reum was, in a becoming manner, erected and consecrated in the centre of his creation, and in a place where he often taught—in front of the so-called *Rundetheile*, or circus, in the Garden.'

The first-mentioned bust was presented by the Cabinet Minister Count von Einsiedel; the latter was erected at the instance and expense of several admirers of the distinguished man.

On the summit of the tree-clad hill, which forms a background to the Academy, stands the monument in question, surrounded by a wide circle of noble trees planted as saplings on that occasion by admiring grateful disciples, as a tribute to the honoured founder of the Academy. Thither the members of the Congress were conducted, many of us knowing not why or whither, and many a quip and jest, and hilarous laugh, seasoned our reasonings by the way; but as we drew near, and realised the scene, every voice was hushed, even the footfall was made in silence profound, and collecting in the sacred enclosure, while more than one was apparently engaged in silent worship, fancy seemed to hear once more the voice, heard by the beloved disciple of our Lord in Patmos: 'And I heard a voice from heaven saying unto me, write: Blessed are the dead which die in the Lord from henceforth; Yea, saith the Spirit, that they may rest from their labours; and their works do follow them.'

CHAPTER II.

THE ROYAL FOREST ACADEMY AT NEWSTADT-EBERSWALDE.

The route which I followed in going to the Congress of German foresters and others held in Dresden in 1881, my attendance at which gave me an opportunity of visiting the Royal Saxon Forest Academy at Tharand, led me through Berlin, and I availed myself of the opportunity to visit the Royal Prussian Forest Academy at Neustadt-Eberswalde. It was one of the first of the schools of Germany established after that of Tharand. It is situated on the Finow, a stream which is here connected by a canal, with the Oder on one side and with the Havel on the other. It is passed by the railway connecting Stettin with Berlin.

The following is a translation of a historical sketch of the parent school, supplied some years ago by Dr Dankelmann, the director of the institution :—

'As early as the close of the eighteenth century there were, now and then, at the University of Berlin (if there happened to be qualified persons), lectures given on the science of forests, without, however, establishing a permanent professorship for this object, or imposing conditions upon candidates for the public forest service for the completion of their studies in forest science. It was then deemed sufficient to be conversant with the keeping of accounts, mathematics, and the science of natural history, thus entirely leaving technical education to be acquired by practice. The number, however, of qualified employées, thoroughly and systematically educated with regard to technical knowledge, growing, in consequence of this system, constantly less and less, it was deemed proper to establish, in 1821, an Academy for forest instruction at Berlin.

'Dr Friedrich Wilhelm Leopold Pfeil, then Oberforstrath, was intrusted with the superintendence of this institution, which, although organically not connected, entered into such association with the university as to employ the professors and means of instruction belonging to the latter, for teaching the fundamental and accessary sciences, while the lectures on the principal studies were given by technical instructors. This organisation, however, soon proved inadequate. On the one hand the much-extended study of the fundamental accessary sciences produced an injurious effect upon the principal studies, and, on the other, there being no suitable forests in the immediate neighbourhood of Berlin, the theoretical lectures could not be explained, nor supplemented with practical illustrations. The more distant, but unfrequent excursions and forest journeys, could not efficiently remedy this inconvenience, and they proved insufficient to secure a close connection between the theoretic study and the living instruction of the forest.

'On the superintendent's advice, based upon these considerations, and strongly supported by the intercession of Wilhelm and Alexander von Humboldt, the Academy was, in 1830, removed to Neustadt-Eberswalde, and named the High Institution for Forest Science. In the immediate neighbourhood of this place there are two large forest districts which offer the students in high degree a fine opportunity for becoming familiar with their various features. Dr Pfeil continued to act as superintendent, and, at the same time, he was intrusted with the administration of the said districts. In addition to Pfeil, who taught the science of forestry proper, there were appointed two other professors, one for the whole department of natural sciences, and the other for both mathematics and geodesy. In 1830 a chair was established for Prussian jurisprudence, with particular reference to forest matters, and, in 1851, a second teacher of forest science was appointed.* Pfeil remained in his position as superintendent till autumn, 1856, when he was succeeded by Oberforstmeister Grunert. On the latter's resuming his former position in the administration of public forests, the direction of the institution was conferred upon Dr Dankelmann, the present incumbent. Since 1866 very important changes have taken place in the organisation of the Academy, with a large increase in the number of instructors. At present there are officiating at the Academy, besides the Director, who occupies the first chair for forest science, two more teachers of this science, a teacher of mathematics, physics, mechanics, and meteorology; one of chemistry, mineralogy, and geognosy; one of botany, one of zoology, and one of jurisprudence; and, in addition, a royal chief forest officer, as assistant teacher of roads, geodesy, and plan-drawing; and also a chemist as assistant teacher of geology.'

The regulations for the Royal Forest Academy at Newstadt-Eberswalde, and that at Münden in Hanover, at present in force, were issued by the Minister of Finance under date of 5th April, 1875. In accordance with these :—

The schools are under the control of the Minister of Finance. The Oberland Forstmeister is curator of both. The staff of teachers in each is composed of a Director, appointed by the King, who is instructor in forest science, a second professor of forest science, a teacher of mathematics, a teacher of natural science, and a teacher of law, in its relation to forests and to game; and permission to any one to act as college tutor (*Privatdocent*) in a Forest Academy may be given with the sanction of the Minister of Finance.

The arrangements in each of these Academies for the study of every department of forest science is complete, but part of an autumn vacation may be spent by the

* Notwithstanding this, those who were destined for the superior functions of inspection and conversation had, besides their two years and a-half at the school, to follow a course of some years at the university.—(*See Revue des Eaux et Forêts*, May, 1876.)

students at one in the practical forest operations carried on in connection with the other.

The course of study extends over two and a-half years, and embraces fundamental science, special science, and accessary science.

Under the head of Fundamental Science are included—

1. Physics, Meteorology, and Mechanics. 2. Chemistry, inorganic and organic. 3. Mineralogy. 4. Land Surveying and Geology. 5. Botany, including the structure, physiology, and pathology of plants; special forest botany and microscope demonstrations. 6. Zoology, including special zoology, with a reference to forest economy and to game, and especially to forest insects. 7. Mathematics, including arithmetic, plane and cubic mensuration and trigonometry, elements of analytical geometry, elements of the higher analysis, land surveying and chart drawing. 8. Political Economy, with a special reference to forests.

The special technical sciences in which instruction is given are these—

1. History and literature of forests. 2. Local or national doctrines of forests. 3. Exploitation of forests. 4. Forest protection. 5. Forest products and forest technology. 6. Forest taxation, mensuration of wood, forest mensuration, and all of those with special reference to Prussian usage 7. Valuation of forests and forest statics. 8. Forest statistics and forest management, with a special reference to the classifying of forests in Prussia. 9. Forest rights, usages, and servitudes.

The Accessary Sciences are—

1. Law, in theory and practice; Prussian law, civil and criminal, and civil and criminal processes. 2. Forest-road making. 3. Game laws and the chase.

The study of fundamental and of accessary science is strictly limited to what may be necessary to a scientific practice of forest economy, but it embraces all that is required for this. The means of instruction are—

1. The Royal forest districts of Biesenthal and Liepe, a *Secherie* near Newstadt-Eberswalde, and those at Gabrenberg

and at Cattenbuhl, near Münden. 2. Seed-kiln at Newstadt-Eberswalde. 3. Botanic Garden, and Arboretum illustrative of Forest Economy. 4. Chemical laboratories; and cabinets of collections illustrative of. 5. Natural Philosophy; 6. Land surveying; 7. Forestry and the chase. 8. A Library.

The course of study extending over two years and a-half, is commenced with the summer session; but students who have no intention of entering the forest service of Prussia may enter either then or at the beginning of the winter session. The summer session extends from Easter till the 20th of August; the winter session from the 15th of October till fourteen days before Easter. The arrangements for lectures during each session is submitted to the Minister of State some weeks previous to the commencement of the session; and it is published for general information.

There are required of applicants for admission certificates:—1. Of having passed with credit through a German Gymnasium, or Prussian High School of the first class; 2. Of not exceeding twenty-four years of age; 3. Of a fitness for a forest life; 4. Of blameless moral character; 5. Of adequate means of support while at the Academy; 6. Of having passed a university examination, or other equivalent examination, in land measuring; and of having spent a seven months preparation in forest work.

Students from the Huntsman's Corps (*Fieldjagerkorps*) required to attend the Academy are required only to produce the certificate No. 3, and to submit to the Director certificates corresponding to Nos. 1 and 6; and of students who do not intend to enter the forest service of Prussia there are required only the certificates Nos 4, 5, and 6.

Forest students and forest candidates, who have completed their curriculum, are permitted, without charge, to go on the excursions, and to avail themselves of the collections, &c., belonging to the Academy as means of instruction, so far as practicable, on authority obtained from the Director; and also to attend particular lectures, &c., as *Hospitanten*—but the Director is authorised to require of such, if he think proper, a fee of 9 marks for every class attended; and others, who have studied $2\frac{1}{2}$ years in a foreign School of Forestry may be admitted to the same privileges as *Hospitanten* on payment of 10 marks to the general fund as a fee for entrance ticket or matriculation.

The entrance fee to either of the Academies is 15 marks, and for transference from the one to the other 10 marks; and the fees for each session are 75 marks. But members of the *Feldjagerkorps*, and of the *Jagerbataillone*, or State-huntsman, required to attend the Academy, and others holding *Ladenberg bursaries*, are exempted from payment of these fees.

Appropriate means of maintaining discipline are prescribed; and regulations are laid down in regard to students leaving the Academy; and bye-laws have been added under the same authority regulating the use to be made of the various educational collections, &c., belonging to the Academy.

Previous to the promulgation of these regulations in 1875 there were in force corresponding regulations promulgated under date of 1st March, 1868. These were then superseded; and under date of 30th June, 1874, there were issued prescriptions for the training and testing of officers employed in the Royal Forest Service of Prussia; but this subject is not one which comes under consideration here, which is solely the educational arrangements in the Forest Academies, by which in part that training was provided for. There is, however, one point on which a word of explanation may be necessary.

According to an Order of the Minister of Finance of 6th April, 1871, and to sec. 1 of the prescriptions referred to—As an examination in land-measuring is required to precede that in regard to practical forestry, admission to that examination must be preceeded by two years occupation with land measurement and levelling, and these two years, in the case of students at the Forest Academy, intending to enter the forest service is, along with seven months attendance at the Academy, to reckon as one year in the two and a-half years embraced by the curriculum.

In accordance with the practice generally adopted by Schools of Forestry in Germany there is issued before the commencement of each session a programme of the studies to be pursued, for the information of any who may have under consideration the expediency of seeking admission, as well as of those who have already entered on the curriculum. The following is a translation of that issued for the winter session 1882-83, at which there were in attendance about 50 Prussian students, besides foreigners.

First section of the course of study, designed for students of the first year who had entered the school at Easter 1882.

I. FOREST ECONOMY.

Culture of Woods.—Five hours a-week : and so with the others. Wood-Cutting.—One hour a - week. Forest excursions.

II. NATURAL SCIENCES.

Meteorology and Climatology.—One hour. Inorganic Chemistry.—Three hours. Organic Chemistry.—One hour. Mineralogy.—One hour. Chemistry applied to Technology.—One hour.

General Botany, Anatomy, and Vegetable Physiology.—Four hours. Structural Demonstrations by aid of the Microscope.—Two hours. Zoology.—Invertebrate Animals. Five hours.

III. MATHEMATICAL SCIENCES.

Repetitions and Exercises in Mathematics.—One hour. Geodesy.—One hour. Political Economy and Jurisprudence, and Civil and Criminal Law.—Two hours.

Second section of the course designed for students of the second year who had entered the school at Easter 1881.

I. FOREST ECONOMY.

Redemption of Servitudes.—Two hours. Exploitation of Woods and Technology.—Three hours. *Rentabilitaets-lehre*, or estate and area, and theory of the greatest return as an investment.—Two hours. History of Sylviculture—Two hours. Cubic Measurement of Woods. —One hour. Road Making, and Establishment of Network of Forest Paths for the bringing out of Wood.—Two hours. Examination on Forest Economy.—One hour.

Forest excursions, with exercises in practice, consisting of management of a regular timber forest; management of a forest by Jardinage; and redemption of servitudes burdening a large forest of woodland.

II. NATURAL SCIENCES.

*Repititorum** of Chemistry, of Mineralogy, and Geodesy. One hour. Practical operations in the application of Chemistry to the analysis of soils.—Two hours. *Repititorum* of Botany.—Two hours. *Repititorum* of Zoology.—One hour.

III. MATHEMATICS.

Elements of the Higher Analysis.—Two hours. Elements of Analytic Geometry.—One hour. Political Economy and Jurisprudence. Commercial Management of Forests.—Two hours. Civil and Criminal Law.—Two hours a-week.

The following is a translation of the Unterrichts-plan or programme of study for the complete curriculum of two years and a-half. It is one of an earlier date, extending from Easter 1870, to autumn, 1873. These are issued annually, but they are essentially the same.

---

* *Repititorum*, as I have already intimated, is a term applied to class examinations, designed less to demonstrate the height of attainments made by the students than their defects; and this less with a desire to expose the deficiency of the student than that of the instruction given, that the teacher may know what he should say more or say differently than what he has said.

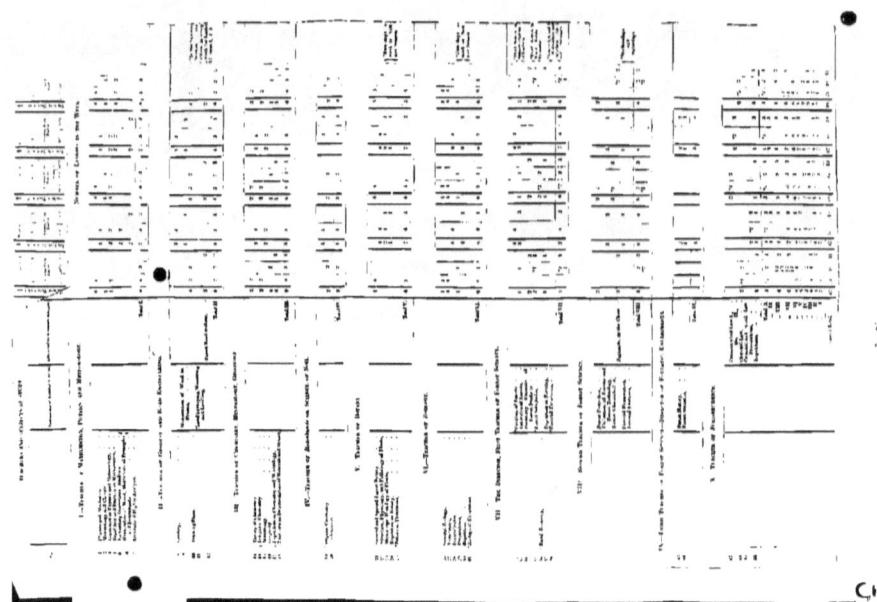

ACADEMY AT NEWSTADT-EBERSWALDE.

The following summary of the instruction given is embodied in a Report upon Forestry prepared under the direction of the Commissioner of Agriculture of the United States Government for 1877 by Dr Franklin B. Hough.

'As it may afford some interest in mentioning the number of hours assigned during the five term-times to the different lectures we give the following table:—

Fundamental Sciences.		Principal Sciences.		Secondary Sciences.	
Objects of instruction.	Whole number of hours.	Objects of instruction.	Whole number of hours.	Objects of instruction.	Whole number of hours.
NATURAL SCIENCES.		Cultivation of forests..........	80	JURISPRUDENCE.	
General and theoretic chemistry	32	Forest implements...........	20	Civil law..........	72
Special inorganic and organic chemistry applied..........	80	Geograph forest botany......	48	Criminal law..........	32
Physics and meteorology......	80	Protection of forests.........	32	Civil criminal law suits and constitutional rights..........	40
Mineralogy and geognosy......	60	Forest usufruct and technology	80	Jurisprudence	36
Definition of minerals and rocks		Forest surveying...........	20	Total..........	180
Reviews for inorganic natural sciences	20	Appraising forests..........	80	Construction of roads......	32
Botany in general, and forest botany in particular..........	16	Calculation of the value of forests and forest statistics..........	32	Hunting..........	32
	64				

NUMBER OF HOURS GIVEN TO THE DIFFERENT LECTURES—Continued.

Fundamental Sciences.		Principal Sciences.		Secondary Sciences.	
Objects of instruction.	Whole number of hours.	Objects of instruction.	Whole number of hours.	Objects of instruction.	Whole number of hours.
Anatomy of plants, vegetable physiology and pathology	60	Administration of forest and hunting	48	Shooting exercises, two hours each	96
Microscopy	20	Redemption of rights of usage	32		
Botanical reviews	20	Forest history	40	Total sum of hours for secondary sciences	340
Botanical excursions, each two and a-half hours	80	Forest statistics	20		
General zoology	16	Review of various forest matters	56		
Vertebrates	80	Examinations	40	Grand Total	2,648
Invertebrates, with special reference to forest insects	80	Forest excursions, each four hours	352	Percentage of fundamental sciences	50
Zoological preparations	16			Percentage of principal sciences	37
Zoological reviews	20			Percentage of secondary sciences	13
Zoological excursions, each three hours	96	Total	980		
Total natural sciences	840				

ACADEMY AT NEWSTADT-EBERSWALDE.

NUMBER OF HOURS GIVEN TO THE DIFFERENT LECTURES—*Continued.*

Fundamental Sciences.		Principal Sciences.		Secondary Sciences.	
Objects of instruction.	Whole number of hours.	Objects of instruction.	Whole number of hours.	Objects of instruction.	Whole number of hours.
MATHEMATICS.				Average per instruction week (21 in winter, 17 during summer): $\frac{2648}{93} = 28.5$ hours, or per day, 4.9 hours.	
Geodesy	72				
Interest and rent account	20				
Wood-measuring	20				
Mathematical reviews and exercises	56				
Surveying and leveling exercises, each four hours	192				
Plan-drawing exercises, two and a half hours	80				
Total mathematics,	440				
ECONOMICAL SCIENCES.					
Public economy and finances	48				
Total sum of hours for fundamental sciences.	1,328				

It may be interesting to learn through what phases the course of instruction has passed from the origin of this school to 1875. They have been as follows:—

Number of hours devoted to instruction.

Programme of subjects.	1834–36.		1844–46.		1860–62.		Course of two years and a half. 1873–75.	
	Hours.	Per cent.	Hours.	Per cent.	Hours.	Per cent.	Hours.	Per cent.
Inorganic natural history	188	6	168	6	220	8	288	11
Botany	396	18	354	14	348	12	244	9
Zoology	326	15	332	18	332	11	308	12
Total natural history	910	39	854	38	900	31	840	32
Mathematical sciences	406	19	618	24	598	26	440	17
Economical sciences	54	2	36	1	36	1	48	1
Total for the fundamental sciences	1,370	60	1,508	63	1,634	58	1,328	50
Law, forest economy	814	38	904	30	992	35	980	37
Law	...	...	152	6	172	6	180	7
Forest construction	...	...	...	...	...	...	32	1
Hunting	40	2	40	1	40	1	32	1
Exercise with gun	...	...	...	...	...	...	96	4
Total for accessary instruction	40	2	192	7	212	7	340	13
General total	2,224	100	2,604	100	2,838	100	2,648	100
Time of teaching per day	4.8	...	4.8	...	6.2	...	4.8	...

' A fact is developed by this table, which is noticed in many other institutions, that the two years' course had become crowded by the unavoidable development of new studies, so that before the enlargement to five semesters, the recitations and exercises occupied 6.2 hours each day, besides the time given to study. This requirement was too much, and could not fail, if continued, to bring lassitude and inattention. The course of law was introduced in 1844, and that of forest constructions in 1873. Professor Mathieu, of Nancy (from whose article in the *Revue des Eaux et Forets*, 1874, p. 155, the above table is derived), remarks concerning the more recent addition of studies as follows :—

'" We would specify among other subjects recently added to the programme of studies at Newstadt-Eberswalde, microscopic examinations of vegetable tissues, and a general knowledge of the lower organisations, which, from their parasitic habits, are a determinate cause of a great number of maladies in plants and animals, and which are likewise agents in fermentation. Furthermore, we might specify the elements of organic chemistry, which are indispensable to an understanding of the laws of vegetable physiology; some ideas of forest statistics, one of the principal and most urgent of the desiderata of every well-ordered administration; a glance at the history of forests, and of the various phases through which the sciences relating to it have passed; and, finally, the elements of meteorology, which, by setting the forest agents to the pursuing of observations of this kind, will lead us to a certain knowledge of the influence still so controverted, as to the influence of the forests upon the climate of a country, and upon the delivery and maintenance of the sources of supply of the water which fertilizes it. All these new ideas are doubtless useful, and may, without difficulty, be included in our course of forest instruction."

'Since 1872 the principal station for experiments relating to forest matters in Prussia, on which there is conferred, at the same time, the management of the transactions of the Association for German Experimental Stations relating to forest matters, is connected with the Academy at Newstadt-Eberswalde in this way, that the latter's superintendent is also the director of the principal station, and that, under his direction, the instructors of the Academy are elaborating the different divisions of the experimental work, viz., the forest technical, the chemical, physical, the meteorological, the zoological observations, and also what relates to physiology of plants.

'This opens, on one hand, a large field of scientific researches to the teachers, putting at their disposal new teaching matter, and gives, on the other hand, to students the opportunity of studying how to prepare the scientific solution of interesting and important problems, and of taking their own share in the respective elaborations.

' The results of active instruction at this Academy during the forty-six years of its existence are highly satisfactory. Almost all the Prussian employées near the administration of public forests—without, however, counting those from the provinces added to Prussia in 1866, and who entered into Prussian service—owe their perfection in forest science to this Academy. Besides a considerable number of private forest officers and forest proprietors of the country have here acquired the necessary skill in administering their own forests or those committed to their charge. Finally, many foreigners have applied themselves at this Academy to the study of forest science. The following table, showing the annual number of students from 1830 to 1876, may be of service in judging of the Academy's operation :—

ATTENDANCE AT THE FOREST ACADEMY OF NEWSTADT-EBERSWALDE.

Years	Semesters.		Years	Semesters.		Years	Semesters.		Years	Semesters.	
	Summer	Winter		Summer	Winter		Summer	Winter		Summer	Winter
1830	39	36	1842	37	42	1854	84	84	1866	66	45
1831	30	29	1843	51	48	1855	83	76	1867	72	79
1832	23	23	1844	51	47	1856	62	65	1868	93	63
1833	28	21	1845	52	63	1857	57	64	1869	64	67
1834	36	30	1846	66	65	1858	72	67	1870	66	(a)
1835	36	29	1847	71	72	1859	68	54	1871	62	66
1836	36	32	1848	68	81	1860	44	51	1872	61	63
1837	33	32	1849	78	83	1861	53	55	1873	57	52
1838	40	41	1850	84	86	1862	47	38	1874	68	45
1839	45	40	1851	80	85	1863	33	32	1875	68	50
1840	40	34	1852	81	80	1864	36	42	1876	66	50
1841	40	45	1853	84	84	1865	57	59	Average	57	54

(a) Closed on account of war,

It is stated from information a few years ago that there were not less than 33 barons or baronets who held appointments in the Crown Forests of Prussia.

The following details of the requirements for employment and promotion in the forest service in Prussia are given in the *Bestimmungen über Ausbildung und Prüfung für den Königlichen Staatsforstverwaltungsdienst*: Requirements for the education and examination of officials in the Prussian State Forest Service. The applicant to be received into the forest service must satisfy the following conditions issued by the Minister of Financ eon 30th June, 1874, with some verbal changes subsequently odered:—

1. 'He must have obtained a diploma of completed study in a gymnasium of the German Empire or in a *Real-schule*. 2. Be not above twenty-two years of age. 3. Have no bodily infirmity which would unfit him for the forest service. 4. Be of good conduct. 5. Give proof of possessing sufficient means to meet the expense of preparation for the work.

'This preparation commences with practical work done in the forest, under the direction of an *Oberforster*, during at least seven months, generally from October to April.

'The design of these preliminary exercises is to make the aspirant acquainted with the work of exploitation, and with the principal kinds of trees, to make him practically acquainted with sylviculture, with the surveillance of woods, and the police of the chase, and at the same time with land surveying, all of which are things which lie at the foundation of his subsequent theoretical studies.

'To be appointed *Forstbeflissener*, or forest-aspirant, an application must be made to the inspector, or to the conservator, of the administrative circuit; this application must be transmitted by the *Oberforster* to whom the pupil desires to be attached.

'The papers to be supplied are five in number. 1. The diploma of study from a gymnasium or *Real-schule* of the first class. 2. Certificate of birth or baptism. 3. A medical certificate. 4. If the aspirant do not pass directly from the gymnasium to the service, a certificate of good conduct from the time of his leaving the gymnasium. 5.

An engagement by the father or guardian of the aspirant to provide for the maintenance of him during at least seven years.

'Further, the *Oberforster* must supply special information, in regard to the family and person of the aspirant; and then if there be nothing to hinder the aspirant being accepted, he receives his appointment from the inspector or the conservator. These have a right reserved to appoint the aspirant to another *Oberforster* than the one he has chosen, and even to remove him during the time of his preparation, after having referred the matter to the Minister of Agriculture, Domains, and Forests.

'If the aspirant on trial prove not quite satisfactory in the triple point of view, physical, intellectual, and moral, the *Oberforster* addresses a report to the inspector and to the conservator, who judge whether the aspirant should continue his studies; in case of a difference of opinion between them the minister decides.

'This stage passed, the *Oberforster* delivers to the candidate a certificate testifying to the time spent in this stage, and to the work done. This certificate confers on the aspirant the title of forest pupil. To continue his studies the forest pupil should follow for at least two years and a-half the course of study of a School of Forestry, or of a Forest Institute annexed to a university; those who may desire to follow that pursued in another school than those of Eberswalde and Münden should previously assure themselves from the office of the minister that the time spent by them at this school shall be reckoned equivalent to the studies prescribed by the regulations; and further they are required to study all the subjects comprised in the programmes of these said schools.

'These forestal studies completed, and, at latest within six years after the commencement of the preparation, the pupil addresses to the minister an application to be admitted to the examinations, and attaches to this the following papers :—1. A *curriculum vitae*, or history of his previous course of life, entirely in his own handwriting.

2. The diploma of study in a gymnasium or *Real-schule*.
3. The certificate of being a forest pupil. 4. The certificate of his having attended a School of Forestry or a University in the course of his studies 5. A certificate that the pupil has taken the required part in works of land surveying, and the preparation of charts, at the School of Forestry or at the University. 6. A chart prepared by the hand of the candidate, of some Royal forest of at least 500 hectares, on the scale of 1 to 5000, and this chart must be accompanied with an attestation that the work has been done entirely by the pupil.

'The design of the examination is to make it be seen that the pupil possesses the general instruction required, and that he has made with success the technical studies prescribed; and to determine further that the pupil is fit to continue his studies.

'The knowledge required at this examination are these:—

' A.—In Special sciences.

' Exploitation, management, and estimation of woods, technology, protection of the State forests, and forestal history and bibliography.

' B.—In Auxiliary sciences.

' 1. Mathematics. Elementary principles of statics and mathematics. 2. Natural History.—Principles of the classification of animals, plants, and minerals. A. Zoology.—Divisions of the animal kingdom; mammalia, birds and insects looked at from a forestal point of view; entomological nomenclature, structure and habits of insects in general, and special study of those which are useless or hurtful to forests. B. Botany.—Classification, description, physiology, and structure of plants, and special knowledge of those which are useful from a forestal point of view. C. Mineralogy.—General notions of geognosy and geology; general idea of the formation and the upheaval of mountains; influence of the subsoil on vegetation, and special study of the minerals and rocks useful to the forester. D. Physics and Chemistry.—

General properties of bodies; views entertained in regard to light, heat, magnetism, and electricity; carbonisation, resin, and tannin.

'3. Legislation and Jurisprudence.—History of Prussian law; notions of civil and criminal law as applied to forests.

'The examination takes place in general once a year, in September or October, before a commission appointed by the Minister of Agriculture, Domains, and Forests. This examination is held, one part indoors, and another part in the forests; if it prove satisfactory, the forest pupil receives the title of Forest Referendary.

'In case of failure he is allowed to recommence his trials, in whole or in part.

'To continue his preparation, the forest referendary should devote himself to personal studies in the forest, and, moreover, take an active part in all forest works, in order that he may acquire, under an *Oberforster*, all practical knowledge relating to forest economy and forest administration. In the first instance, he is free to choose the circuit in which he wishes to prosecute his studies; but the Minister reserves the right to send him officially to any specified circuit.

'The *Oberforster*, near to whom the forest referendary is sent, is his immediate superior, and the referendary should take for his guidance in the service the instructions issued to forest overseers. The duration of this stage imposed on a forest referendary is at least two years. He should pass eight successive months, which should always comprise the interval between December and April, in discharging the duties of a forest guard in the same circuit, and in a particular part of the circuit. This part is chosen by the *Oberforster* according to the indications made by the inspector, and the candidate should give himself entirely to all the works of the guards engaging in the surveillance, as well as in the exploitations, preparation of estimates, measurement of trees, sales, and the cultural operations going on.

'During these eight months he cannot be employed in the office of the *Oberforster*.

'The referendary ought then to visit different circuits: the design of these visits being to make him familiarly acquainted with all the kinds of trees growing in the forest, to give him explicit conceptions of different modes of exploitation and management, and in fine, to give him practice in all kinds of forest business by making him take part in all the operations of an *Oberforster*.

'During this stage the referendary is required to keep a journal. This journal ought to indicate the circuits in which he has had a charge, their situation, their soil, and the exploitations and works of culture in which he has had to take part, &c.

'It ought, moreover, to contain notices of remarkable facts which have struck the referendary, and the observations which have been suggested to him by the study of the forest, and by the works which he has had to do in the office of the *Oberforster*.

'The journal should be sent to the *Oberforster* on the first of every month, and submitted to the superior agent in the circuit, if such there be.

'In fine, when the referendary leaves the circuit, the *Oberforster* should indicate the date of his departure, and give testimonials of his conduct. If there be occasion for observations in regard to faults, to want of punctuality and obedience on the part of the referendary, or especially if he has shown a real incapacity for the work of forest service, the *Oberforster* is bound to make his report of his to the inspector and to the conservator.

'The Minister of Agriculture and Forests can exclude from the service any forest referendary who may have manifested gross misconduct or negligence, or any candidate whose progress may be considered unsatisfactory.

'Every *Oberforster* ought to send to the inspector, at latest on 5th January in each year, a statement of his opinion of the candidates who have passed in the course of the preceding year more than four weeks in the circuit. The inspector adds to this his own observations. When the candidate has discharged the duties of an overseer, the inspector should give the results of the examination which he has made of the district entrusted to the management of the referendary. These documents are sent by him to the General Directory before the 15th January; they are collated and compared with those furnished by the conservator, and are then sent to the Minister to form the file of papers relating to the candidate. When the referendary has completed his course, done all the prescribed works, and satisfied the requirements of the military service, he may address to the Minister an application to be allowed to pass the State examination; the time allowed for this is five years from the passing of the last examination.

'To this application are attached the following papers: 1. A *curriculum vitæ*. 2. The diploma of study at a gymnasium. 3. The diploma of forest pupil. 4. The certificate of diligence in the course of a School of Forestry. 5. The journal. 6. Lastly, for candidates who belong neither to the corps of *feldjäger*, nor to the batallions of chasseurs, a document attesting that they have satisfied the military service.

'When there is nothing to hinder authorisation being given, the person named is sent before a commission who inscribe it, and fix for him the date of his examination.

'This examination is conducted according to the instructions and regulations of the minister, partly indoors, and partly in the forest. The latter is by far the more important, as it determines whether the referendary has acquired practice and knowledge of administrative questions.

'The examination turns on all parts of forest science and of forest economy in their connection, on the application of special law and common law to forest matters, and on the police and administration of the chase.

'The referendary having been subjected to this examination, at once receives from the commission the title of

Forst-Assessor, and is inscribed on the roll of officials going through their course of training.

'If the referendary do not pass the examination with success the commission decides whether or not he shall recommence his trials in whole or in part after a delay of at least six months, but which must not exceed twenty-four months.

'The Forst-Assessor is employed in the royal administration so far as is practical until he receives his appointment, and he is bound to apply himself to the forest works which the minister may entrust to him.

'If the Forst-Assessor undertake the administration of communal forests, of public establishments, or even those of private persons, he ought to communicate this to the minister; and this undertaking is not in any way a reason for excluding him from the royal service; but it is clear that the years spent thus, are not to be reckoned to him as years spent in the service.

'And in case a Forst-Assessor after a certain lapse of time passed thus beyond the royal service, should refuse a work which the administration would give to him, he may, on the proposition of the minister, be removed from the roll of officials going through their course of training.

'Each Forst-Assessor is bound to make known, through the *Oberforster*, his presence to the inspector and to the conservator of the circuit in which he finds himself, and whether he belongs to the royal service, or he be administering private forests. Likewise on each change of residence he should make a similar communication to the same agents.

'In order to acquire a more extended instruction, and perfect themselves in the general practice of business, aspirants to the forest service should, beyond their technical studies, go through a course of law and of political economy at a University. The candidate is free to make choice as to the time at which to pursue these studies, as that which may best suit him while prosecuting his preparation; but it is preferable that he should take them up while he is a Forst-Assessor.

The Forest-Assessors who, besides the ordinary prescribed forest studies, give themselves for at least two half-year sessions to the studies of these political sciences, can, after having been attached for one year to a Directory of Finance, address to the Minister an application for permission to submit to an examination on the matters spoken of; which application should be accompanied by a certificate of his having followed a course of study at a University. This examination is conducted before the superior commission of forests, by the Minister-adjunct of the special examiners for legislation and political sciences. It turns on the applications of civil law in Prussia to the administration of forests, and principally on the administration of law and political economy. But this is no longer required absolutely.

The trials ought to show whether the candidate possesses the knowledge necessary to enable him to discharge in a satisfactory manner the duties and functions of a *Member of a Forest Directory*. The Forest-Assessors who pass this trial successfully receive from the Minister the title of *Oberforster*. The inspectors, or *Först-meisters*, are chosen from among the *Oberforsters*, who must have distinguished themselves in their service, and preferentially from amongst those who have passed the last mentioned examination.

Captain Campbell Walker, formerly deputy-inspector of forests at Madras, writes of a visit paid by him to Newstadt-Eberswalde :—

'I visited the Forest Academy at Newstadt-Eberswalde, and had a most interesting conversation with the Director, Herr Ober-forstmeister Danklemann, on various subjects connected with the forestry in Europe and India. He is assisted by a staff of seven professors, with assistants, and there is an Experimental Garden attached to the Academy, with Oberforster Berubard in charge of the strictly technical portion, and other gentlemen for the meteorological, zoological, and chemical sections. The number of students at the Academy averages 65. Oberforester Bernhard kindly accompanied me round the gardens, and pointed out everything of interest, including a building where the seed is dried and separated from the cones, known as a "*Sammendarre*," extensive seed beds of spruce and fir sown in parallel lines, with the help of boards specially adapted for the purpose, which insure regularity, and the seed being all the same depth; seed beds of willow, and treatment of the seedlings when transplanted; and examples of trees of every description for botanical study, including many of the rarer description for the more advanced students.

'Professor Dr Altum, the successor of the well-known entomologist Ratzeburg, author of a large work on insects destructive to trees and timber, accompanied me through the museum, which is rich in specimens of all sorts of birds, animals, and insects found in the forests, very neatly arranged in cases. Where the animal or insect does damage to trees, specimens of the branch, bark, leaf, root, or cone, in a healthy state, and after being attacked, are exhibited close to each, so that the student can see at a glance the nature of the damage, and connect it with the animal which causes it. Thus we have squirrels, rats, beavers, and mice, set up to represent nature, gnawing the barks, grubbing at the roots, &c., &c. Insects are shown in several stages of their existence, larvæ, chrysalis, caterpillar, moth, with their ramifications in the stem or branches of the tree. These, with specimen blocks of almost all descriptions of timber, form a most instructive and interesting collection, in which much time could be spent with advantage.

'Nothing struck me as more remarkable than the extent and varied nature of the studies required from the forest candidates or probationers in Prussia, and the number of years they are content to spend, first in studying, and then in waiting for an appointment. The would-be Oberforster, which is the lowest of what we would call the "gazetted appointments," must, after passing certain terms at a Government school of the first class, spend a year with an Oberforster in a revier, and then pass an examination as forest pupil, after which there is a two years' course at a Forest Academy, and an examination in scientific forestry, land surveying, &c., on passing which the pupil becomes a "*Forstkandidat;*" then another two years' practical study, during at least nine months of which he must actually perform the duties of a forester, after which comes the final Government examination, on passing which he enters the grade of Oberforster-kandidat. The difference betwixt the two examinations is explained to be that the first tests the candidate's knowledge of theoretical forestry and cognate sciences, whilst the latter tests his ability to apply what he has learnt, and capability for employment as Oberforster and in the higher grades.

'After passing the final examination, the Oberforster-kandidat is employed as an assistant in the academies and control offices, in making forest surveys and working plans, and sometimes acting in charge of a revier, receiving certain daily or weekly allowances whilst so employed. After five or six years of this probation, he may look forward to being permanently appointed.

'Thus we have at least five years spent in study, and another five years spent in probation; the former without any pay, and the latter only with meagre allowances whilst actually employed, before the would-be first officer is installed; and the time is generally much longer. Yet so great is the desire for Government service, and particularly forest service, in Prussia, and indeed in Germany generally, that there is no lack of competitors.'

The impression made on my mind was similar. I was struck with the completeness of the collections in the several museums. The Aboretum, or Forest Garden, is extensive, but it appeared to me that no use was being made of it, beyond what could be made of one much less extensive. The walks and drives seemed to minister greatly to the amenities of the town, which is much frequented in the summer months by families lodging there, but at other times resident in Berlin; and though utilised for the instruction of the students, this appeared to me to be done more because they were at command, than as necessary and requisite.

I made inquiry here, as I did also elsewhere, in regard to the design of giving instruction in rifle shooting, and in much beside relating to the chase; and the information I received in reply was similar to what I received elsewhere, which was substantially, that it was not without its use, which was explained; but that it was more as an accomplishment than as a necessary qualification for forest management that such instruction was given; and it had been observed that foresters who took an interest in hunting took more heartily to life in the forest, and felt less of the *ennui* and restlessness, and desire after city life, from which some others suffered.

There are connected with the Academy, besides the Forest of Eberswalde, three others, with a total area of 18,606 hectares, of which 17,148 are under wood. Of these of timber forest—

      447 are of Oak.
  2,272 Beech.
      217 Alder and Birch.
13,721 Pine.
       29 Fir.
      220 Plantations.

Of coppice wood their are 242 hectares.

The ground is of Tertiary formation, Diluvium, and Alluvium. The contour of two is hilly and almost mountainous.

The garden illustrative of forest botany is 190 hectares in extent.

The Experimental Garden, illustrative of different methods of annual plant culture, which, is 484 hectares in extent, with upon an average two millions and a half of plants;

and in Chorin, one of the forests, there is an Aboretum of 8 hectares.

Connected with the Academy is one of the most important meteorological observatories in Germany.

The museum was founded by Dr J. T. C. Ratzeburg, at that time Professor of Naturwissenschaft in the Academy, a distinguished entomologist, and author of a valuable work entitled, *Die Waldverderber und ihre Fiende, oder Beschreibung und Abbildung der Schaedlichtsten Forstinsecten und der uebrigen schaedlichen Waldtheire, &c.* It is rich in specimens of all sorts of quadrupeds, birds, and insects found in the forests, and when they are injurious to trees, there are specimens of branch, bark, leaf, root, and cone—both in a healthy state and in the injured condition, enabling students to see at once the effects, and the animal by which they were produced. Insects are shown in the several stages of their existence—larva, chrysalis, and moth—with the erosious produced by each on leaves, branches, stems, and bark of the trees infested by them.

From a report made by Dr J. A. Warden, a member of the Scientific Commission of the United States, to the International Exhibition at Vienna, in 1873, the Academy cost the State 12,500 thalers, or well nigh £2000 per annum.

There were issued by the Minister of Finance, under date of 5th April, 1875, a series of statutes for the regulation of students, and appended thereto regulations relative to their studies and regulations, relative to the use to be made of the library, museum, &c. Subsequently there was issued a programme of course of studies to be followed; and on 16th October, 1882, a supplementary notice in regard to the examinations, to which students were to be subjected on land surveying and mensuration. The latest regulations in regard to the preparation required for the forest service were issued in August, 1883.

The number of students at Eberswalde in the summer

session of 1885 was 140; and in the winter session 1885-86, 148, of whom in the former 46, and in the latter 47, were not studying with a view to entering the Prussian forest service.

The staff of teachers in actual service numbers 11, namely, along with the director, 10 professors or docenten, of whom 5, including 3 in charge of oberforsteries, and the director of technological experiments in the station for forestal experimental research, give instruction in forest science; one in chemistry, mineralogy, and geonosy; one in statics, one in botany, one in zoology, one in physics, and mathematics, and one in jurisprudence. All of whom are provided with the necessary assistants.

As forest districts for instruction and excursion, four oberforesteries of the Government circuit of Potsdam-bhiesenthal, Chorin, Eberswalde, and Freienwalde, are placed under the technical administration of the Director of the Academy.

CHAPTER III.

THE ROYAL FOREST ACADEMY AT MÜNDEN.

THE Royal Forest Academy at Münden in Hanover was inaugurated 27th April, 1868, under Dr Gustavus Heyer as Director, and was richly equipped by the Prussian Government when Hanover became connected with Prussia. Münden is situated at the confluence of the Werra and the Fulda, whose united waters here take the name of Weser, which is navigable from this point to the sea.

It is the site of an old castle or Schloss, built in 1566 by Duke Erith II., which was formerly a residence of the Guelphie ancestors of the Royal Family of England. It has now been used for a long time as a magazine. The scenery around the town is pleasing, and has been considered not unlike that of the vale of Llangollen in North Wales.

For some years British candidates for appointments in the forest service of India were allowed to pursue their preparatory studies here.

The educational arrangements, and the course of study and of training, are similar in all respects to those at the Forest Academy at Newstadt-Eberswalde in Prussia. In both they are in accordance with the regulations issued by the Minister of Finance, under date of 5th April, 1875, and 1st August, 1883; and the course of study is similar. Like that at Eberswalde, this is subject to the general sunpervision of the Minister of Finance.

By Dr N. J. C. Müller, Professor of Botany in the Academy, I was courteously supplied some years since with the following information:—It was first opened in 1868. The fees are 150 marks a-year. The course of study embraces five semesters, or half-yearly sessions, three summer and two winter sessions. Aspirants for employment under the forest service are admitted only at Easter, students from other Schools of Forestry at Easter, on the Monday after Easter week, and at Michaelmas (15th October).

Students must not be above twenty-five years of age, and must hold a certificate of having passed the final examination at a gymnasium or *Real schule* of the first rank; testimony in regard to the previous seven months having been spent in forest work; testimony to his good behaviour and to his means of livelihood while prosecuting his studies being provided.

Of the students in the Academy on 31st December, 1881, there were—

    Free students, . . . 5
    Paying half fees, . . . 7
    Paying whole fees, . . . 69
       In all paying students 76.

Of these there were—
Subjects whose parents were engaged in husbandry, 5
Do. engaged in other callings, . . . 71
Foreigners, ... 0

The number of those who had been educated there since the organisation of the Academy were—

    Subjects, ... 629
    Foreigners, . . . 23

The area of an Experimental Garden was 5 hectares; the grant from public funds, 57,440 marks.

The Director of the Academy gave instruction in forest science; besides whom there were five professors and assistants giving instruction in mathematics and land surveying, geology and mineralogy, chemistry and physics, forest exploitation and botany.

In the teaching of botany there were devoted four hours a week to the morphology, biology, and classification of plants; two hours a week to practice in the classification and the microscopic study of plants; and a course of demonstration and microscopic studies, occupying in all ten or twelve hours in the session. There were botanical excursions of half-a-day weekly. Three hours weekly in the winter session were spent in the study of the structure and physiology of plants. One hour weekly in microscopic demonstrations. And one hour weekly in winter in *Repititorum*, or examinations in botany.

The designation of the institute is 'The Royal Forest Academy.'

The attendance of students at the Academy from 1868 to 1876 had been:—

Years.	Summer semester.	Winter semester	Years.	Summer semester	Winter semester
1868	44	52	1874	113	86
1869	60	61	1875	106	61
1870	62	75	1876	78	
1871	64	78			
1872	81		Average	78	70
1873	83	74			

I enquired what reasons were assigned for the maintenance of two forest institutes in Prussia—one here and the other at Newstadt-Eberswalde. The reasons stated to me seemed to centre themselves chiefly into considerations of convenience; but amongst others it was stated that in the one district the forests were in a great measure forests situated on *Tiefebene*, or plains of but slight elevation above the sea level, and in the other district the forest are in a great measure forests situated on mountain ranges; and some advantage was gained by special studies, appropriate to each, commanding special attention in the different schools.

An important element to be taken into account in judging of the appropriateness of scholastic arrangements for the study of forestry with the view to entering the forest service of a State, is the number of men required for that service. The writer of an article on forest management in the *Edinburgh Review* [No. 290, p. 373] states that 'the staff for the administration of forests in Hanover consists of two branches, which may be described as preparatory and administrative. All preliminary arrangements on taking a piece of forest land into culture by the State are conducted by the *Einrichtungs-bureau* or survey office. This consists of a *Verstand* or superintendent, draughtsmen, and clerks, who are generally practical foresters; and a staff of surveyors and valuators, who are generally candidates for the office of *Oberforester*, the third grade in the system of permanent administration. The surveyor surveys the whole tract of forest, and delineates, with the aid of the valuator, the blocks or subdivisions into which it is to be divided for permanent culture. A detailed plan is drawn up for the future management, pointing out the mode in which the successive periods are to be worked off, the roads which it will become necessary to make for transport, and the usual details of the condition of the forest. This plan, together with a complete code of rules, is handed over for the guidance of the permanent forest officers.

'The permanent administration consists of one *Forst-director* and *Oberforst-meister*, who is also a counsellor; 20 *Forst-meisters*, in charge of circles or divisions, who form also a consultative council; 112 *Oberforsters* in charge of districts of about 17,000 acres each; 403 foresters; and 343 overseers and under-foresters, who watch the forests, and supervise the work executed by contract or by day labour. A cashier is attached to each over-forester, who receives and disburses all money in and from the forest cash chest, on the orders of the over-foresters. A perfect financial check is thus maintained under the control of the forest master. The duties of these officials are confined to superintendence. The over-foresters spend the greater part of their time in the forest supervising the actual operations. So regular and efficient is the entire system that the state of each block of the forest is generally found to be in accordance with the programme laid down on the original working plan.'

To make more clear what is referred to in the last sentence, it may be necessary to bring forward a statement, by which are preceded, the statements made:—
'The aim of scientific forestry in its present most advanced state, is to convert the irregular growth of woodland district into what is called a *Geschloss Bestand*, or compact forest, divided into district blocks of trees of equal age. The usual *Umtrieb*, or rotation for beech, and *Hochwald*, or high forest, in Hanover, is 120 years. The forest is so divided that there shall be as nearly as possible six equal areas allotted to as many periods of twenty years' growth. Thus, one block will be full of trees not exceeding twenty years old; a second, of trees from twenty to forty years old, and so on. When a block arrives at the last period felling commences by a *Vorbereitung*, or preliminary clearing, which is little more than the ordinary thinning carried on from time to time in former periods. The beech in these woods only ripens its seed every third or fourth year. After the first seed year in the final period, a *Lichtenschlag*, or clearing for light, takes place, in order to afford light for the germination of young seedlings; the finest trees being left standing. When the ground is well covered with seedlings the old trees are felled, and carefully removed; and the block recommences growth. The tendency to a gradual removal of the old trees appears to be on the increase, so as to make the culture approach as nearly as possible to the natural growth of a wild forest.'

The twelve provinces of Prussia, several of which represent kingdoms, are divided into thirty *Regierungsbezirken*; and to each of these is appointed an *Oberforstmeister* to represent the forest department in the council of the local *Regierung*, or administration; the *Forstmeisters* number 108, each in charge of a division, with an average area of 25,000 hectares; there are 706 *Oberforsters*, with charges averaging 3000 hectares in extent, to each of which is attached a *Forstrendant*, or collector of forest revenue, and there are 3,646 *Forsters*, or overseers, with ranges of from 500 to 1000 hectares, in the forest service of the country.

At the Academy the number of students in the summer session, 1885, was 57, and in the winter session, 1885-86, 41, of the former of whom there were 9, and of the latter 6, who were not Prussian subjects.

Of the staff of teachers, 11 in number, there were, besides the director, 10 professors : four for forest science, of whom three had the direction of oberforsteries; one for mathematics and physics, one for chemistry, mineralogy, and geonosy, one for statics, one for botany, one for zoology, one attending from the University of Goettingen for political economy and ficancial science, and likewise one for jurisprudence, all with the necessary assistants. The forest districts appropriated for instruction, and placed under the direction of the Director of the Academy were the oberforsteries of Cattenbühl (in the province of Hanover) and Gahrenberg of the Government circuit of Cassel.

CHAPTER IV.

THE GRAND DUCAL FOREST ACADEMY IN EISENACH.

MY return journey from Dresden, after my visit to Tharand, brought me through Leipsic, Gotha, and Eisenach.

At Eisenach, in the Grand Duchy of Saxe Weimar, there was established, in the first decade of the present century, a Forest Institute, or School of Forestry, which may claim to be considered the oldest existing institution of the kind in the world, though Tharand may justly claim to be considered the representative of the earlier school which was originated at Zillbach in 1795. Tharand only celebrated her own jubilee in 1866, while Eisenach, in the spring of 1880, celebrated, not her centenary indeed, but the close of the hundredth session of the institute.

In a memorial statement issued on the occasion by Dr Carl Frederick Augustus Grebe, the Director of the Institute, and Oberlandforstmeister of the Grand Duchy, it is stated:—

'The origin of the School of Forestry at Eisenach dates from the first decade of the present century. Heinrich Cotta had previously established, as is known, a Forest Academy in Zillbach in the year 1795, and maintained it till he was called to Saxony in the year 1810. G. Koenig sought to supply what was thus withdrawn from the arrangements for training young foresters for the work in which they were called to engage. He had laid the foundation of his knowledge of forest science under the guidance of Cotta at Zillbach, in the years 1794-1796, and subsequently qualified himself fully for the work, partly by acting as assistant forester—under, amongst others, Oetelt in Ilmenau,—and partly by taking part in the

Prussian arrangements for forest management. He was, in 1805, as forester, appointed an official of the forest administration of Ruhla; and here he commenced the work of tuition in forestry by receiving young foresters into his house as students in forestry. To these he gave practical instruction in all matters pertaining to the management of forests; and in the winter months he gave to them oral discourses on the more important branches of forest science; and not only natives of the Grand Duchy, but many foreigners were received thus into his house as students. This was the origin of the Forest Institute of Eisenach.

'A more formal character was given to this instruction in 1813. Koenig solicited, through his official superiors, permission to organise and establish in Ruhla a Theoretic and Practical Institute of Forest Science; this was readily granted by Duke Carl Augustus on the 11th January, 1813, along with the additional permission to arrange for this use the spacious forest lodge of Rhula; and on the same occasion, under date of 5th January, 1813, Keonig was appointed *Oberforster*.*

'In regard to the instruction given in the private School of Forestry opened by Koenig, detailed information is given in Koenig's first published work, *Anleitung zur Holtztaxation*, Gotha 1813.—Introduction to forest taxation, or estimate of the cubic measurement and probable annual production of wood in a forest. According to what is stated there, young candidates for employment in the forest service were gradually thoroughly instructed in everything relating to the management of forests and game. After this they were, in some special forest district, instructed in the practical application of what they had acquired. All which was so done as to prepare them

---

* A large granite block, erected as a memorial stone in the Gloeckler district of the Ruhla Forest, bears on its southern side as an inscription : *In dem Jahren, 1809-1812, von L. V. G.* (Louis Von Gross), *A. V. H.* (August Von Hopfgarten), *L. V. H.* (Ludwig Von Hopfgarten), *H. H.* (Heinrich Hopfmann), *F. H.* (Ferdiand Hagemann); and on the eastern side :—*1813. Wurde Hier Gepflanzt fuer 1871.* But it is alleged that this is misleading, as a private forest educational institute was organised and established by Koenig in 1808.

efficiently for the work to which they aspired. Within doors, and more especially in winter, from three to four hours daily were spent in theoretic instruction, with a view to the practical application which was to be made of this, the greatest importance being attached to mathematics. Information as to what was done from this time onward is not at command; but it is known that after the establishment of the Grand Ducal Forest Taxation Commission, in the year 1831 (with the direction of which Koenig was entrusted, he having been meanwhile, on 27th April, 1819, appointed Forstrath, or Forest Counsellor). theoretical instruction was given only in the winter half-year, and the students belonging to the Grand Duchy found their principal employment in surveying and making measurements, and in the preliminary work required for the taxation and management of the forests of the Grand Duchy.

'In the year 1819 the Grand Duke Carl Augustus entertained an idea of establishing, in the Grand Duchy, instead of this private School of Forestry of Koenig, an independent State School of Forestry. Koenig having been applied to to supply information in regard to what would be required, submitted a detailed plan for such an institution; but, for financial reasons apparently, the measure was not carried into effect. We must forego the satisfaction we might have promised ourselves from considering minutely the interesting proposals of Koenig, but we may remark that Koenig at that time, in regard to the question of a site for the projected State institution (for which Ruhla, Berka, Ilm, and Eisenach, had been named), pronounced decidedly in favour of Eisenach; and this he did without hesitation or qualification; before everything else he desired for candidates for the forest service a superior general preparatory instruction, and for forest officials an improved social position.

'Immediately on the accession to power of the late Grand Duke Carl Frederick, in January, 1828, he required of Forstrath Koenig to draw up a scheme of instruction appropriate for a Forest Institute in Eisenach; and there was submitted by him a detailed scheme of instruction on the 1st November following.'

Dr Grebe gives a detailed outline of the programme proposed by Koenig, and he goes on to remark:—' All that Koenig asked from the State, beyond the building, was an annual grant of 100 thalers, and that principally as a means of procuring such teaching appliances as books and instruments, and collections of natural objects. The scheme commanded high approval, expressed in a ministerial order of 4th July, 1829, which was issued with the following specifications:—

'1. The Forest Institute of Forstrath Koenig to be erected at Eisenach is, and continues to be, a State-supported private enterprise.

'2. The support afforded by the State shall consist: (*a*) In permission to make use for purposes of instruction in the Institute of the staff of instructors employed by the Forest taxation commission. (*b*) In granting a building suitable for the purposes of the institution, or the means of hiring such. (*c*) In an annual cash payment of 100 thalers. (*d*) The use as training forest of the Grand Ducal Forests of Eisenach, Wilhelmsthal, and Ruhla; and it is granted to Forstrath Koenig, in the interests of instruction, to have the control of the management of these forests. Attention shall also be given in the appointment of forest officials, especially in Eisenach, to select officials apt and qualified to teach. (*e*) The Forest Institute shall have the use of the botanical grounds, in the Karthausgarten, at Eisenach and Wilhelmsthal, for purposes of instruction in forest botany.

'3. Persons engaging in the forest and game services of the Grand Dukedom must have attended the Forest School at least one year; and can neither enter the Jäger corps nor otherwise be employed in the forest service, if they have not left the School of Forestry with a good certificate.

' At the same time there was required the preparation by Koenig of regulations relative to the preparation which should precede admission into the Grand Ducal Forest Service, more particularly in regard to the instruction of candidates, and more especially their instruction in forest science; regulations in regard to the admission of students to the School of Forestry, and their leaving it; and regulations in regard to the practical training of candidates for employment in the service.*

'On the basis of this arrangement, Koenig, after having procured a house of his own in Eisenach (Schmelzerstrasse No. 14), opened the Forest Institute at Easter 1830, in accordance with the approved programme submitted by him, and continued till his death, 22nd October, 1849, he having meanwhile been, on the 15th August, 1837, appointed Oberforstrath.'

During the winter session following his death, the direction of the Institute was entrusted to the oldest of the teachers, Sculrathjobst, and in Easter 1850, it was undertaken by Dr Grebe, the present director, who was recalled from Griefswald to undertake, along with the direction of the Grand Ducal Forest Taxation Commission, the direction of the *Forstlehranstalt*, which was at the same time transferred to the more spacious Grand Ducal building, Frauenberg.

Details of the educational arrangements and appliances of the Institute are given. The branches of forest science in which instruction was required to be given, in the most thorough manner and to the fullest extent, are these :—

1. Introduction to the study of forest science, with a glance at existing Schools of Forestry. 2. History of forests: a condensed survey of the chronological development of forest property, of forest economy, of forest science, and of forest literature. 3. Forest culture in the most comprehensive application of the term, with Stumpf's *Lehrbuch des Waldbaues* as a text book, but with extensive supple-

---

* The regulations submitted by Koenig were approved by the supreme authority, and published on the 16th February under the title *Vorschrift Wegen Bildung der Bewerber um Forstdienststellen im Grossherzogthum Sachsen-Weimar-Eisenach*, Proposals in regard to the education and training of candidates for the Forest Service in the Grand Duchy of Saxe-Weimar-Eisenach; and they continued to be acted on till the subsequent issue under date of 8th February, 1854, of the Order of which is now in force.

mentary information. 4. Forest protection and forest management, with *Koenig und Grebe's Waldschutz und Waldpflege* as a text book. 5. Forest exploitation, with *Koenig und Grebe's Forstbenutzung* as a text book. 6. Forest management and regulation of amount of produce to be withdrawn from the forest. (*a*) Preliminary work: Forest surveys and measurement; description of the site and condition of the wood; with statement of the cubical measurement of the existing wood, and of the probable annual production by growth. (*b*) Basis of management: Selection of kind of wood and of *regime* to be followed—that of coppice wood, timber forest, or combination of the two; determination of duration of cycle of operations to be followed; the renovation of the forest and subsequent culture to be followed. (*c*) Method of exploitation; partition of the forest into divisions for successive fellings; application of these to the *fachwerksmethode* of exploitation with the maintenance of forests in good condition; and preparation of plans of operation. (*d*) Determination of produce to be obtained and of the utilization of the remainder. (*e*) Securing of sustained produce; bookkeeping and revision of programmes of successive operations in subsequent years. As the basis of instruction under this last head there are used *Koenig's Forst Mathematik* and *Grebe's Betriebs-und Ertragsregulierung der Forsten.* 7. **Estimation of the value of** the forest, with a special reference to financial operations, to sales, exchanges, exappropriation and the determination of compensation to be given and required for damage done with *Koenig's Forst Mathematik* as a text book, with supplemetary additions. 8. Forest economy in its application to State forests; general principles based on political economy, financial and police science, the relative importance of forests in national and State economy; forests in relation to different industries; the area and distribution of forests, local and general; deficient and excessive supply of forest products; **what sites are most favourable for the practice of forest economy; what measure** of State control or of interference with all forests, so far as to secure their conservation and the advancement of forest culture, by the abolishing of servitudes and other hindrances to this, and the advancing of the required pecuniary means, &c., is expedient; and, what are the principles upon which a Government should proceed in the administration and management of State forests what superintendence a State should exercise over forests belonging to communes, to endowments, and to private parties; the training of forest officials, &c. 9. Organisation of the forest service, and documentary correspondence relating thereto. Instruction is also given in regard to the method of conducting judical proceedings and office or counting-house work.

'The scientific studies embrace mathematics in the several departments applicable to forestry; natural philosophy, including inorganic, organic, and agricultural chemistry; mineralogy and elements of geology; physics and meteorology; botany in several departments, and agriculture; zoology, with special attention being given to entomolgy; forestry in all its departments; and jurisprudence.

'The full course of study extends over two years. The studies are so arranged that in resuming in one session the study of any science begun in the preceding session —by a review of the more important principles, and by retrospective questions relative to what has been previously studied, and more especially by examinations on the practical application, which may have been made, of what has been taught—the student can, at the commencement of each session, resume his studies without any fear of interruption to his course of study. The means employed in communicating instruction are: Lectures on the several subjects of study, examinations, practical applications of what has been acquired, and excursions.

'1. Lectures.—The living voice is found in practice to be the most stimulating and most efficient medium of communicating instruction. Free delivery of lectures, founded on the statements made in appropriate text books, is the method of teaching which is generally adopted, and only in so far as the text book may require, some supplementary statement is recourse had to dictation. The lectures on the different subjects of study are given in the forenoon, in the hours from 7 to 9 and from 10 to 12.

'The subjects are so arranged that of the twenty-four hours weekly thus occupied, upon an average from nine to ten hours are devoted to forestry; from seven to eight hours to physical science; from five to six to mathematics; and about two hours to training in judicial procedure.

2. Examinations.—These have proved to be a means of instruction no less efficient, in as much as they, when properly conducted, reveal what deficiencies in the instruction given require to be supplied, give opportunities for more ample explanation or illustration of difficult subjects, assist greatly the weak, and prove to all a wonderful stimulus to the prosecution of studies. To examinations on each of the subjects of study there is devoted at least one hour a week; and towards the close of each session usually several hours a week are spent in examinations on different subjects.

'3. To practical applications and excursions are devoted, without exception, every afternoon after two o'clock.

'(a) Summer Session.—In the summer session either three or four afternoons in every week are devoted to exercises in surveying, that expertness may be acquired in the handling and use of the instruments, and an acquaintance with the different methods of measuring extensive plains, and limited patches, of taking levels, and altitudes, &c. In favourable weather the results to be obtained are wrought out in the class-room by logarithms, and trigonometrical calculations, and the preparation of charts and diagrams.

'(b) One afternoon in the week is devoted exclusively to forest excursions; the first of these is employed in a general survey of the conditions of the ground, and of the forest trees, &c., in the wood appropriated to the instruction of the students; in succeeding excursions each is devoted to the detailed study of some one object. And it is sought so to arrange these that the excursions shall be subservient to the instruction of the students by sight, such, for example, as the forestal peculiarities of different kinds of trees; the different ways of managing forests; the determining of sites for fellings, clearings, and thinnings, seed beds, and nurseries; different methods of culture; the measurement of trees, and estimation of their increase by growth; forest road-making, &c., combining, as much as possible, theoretical and practical instruction, that these may go hand-in-hand together. And in order to every facility being given for this mode of instruction, to the Director is committed the unlimited direction and control of the forest production of the forests assigned to the school for purposes of instruction.

'Besides the regular afternoon excursions, there are also made regularly occasional longer excursions into the neighbouring forest districts, partly to see the forestal peculiarities of the different forest sites—gneiss, mica slate, and porphyry, in the Ruhla forest; sechstein, variegated sandstone, and basalt, in the Markfuhl forest; mussel chalk, lias, and keuper, in the Kreusburg forest, &c.— partly to obtain illustrations of those forms of management which are not to be seen in the forests in the vicinity of Eisenach, such as low coppice, medium coppice, conversion of medium of mixed coppice in timber forests, second growth of timber forests, the management of mountain firs, &c., with the different devices practised in the conducting of successive fellings, &c.

'(c) Moreover, there is in every summer session a complete regulation management, for an appropriated portion of Eisenach forest, gone through with all the preparatory work, exclusive of measurings, which would consume a great deal of time; and, in this simple work, the peculiarities of the different methods of taxation and management are illustrated. This work serves, moreover, as the basis of a detailed example of estimating the value of a forest. While these more extended practical trainings are going on, lectures are entirely suspended.

'(*d*) On one afternoon weekly, during the summer session, there is an excursion for the study of natural history, more particularly of botany and geology, for which the vicinity of Eisenach, with its manifold rare geological formations, and its corresponding rich flora, presents an excellent instruction ground. On the conclusion of these natural history excursions, every summer session there is carried out an excursion extending over some days, into the geologically interesting parts of the Thuringian forest, under the guidance of the teachers in this department of study.

'(*e*) In the winter session there are, on every second afternoon, exercises in mathematics, repetitions, or examinations, forestal calculations, geometrical problems, &c., for practice, for assistance to the weak, and for the completing of the course of instruction of any who have not entered the school at the commencement of the course. Two other afternoons are set aside for practice in chart drawing. The excursions in the forests are confined to visiting fellings which are being carried on, in order to have here practical illustrations of some of the more important operations connected with fellings, such as the act of felling, trimming, preparing, and measuring logs, &c.'

Dr Grebe says ' the systematic illustration and extension of theoretic instruction, by direct inspection and practice, we consider, after well nigh forty years experience, to be by far the most efficient and profitable mode of instruction, and one which cannot be compensated by any other method of instruction which may be adopted in a School of Forestry. The possibility of making available, for purposes of instruction, the various incidents occurring constantly in the management of a forest, such as the annual preparation of schemes of exploitation and of culture, the determination of sites of fellings, of thinnings, and of preparatory clearings. The work connected with seed beds and nurseries, sowings and plantings, and the preparation of inventories, and estimates of the cubic measurement of wood in a forest, and of the probable annual increase, by properly qualified agents, for the administration and management, the conservation, exploitation, improvement, and extension of existing forests.'

The experience of Dr Grebe, to which he appeals, shows what advantage may be found in having forest operations daily under review by students; and of having every facility for taking immediate advantage of incidents as they may occur in connection with the management of a forest attached to a school. But it may be found that others, either losing sight of these, or in full view of these, consider that the advantages derivable from having a School of Forestry in connection with a University, or some other site of learning, more than counter-balance the advantage of having an independent site for such an institute : seeing that facilities can otherwise be obtained for the study and practice of the application of the instruction received in school. And, without prejudice to the statement made by Dr Grebe, it may appear that others, with like facilities to those enjoyed by him, have attached more importance to other arrangements for securing the same advantage to students. My sympathies are with these; but I consider it a good preparation for entering upon the account to be given of the discussions which have taken place on this point, for the reader to give its full weight to this testimony by Dr Grebe.

Growth, descriptions of the contents of the forest, and all the work in a model forest required to secure the continuous uninterrupted work which has to be done, can, he alleges, only be secured in an independent institute—and never in the complex system of education carried on in a University. A circumstance, this he adds, of great weight, which has been too much overlooked in the controversy which has been going on for some time in regard to the proper site for a School of Forestry.

We are about to enter on the consideration of the controversy to which Dr Grebe refers. His allusions to it burst upon us like the boom of the first cannon fired at dawn of a day of renewed strife in the assault and defence of some fortress, upon the scene of which we have come overnight, and we shall soon be looking upon the contending foes in the thick of the battle; each party and each combatant contending for what he believes to be the just, the true, and the best—the best for all, and best for the interests of Europe and of the world; in so far as these may be involved in preparation for work.

The most important and most extensively used means of instruction in the Eisenach institution, are the forests attached to it; and next to these, among such means may be reckoned the library and the museums.

'1 What is reckoned here an indispensible appendix to a School of Forestry is a forest for field instruction. Here there are, in the first line, the Grand Ducal *forest reviers* or districts of Eisenach, Wilhelmsthal, and Ruhla; and more distant, but still adjacent, being upon an average within range of a day's tour, the forest districts Marksuhl, Frauensee and Kreuzburg, in the Grand Ducal forest.

'The first-mentioned comprise an agregate circuit of 61,146 hectares; and extends partly over existing members of primitive rocks—granite, gneiss, mica slate, porphyry, &c.—partly, and that for the greater part over the red clay, and lastly, partly on the borders, over different members of the Sechstein formation, with an unusually varied and complicated earthy covering. The second class of forests named, presents, on the other hand, in Marksuhl and Frauensee, different localities of coloured sandstone, with basaltic eruptions of Muschelkalks in Kreuzburg, and of Keupers and Lias. With the exception of the latest formation, there are also within reach of a day's excursion represented all formations providing a field full of instruction in geology, rural economy, and more especially in forest economy, such as is hardly to be found combined anywhere besides.

'These diversified conditions present for botanical study a very rich flora; and, above all, a very varied condition of forest existence. The higher lying parts of the Ruhla forests have quite a mountain character, with a preponderating covering of coniferæ, and supply an opportunity of studying the characteristic of this kind of wood; the phenomena of windfalls, and injuries done by frost and snow; the felling of such, and the manifold devices used for the protection of forests against such calamities; and the regulation of the succession of fellings practised. In the forests of Eisenach and Wilhelmsthal there predominate timber forests of beech. These supply, in great variety, illustrations of the felling of timber, with provision for the natural reproduction of the forest; and therewith are found illustrations of the process of converting broad leaved forests into forests of coniferæ; also, of the measures taken to promote the growth of seedlings and saplings, by the destruction of injurious weeds, and by successive thinnings. And again, altogether different is the tree growth and the treatment of this on the coloured sand stone of the Marksuhl forest, and on the Muschelkalk of the Kreuzburg forest : in the first of these are located the seed beds and nurseries, while in the latter are very instructive representations of the middle timber forest, and of the conversion of such into timber forests, and of the treatment of mixed timber and coppice woods.

'2. The library of the institution has a tolerably complete collection of all works treating of forestry, and of the more important works treating of mathematics, natural history, and political economy. It comprises, for example, about 2100 independent writings; and a considerable portion of the grant from Government is spent on the maintenance and increase of the library. The use of the library is, as may be understood, open to the students under prescribed rules.

'3. In the museum are provided collections of different kinds: (*a*) A pretty complete collection of all mathematical and metrical implements in use in forest economy; the latter, for example, comprising several specimens of each for use in practical instruction in surveying, for training in which the students are divided into sections. (*b*) A pretty complete collection of implements and of models, especially of such as pertain to the culture of seedlings and trees, the transport of wood, the economic use or sale of wood, and the improvement of forest products—including models of buildings, bridges, and sluices, of appliances for the procuring of secondary products, charcoal-kilns and kilns for the manufacture of pitch, tar, lamp-black, &c. (*c*) An instructive mineral and geological collection. (*d*) A rich herbarium, comprising the more important kinds of exotic woods; a collection of models of the more important fungi—Her Royal Highness the Grand Duchess of Saxony having presented to the institution a valuable collection of the same, known as "The Arnold Collection of Models;" and collections of seeds and of different kinds of wood. (*e*) A collection of the more important insects, and specimens of their destructive work.

'But the collections of objects of natural history, through limitation of space and of funds, are somewhat limited, and cannot be compared with those in some of the larger forest academies. They are confined to what are deemed absolutely indispensable for purposes of instruction, and they only suffice for this through the richness of the surrounding country in geological and botanical specimens.'

With regard to the expense of maintaining the institution, it is stated that, according to an arrangement in the finance department of the Ministry of the State of the Grand Duchy, there is given to the institute only an auxiliary pecuniary contribution. This has been for the twenty years—1830-1849—5593·37 marks, a yearly average of 280 marks; for the thirty years—1850-1879—

50228·29 marks, averaging 1668 marks a year; for the fifty years—1830-1879—55821·66 marks, on an average 1116 marks a year.*

These contributions are used mainly in aid of salaries paid to individual teachers, and the maintainance of educational appliances, namely, the library and collections of objects—on the latter, for example, have been expended, since 1850, not less than 17,541 marks or about thirty-five per cent of the whole. But in connection with this it should be borne in mind that the Director of the institution is at the same time president, and the teacher of mathematics is a member of the Grand Ducal Forest Taxation Commission, and the payment of the salary of the former has been entirely, and that of the latter to a great extent, taken over by that court; and about half of what is thus paid may be considered expenditure on the institution.

The conditions on which students are received into the institution vary according as they may be aspirants for employment in the State Forest Service of the Thuringian States—those in the Grand Duchy of Saxe-Coburg Gotha, in the Duchies of Saxe-Meinigen, &c., and in the principality Swarzburg-Rudolstadt, and Saxe-Sondershausen—or aspirants from other countries—or, lastly, are received as hospitanten.

According to existing arrangements, there are two instructors in forest science; the director, who is first teacher in this department, and a teacher of mathematics; two of natural science; one assistant as a teacher of political economy. There is required of students at admission the exit certificate of a gymnasium or of a *real-gymnasium*, and one year's preparatory study. The course embraces two years; but aspirants are free to attend some other

---

* In this last amount are included contributions which were made from State funds on the occasion of the Congress of the foresters of Thuringia being held in Eisenach in 1858, and of the Congress of the foresters of Germany being held in Eisenach in 1876.

School of Forestry. Annually, at the close of the winter session, there is held a *Tentamen*, which extends to all the branches of instruction in forestry. Special stress is laid on mathematics, but without including the higher departments of that science. As forests appropriated to instruction, there are, as has been stated, the six forest *reviers* or districts of the Eisenach inspection, with which the Director is entrusted.

The number of students in the summer session of 1885 was 168; in the winter session of 1885-86, 71; of whom, respectively, 12 and 13 were from the Thuringian States.

The institution founded by Koenig in 1808 at Ruhla was originally a private enterprise, and such it remained till 1830, when it became a State establishment; and such it has remained.

Eisenach is the site of the palace of the Grand Duke of Saxe Weimar, and here, in the Wartzburg, Luther was imprisoned. A relict of his imprisonment is shown to travellers, in a black smutch upon the wall of his cell—produced, it is said, by the ink in the inkstand, thrown at the head of an apparation considered by him to be the devil.

We are here in the centre of a forest region, to the north-east are the Hartz mountains, also associated with tales of diablery, and covered with the remains of the Thuringian forest; while to the south stretch away successive vestiges of the Black Forest, scarce less interesting to the worshipper of ancient remains.

A guide book well known to travellers tells:—

'The Thuringian Forests.—The Thuringarwald is a hilly, wooded tract of country, extending from the sources of the Werra, north-west to near Eisenach. It is a part of the ancient Hircynian forest, and is about 70 miles long, and a breadth varying from 9 to 16 miles. It is thinly peopled; but it is rich in metals, particularly iron and cobalt. Its highest peaks range from 2000 feet to 3200 feet. It is covered with fruits in almost every direction.

It is traversed by only two great roads. It gives rise to a number of streams which flow into the adjacent plain, and eventually into the Main, the Weser, and the Elbe.'

By proceeding from Eisenach to Frankford an opportunity of visiting several outlying portions of the Thuringian forest may be had. From Gotha the Hartz mountains may easily be reached. This was my route on the occasion of a previous visit to Eisenach.

Shortly before crossing the boundary of Hesse Cassel, in travelling to Giessen, the traveller passes through Marburg, a town on the Lahu, built on the slopes of a hillside, and the site of the first university founded in Germany after the Reformation. It was founded in 1527. It has, or had, forty professors, but not a proportionate number of students.

On the Schlossberg rises proudly the ancient *Castle of the Landgraves of Hesse*, a structure of the chivalrous ages, now dismantled, commanding a fine prospect.

The houses inhabited by Luther and Zwingleu during the theological discussions which they carried on in the presence of the Langraves of Hesse, still exist; but it is Giessen which is now our destination.

CHAPTER V.

FORESTAL INSTRUCTION AT GIESSEN IN HESSE-DARMSTADT.

The several Forest Academies which have been brought under our consideration, thus far are all of them properly designated Forest Academies. They are technical institutions, designed exclusively for instruction in forestry, and fulfilling for a time, and that a long time, that function alone. The study of rural economy was prosecuted in the same institution as the study of forestry in the Saxon Academy at Tharand; but, since 1870, it has not been so. At Giessen there was formerly such an institution, but it has been combined with the University which is there —a University well known by name at least in Britain, as the seat of learning in which Liebig and his disciples pursued their researches in agricultural chemistry, with great benefit to the nations. And then there is brought before us another phase of Schools of Forestry.

With regard to the School of Forestry in Giessen, as with regard to that at Eisenach, I have to state that I had only one evening, or rather part of an evening, and the early morning of the following day to spare for seeing the interesting town in which it is situated; and beyond seeing the locality, I could not, by personal observation, or enquiry at the honoured officials entrusted with the instruction of students, make myself acquainted with the existing arrangements in connection with this; but what I thus missed learning on the spot, was subsequently supplied by correspondence with Dr Hess, the professor of forestry in the University, and by published and official information supplied to me by him.

FORESTAL INSTRUCTION AT GIESSEN.

Giessen may boast of being the site of one of the original Schools of Forestry, established a hundred years ago, inasmuch as from 1795 till 1825, forestry appear to have been taught in the University as a branch of the instruction given in the study of political economy.

From the introduction to a pamphlet, written by Dr Hess, on the organisation at present existing for the study of forest science in the Ludwig University of the Grand Duchy of Hesse, in Giessen, published in 1877, it appears that the School of Forestry of Giessen was first established as a distinct institution, by Ordinance dated 24th March, 1825. The first director was Dr Johann Christian Hundeshagen, to whom was given the titular rank of Oberforstrath, and who held the appointment of ordinary professor in the University. Dr Hundeshagen had, from 1818 to 1821, laboured in Tübingen as Professor of State-Forest Management; in 1821 he was called to the office of Director of the *Forst-Lehr-Austalt* of the Electoral Principality of Hesse at Hersfeld, whence he was called, and transported to Giessen by Decree of 19th May, 1824. By Decree of 24th March, 1824, Carl Heyer, then *Revierforster* at Greinberg, was nominated provisionally as second teacher in the institute. Dr Hundeshagen announced two courses of lectures, and one *Examinatorium* in the winter session 1824-25, but whether these were actually held does not appear from the records. The records preserve also both a manuscript and a printed list of lectures, for the summer session of 1825. But after giving the prescribed notice, the proposal to lecture on forest science came to nothing, and he delivered only his course of lectures on rural economy (*Lande-wirtschaft und Lande-wirtschaftlisihe Polize.*) And in the winter session, 1825-26, the course of lectures on forest science had the same fate. In the course of these three sessions there only appeared as students one Hessian, Gustav Hoffmann, from Büdingen, and two foreigners.

It was not till the summer session of 1826 that the

lectures on forestry were fairly established. In this
session Dr Hundeshagen lectured on *Forst Benutzung* or
exploitation, and *Forst-Schutz* or conservation ; and Carl
Heyer gave instruction in forest botany and *Waldban*.
The latter appeared in the class-room only occasionally,
while he gave himself mainly to his functions as
Revierforster in the town forests of Giessen and other
communial forests ; and to him, on this account, it was
generally given to go on excursions with the students, and
to give to them practical instruction in the forest. These
seem to have been first entered on in the summer session
of 1827, when ten new students enrolled themselves.
Here many students of previous years still remained.
What number of students attended during any one of the
earlier sessions does not appear from the records.

By Decree, bearing the date of 20th September, 1827,
Dr Johann Ludwig, Klauprecht, who had previously
taught forest science, mathematics, and forest natural
history in Asschaffenburg—the Forest Academy of
Bavaria—was licensed or installed as *Privat-Docent*, or
college tutor in Giessen, more especially for forest
science ; and he began his lectures in the winter session
of 1827-28.

The relative duties of the two recognised teachers in the
forest institute, Hundeshagen and Heyer, was further
regulated by instructions issued 17th November, 1830,
and the curriculm was fixed as comprising three sessions.
As subjects of lectures, besides practical instruction to be
given by them, there were prescribed *Forstans Lattungs-
Kunde*, or instruction regarding the duration of continuous
supplies to be expected from forests in a given condition,
together with forest botany, *Waldban* or Sylviculture, and
Forst-Schutz, or forest conservation. Meanwhile Heyer
had been promoted by Decree of 28th December, 1829, to
be forest inspector at Giessen, together with his appointment of second teacher in the institute. But shortly
thereafter, in consequence of various misunderstandings
between the two teachers, by Decree of 12th April, 1831,

he was released from both appointments that he might enter on the office of *Forst-Meister* in the service of Graff-von Erbach-Fürstenau. And on his own application, Hundeshagen was, by Decree of 14th June, 1831, relieved of the direction of the forest institute, and it was arranged that the teachers and students of forest science should stand in every way in the same position and relation as teachers and students in the other departments in the State University.

'By this measure,' says Dr Hess, ' the Forest Institute, which had existed for a few years as a distinct establishment associated with the High School, was elevated in every way; and instruction in forestry became completely incorporated with the instruction given in the University. This arrangement continued unchanged; and the terms *Forstinstitut* and *Director des Forstinstitut*, when they are used, have a reference only to internal arrangements. He writes :—

'The *Forstgarden* of the *Institut*, which was transferred to the University at this time, continued to require and to receive appropriate management and superintendence as an important means of instruction; and the forest museum, or collections of products, implements, &c., must be maintained and increased. There are many grants for these purposes to be expended. The sums expended for the utilisation of the aids to instruction, for the annual outlay on the management of the Aboretum, for the engagement of labouerrs, and assistance when required in the practical services and the excursions, &c., must be regularly calculated and accounted for, and there is much correspondence necessarily connected with all of these matters. These business arrangements are laid upon the first teacher for the time being, and are attended to by him as Director of the Academy Administration Commission. But the term Forest Institute and the Director of the Forest Institute have nothing to do with the instruction in forestry which is given.'

Such are the statements of Dr Hess in regard to the historical development of the Giessen School of

Forestry, and he goes on to state that Dr Hundeshagen, after ceasing to be director of the institute, confined himself to the duties of his professorship of forest science. Oberforster Dr August von Klipstein stepped into the place of Dr Carl Meyer, and by Decree of 12th November, 1831, he was nominated as second teacher of practical forest science in the University of the State, which position he held till 1836, when, by Decree of 31st October, he was appointed Ordinary Professor of Mineralogy in the State University.

Dr Klauprecht, who, in connection with Hundeshagen, had continued to give instruction in Forestry, was, by Decree of 5th June, 1832, nominated Extraordinary Professor of Forest and Political Economy; but by Decree of 20th November, 1834, he was released from this that he might be free to accept a call to the Polytechnicum at Carlsruhe, which had been given to him.

In the same year, on the 10th February, Hundeshagen died, in the 51st year of his life; greatly honoured by his associates in the University for his profound learning, the more commendable that his life was somewhat embittered by nervous irritability arising from disease; and the loss sustained by the University through his death, was deeply felt.

He was succeeded as Professor of Forest Science by his former associate—Dr Carl Heyer. With him was associated Dr Carl Zimmer; and he attended mainly to the theoretical, while the latter attended mainly to the practical departments of their subject. Finding himself unable to attend to his own satisfaction to his duties as professor, and to those of forest inspector, to which he had been appointed with the rank of *Forstmeister*, he got assistance in the discharge of the latter duties; and subsequently his son, Dr Gustav Heyer, became successively lecturer and successor of Dr Zimmer in his professorship when he died, and after the death of his father, Professor of Philosophy, and Extraordinary Professor of Forest Science.

With him was associated Dr Edward Heyer as second teacher of forest science, till, in 1868, Dr Gustav Heyer was called to the newly-established Royal Prussian Forest Academy at München.

This led to the appointment of Dr Hess, who, in the discharge of his duties, found that the assistance given by a teacher holding an official appointment as a State forester was productive of serious inconvenience, arising in part from the circumstance that the University was under the superintendence of the Minister of the Interior, while the forest administration lay with the Minister of Finance. The Senate of the University, at his instance, solicited, through the Minister of the Interior, the establishment of a special Extraordinary Professorship of Forest Science, 'free from the distracting influence of a forest charge', and, in consequence of this, Forest Assistant Dr Tuisco Lorey, of Darmstadt, now Professor of Forest Science in the University of Tubengan, and Director of the station for forestal experimental research there, was, by decree of 13th October, 1873, nominated Extraordinary Professor to the Faculty of Philosophy, and second teacher of forest science.

In addition to what interest may attach to these details in themselves, they acquire some interest from the circumstances that the expediency of combining Schools of Forestry with educational institutions of a more comprehensive character, instead of organising and maintaining them as separate establishments, was becoming one of the questions of the day amongst forest officials on the Continent of Europe, and may be one of some importance to those who may be disposed to advocate the establishment of Schools of Forestry elsewhere. There are national usages giving form to the evolution or development, but the general principles underlying these may be discerned; and now only can the school be considered as having attained its special development.

Dr Hess has laboured zealously to perfect, if possible, the course of instruction in forestry, scientific and practical, which is given at Giessen. Of the scheme of instruction which is at present being carried out, the following, embracing the time from Easter 1877, to Easter 1879, are details as given by him :—

During the summer session of 1877, or the first session of the course, daily from 10 to 11, or from 10 to 12, so as to secure eight hours a week for the purpose, instruction was given by him in the encyclopædia and methodology of forest science, in connection with a historical introduction, and with a special reference to forest statistics, for forest economists, rural economists, and financers; and the Saturday afternoons were devoted to a course of practical instruction in *Waldbau*, or Sylviculture.

During the same session Dr T. Lorey, the second professor of forest science, twice a week. from 2 to 4 o'clock, gave instruction in forest road making, and spent with the students the Wednesday afternoons in excursions and demonstrations, and on one day in the week, from 11 to 1, in a *Repititorum*, or examination, on the application of geodesy, or land-surveying, to the special requirements of forest measurement and forest divisions for culture and exploitation.

In the summer session of 1878, the third of this course, instruction was given by Dr Hess one hour on five days of the week, on *Waldbau*, or Sylviculture, with practical exercises and excursions, to which were devoted the Saturday afternoons; and by Dr Lorey instruction was given for one hour twice a week on *Forstaushaltungskunde*, or the time which forests in given conditions will hold out in yielding products of a given quantity. And on three days a week one hour was devoted to a *Repititorum*, relative to forest road engineering, to the study of which Wednesday afternoons also were devoted.

In the winter session of 1878 Dr Hess gave instruction for one hour, five days a week, on forest conservation, *Forst Schutze*, and on *Forstbenutzung*, or exploitation, with practical exercises and excursions, to which the Saturday afternoons were devoted.

Dr Lorey, on four days a week, gave instruction for an hour on wood mensuration, in connection with forest surveying, &c.; the Wednesday afternoons were devoted to the latter, and on Saturday two hours were spent by him in giving instruction in matters relating to the chase.

In the winter session of 1878-79—the fourth of the course, Dr Hess gave instruction for one hour, on four days of the week in *Waldertragsregelung*, or regulation of the produce of forests so as to secure sustained production; and one hour a day, on two days a week, to instruction applicable to the management of State forests; and a practical course of instruction in *Forstbenutzung* or exploitation, to which were devoted the Saturday afternoons.

Dr Lorey, in the same session, gave on two days a week, two hours' instruction in *Waldwerthrechnung*, or the estimating of the value of forests, and in forest statistics; and two hours on Tuesday to a *Repititorum* relative to exercises in wood measurement, to which Wednesday afternoons were devoted.

Full courses of lectures were given every year by professors in the University on the following fundamental and accessary subjects pertaining to forest science—Mathematics, geodesy or land surveying, physics, chemistry, zoology, systematic botany, physiology of plants, mineralogy, geognosy or physical geography, geology, political ecconomy, law in its various applications, civil engineering, technology, &c.; besides which, lectures were given by professors and University tutors on mineralogy, law, architecture, and civil engineering and on the following subjects in botany in reference to the special requirements of the forest department of study:—

1. An exposition of forest plants.
2. Discussion of diseases of cultivated plants, with a special reference to lignous vegetables.
3. Mineralogy and soils, in relation to woods and forests.

4. Forest laws.

5. The drawing of diagrams, &c.

6. And agricultural analysis, &c., in the laboratory for rural and forest conomy.

And in every session an introductory lecture, open to all, was delivered by the forest teacher.

The study of forestry was included in the Faculty of Philosophy. As has been intimated, their were two professorships of forest science, a first and a second; the former an ordinary, the second an extraordinary professor, being so appointed in accordance with a usage in Germany—both being independent, but the ordinary professor only having a seat in the *Senatus Academicus*.

In a *Verzeichniss*, or notice of the lectures and practical exercises in the department of forest science, and fundamental and accessary sciences pertaining to it, to be held in the University, arranged as a *Lehrplan*, showing on what days, and at what hours, in all of the sessions in the course of study from Easter 1881, to Easter 1883, issued by Dr Hess, these would be held—there are given the classes held by between twelve and twenty different professors which may be attended without interfering with each other; and in a preface he gives to students, who at Universities on the Continent have much greater liberty in regard to attending or absenting themselves from class lectures than is the case in Scotland, his advice in regard to the course of study which they should follow with a view to the acquisition of instruction in forest science. In this he says: -1. 'If it be at all possible, the lectures on mathematics, physics, chemistry, and land-surveying, should be attended in the first session, and even before entering on the special studies of the department, if this be practicable, in order that the preliminary examinations which may be passed by candidates without having attended a University for any specified period, may be undertaken as soon as possible.

2. 'With advantage, other lectures in fundamental and

accessary sciences may be attended during the first session: such as botany, theory of political economy, and with this the science of finance, jurisprudenc, and forest law; and the encyclopædic study of rural economy and other accessary studies had better be deferred to a subsequent session.

3. 'The Forest Science lectures, according to this programme, will be most advantageously attended in the second year of the course; it would, however, be expedient for students commencing at this time, Easter 1881, to attend at least the encyclopædic lectures on forest science at once, as these are not again delivered until the summer session of 1883; and moreover, they will thus be placed in a position to undertake their true professional forestal studies in any subsequent session which they may choose.

4. 'The attendance on the practical forestal course of instruction, relative to sylviculture, forest exploitation, the making of the forest roads, the science and practice of measuring timber, &c., with or without attendance on lectures, presents itself for the same reason as a course of instruction to be followed from the very commencement of the course. This course of study is, in other lands, required as a preliminary to entering a forest institute.

5. 'It is greatly to be desired that the students, with a view to the utilisation of the advantages for general culture, which the University offers in such abundance, in comparison with the isolated Schools of Forestry, should not rest satisfied with attending those lectures which relate to subjects embraced in *Hochschule* or State examinations: but that they should also attend the lectures in the departments of forest zoology, history, and philosophy strictly so called.'

It is added that the professors of forest science will always be ready to give information and advice to students in regard to their studies; and there is appended to the programme a list of treatises on different subjects of study recommended to students.

At Giessen, as at several other Universities in

Germany, it has long been the custom, and was the custom then, that there is no required course of study prescribed. Every student is free to choose what course of lectures he may wish to attend. He has only personally to wait upon the teacher whose class he desires to attend at the commencement of the session, and enrol himself on the class list.

Without special permission of the teacher no one can attend as a visitor above three times, and attendance beyond this is considered equivalent to a declaration of a purpose to attend as a regular student; but it does not relieve him of the necessity of formally announcing this to the teacher. And on demand every student receives a half-year's certificate in regard to the regularity, diligence, and improvement with which he has attended the meetings of the class.

The summer session begins, or did then, between the middle and the end of April; the winter session at the end of October.

The educational helps in the study of forestry consisted of:—

1. Collections of wood, charcoal, seeds, insects, birds, beasts, foods, stones, implements, models, &c.

2. The academy forest garden, or arboretum, 6 hectares, or 14 acres in extent, with a special forest museum and overseer's dwelling, all under the superintendence of the forest teacher.

3. The forests of Giessen and Schuffenberg, both in the immediate vicinity of the town.

And the helps in the study of general science were these: —A chemical laboratory; cabinets of physical, meteorological, surveying, mathematical, technological, and mineralogical apparatus and substances; a botanical museum; a botanic garden; the institute of rural economy, the institute of fine arts, the institute and cabinet of zoology and comparative anatomy, the cabinet of art, science, and antiquities, &c., &c., and finally the University library and reading-room.

The forest exercises and excursions conducted by the two teachers had for their object the execution of work required in the management of forests connected with sowing and planting, the determination of sites of fellings, and the actual felling of trees; or the execution of appointed exercises in land mensuration, in forest surveying, levelling, and staking out of forest roads; or the professional inspection of characteristic or typical management of forests in the vicinity, oak coppice, beech timber-forests, pine clearings, &c. Of these excursions and exercises, or at least of a portion of them, a formal report was required from the students; beside which, in every summer session, a vacation tour, extending over eight days or a fortnight, was made under the guidance of one or other of the teachers, to some of the larger forest districts at a greater distance.

The fees for attendance throughout the session for a course of lectures, which occupied from two to three hours a week, was eleven marks; if it occupied from four to six hours a week, sixteen marks; if from seven to nine hours a week, twenty-one marks. The mark is equivalent to a shilling.

For a course of lectures, with which excursions and associated experiments were combined, at least double these fees were payable. Attendance a second year on the same course was charged only half the amount of the first fee.

In order to matriculation a native of the principality was required to produce —

(*a*) A *Maturitätszeugniss*, or certificate of complete attendance at a gymnasium or at a *real schule* of the first order—that is a school in which not only languages but the arts and sciences are taught—or of some equivalent institution.

(*b*) A dismissal or exit certificate of some previously attended University or professional educational institute; —and as *licenciates*, might be received those who, in lack of such certificates, produced corresponding certificates in regard to their general education.

A foreigner required, besides the education necessary to understand the academy lectures on general science, only a credible statement from his parents or guardians of consent to his attending the University, and a certificate from any educational institute which he might have previously attended.

Dr Hess has zealously and successfully made use of the press to create, sustain, and intensify an interest in their professional work amongst students who have come under his influence, and to diffuse a corresponding interest in this amongst others; and thus he has done much to promote the study of forest science, and to facilitate this by aspirants for employment in the forest service of the State.

In 1873 he published a scheme of lectures on the encyclopædic and methodology of Forest Science * with copious—I had almost said innumerable— citations of the titles of books, in which the subjects of different chapters are treated of. I do not know of a more valuable repertory of the same, and from statements in the preface something may be learned of the conditions of forest science at the time he entered on his professional duties.

In this preface, while stating that there did not exist any such work which could be said to supply a simple and exclusive encyclopædic view of forest science, which could be made the basis of acadium study, he says in regard to the methodic scientific of forestry, that the work of the immortal Hundeshagen, of which an edition had been published by Klauprecht, must ever be assigned the first position.*

[Hundeshagen: Encyclopædie der Forstwissenchaft, Herausgegeben von Klauprecht 3, Abtheilung, Fubengen.

1. 'Abtheilung: Forstliche Productionslehre, 4 Auflage, 1842.' (1821);

---

* *Grundriss zu Verlesung über Encyclopædie und Methodologie der Forstwisenchaft &c.* Giessen: *J. Recher'sche, Buchhandlund,* 1873.

2. 'Abtheilungen : Forstliche Gewerbslehre, 4 Auflage, 1843.' (1822);
3. 'Abtheilung : Lehrbuch der Forstpolizei, 4 Auflage, 1859.' (1831).]

'The contents of this work, however, are to some considerable extent antiquated, having been published previous to the later forward bounds made by forest science—since it has become an essential of all true progress to take into account mathematical data, to which formerly less attention could be given.

The *Grundriss* of Cotta,* and the generally commendable, and, in some of its parts, most excellent and elaborate Lehrbuch of Fischbach [Fischbach, C. : Lehrbuch der Forstwissenschaft, 2 Auflage, Stuttgart, 1865,] are, at least for the requirements of students at Giessen, insufficient, mainly on this account that they treat the department of forest mathematics with neglect. In neither is the subject of forest statistics treated of, and this on the ground, it is alleged by Fischbach (p. 82), that this department of forest science is, or was at the time he wrote, as yet too imperfectly developed, and for beginners, moreover, difficult to be understood. And the scheme of lectures had been prepared with a special view to the requirements of students of forest economics and of finance, it being his opinion that after the knowledge of *Betriebslehre* exploitation, and especially of statistics, if not to be placed in the same category, there is scarcely a more important, or indeed more interesting branch of study than the science of production.

'The *Forstwirthschaft* of Pfeil, edited by Prissler [Die Forstwirthschaft nach rein Practischer Ansicht, 6 Auflage Herausgegeben von Prissler, Leipzig, 1870,] comes very near to supplying what is wanted in a preparatory school, in which the object is to instruct the students how to obtain pecuniary returns from an appropriate management of forests, and in a school of financial economy;

---

* Cotta, H. : *Grundriss der Forstwissenschaft*, 6 Auflage, Herausgegeben von Seine Euklens Heinrich und Ernst von Cotta. Leipzig, 1872. (1831).

but, as its title indicates, it was designed to supply a desideratum other than that which is under consideration. As a handbook supplying the information generally required by those who are, or purpose to be, forest managers, it will do good service; but it is not suitable as a manual of instruction for academic lectures, and objection may be taken to the plan of the work.

'Hartig's *System und Aleitung zum studium der Forstwirthschaftslehre* [Leipzig, 1858], contains many excellent thoughts, but the peculiar form and manner of the entire grouping is so very different from the system of the course of instruction in forestry followed in the School of Forestry at Giessen that I cannot base my course of instruction upon it. The same remarks may be made in regard to the last edition which has appeared of G. L. Hartig's *Lehrbuh für Förster* [10 Auflage, herausgegeben von G. L. Hartrig. Stuttgart, 1861,] the first volume of which scarcely comes within the designation *Fachwissenschaft*. The *Forstlehre* of Grunert is calculated to meet the requirements of Prussian foresters. Also, the old *Lehrbuch für Förster* of G. L. Hartig, revised by Berggreve [1871], can only be viewed in this light; and, lastly, the *Forstencyklopädie* by Püschel, in consequence of the alphabetical arrangement followed, can only be used as a book of reference.'

He says it was thus that it was rendered necessary for him to prepare a *Forest Encyclopædia* of seven volumes, the publication of which was necessarily deferred; and that the brochure, which was little else than a table of contents, was published for the assistance of his auditors. Fundamentally, the system first used was that of the Hundeshagen school; but in the working out of the several parts he had followed the two Heyers, Carl and Gustav. In the discussion of forest police, of which he had only to treat within the narrow limits of *Privatforstwirthschaftslehre*, he had not followed the limits of any particular school, and the same might be said in regard to certain portions

FORESTAL INSTRUCTION AT GIESSEN. 113

which he had introduced in the introduction, and in the parts relating to statistics.

With regard to the several works cited, he says he would by no means have it understood that these are all the works published on the matters to which they severally referred. To beginners the teacher, according to my mind, says he, should only recommend tried leaders. This volume, as stated, was published in 1873.

In the periodical, *Deutsche Zeit-und Streit-Fragen*, for 1874, published in Berlin, is a paper occupying two entire numbers, entitled *Die Forstliche Unterrichtsfrage*, by Dr Hess, in which are given details of the previous history of the question whether Schools of Forestry should be associated with Universities and Colleges, or be maintained as independent institutions; reasons for the combination of the Schools of Forestry with the *Hochschulen*; statements of the advantages offered by Universities for giving instruction in forestry and forest science, and a review of objections to the measures which have been raised.

To this subject much attention has been given of late years; and the combination of arrangements for the study of forestry with those of existing Universities, and similar institutions, should not be considered an innovation, but a return to an early practice. It was [in the University of Berlin that forestry was first taught in Prussia, and thus was it in Giessen. And in view of that early arrangement, not only may Giessen claim to have been the first University in Europe in which this arrangement has been restored, but it may lay claim to be considered the first, or one of the first, Schools of Forestry established in Europe, taking precedence both of that founded by Cotta in Zilbach in 1795, and of one founded in Hungen by Martio in 1791, and long before that giving origin to the Academy in Eisenach. In a volume published by Dr. Hess in 1831, entitled *Die Forstwissenscaftlichen Unterricht an der Universität Giessen in Vergangenheit und Gegenwart:* Instruction in forest

I

science in the University of Giessen, in the past and in the present—he divides the past history of instruction in forestry in the University of Giessen into three periods—the first of which he designates that of instruction in forest science in the University in connection with political economy, which he states to be the period comprising from 1788 to 1824; the second period in which this was taught in a special School of Forestry from 1825 to 1831, a comparatively short period of six years; the third period that of the existing university forest instruction from 1832 to 1881 inclusive, comprising half a century.

In this volume are given details of the existing arrangements for the study of forestry; of the expense of the organisation and the instruction imparted; and of the duties of the teachers, with tabulated statements of the nationalities of the students in each session since 1825 to the present time, and of the College attendance, and present professional position of all surviving students.

In 1876 he published a Scheme of Lectures on Forest Economy. And, in the same year, he published an introductory lecture, delivered before the University, *Uber die organisation die forstlichen Versuchswesens:* On the organisation of forestal researches—a matter which has of late years commanded much attention.

He had previously published pamphlets on the same subject in 1870 and in 1872. He has issued also numerous fly leaves for the guidance and help of students and forest officials in making observations prosecuting experiments and calculating results in furtherance of the advancement of forest science, and larger works designed to advance the same.

The instruction at Giessen is regulated by order of 31st July, 1879, with alterations according to order of 22nd December, 1883. As has been intimated, there is no special forest district for purposes of instruction but forests around Giessen, and the railway combinations afford excellent facilities for reaching these. The number of students in the summer of 1885 was 44; in the winter of 1885-86, 47; of whom 7 were not Hessian subjects.

CHAPTER VI.

THE ROYAL BAVARIAN CENTRAL FOREST ACADEMY AT ASCHAFFENBURG, AND CLASSES FOR THE STUDY OF FORESTRY IN THE ROYAL LUDWIG-MAXIMILIAN'S UNIVERSITY IN MUNICH.

THE University of Giessen in Hesse Darmstadt, has became famous through the result of researches by Professor Baron von Leibig, and the numerous students whom his enthusiasm, and science, and skill, attracted to the laboratory under his charge; and the Royal Bavarian Central Forest Academy at Aschaffenburg has been made famous by the researches of Professor Dr Ernst Ebermayer, who here laboured as professor, and here began and conducted observations and studies of climatology in connection with the meteorological influences exercised by forests, which have commanded a world-wide commendation.

I have not had an opportunity of visiting Aschaffenburg, having passed through Bavaria much further to the south, *via* Munich, *en route* to Vienna, to visit the International Exhibition held there in 1873; but the history of forestal studies in the Academy has been long known to me.

Aschaffenburg is situated in the northern part of Bavaria, and is easily reached by railway from Darmstadt, or from Frankfort. It is a town which has had its origin traced, or at least attributed, to its having been the station of the 10th and 23rd legions of the Roman army.

The School of Forestry designated *Der Königlich Bayerischen Central-Forst-Lehranstalt*, stands in the Alexandra Strasse. It is a three-storied building of freestone,

130 feet long, standing in an open court; and behind this is the botanic garden.

On the ground flat are two large lecture rooms, a chemical laboratary, a hall containing objects and equipments connected with the chase, and a collection of models, with apartments for the use of the house steward and the beadle. In the second storey there is the business room of the director, the office of the actuaries, a lecture room, a large room for the drawing classes, the library, a hall containing mathematical instruments and apparatus pertaining to natural philosophy, &c.; and in the third storey are six halls containing other collections of objects and apparatus used in the institution.

As may be gathered from some of these statements, there is, or was, for I write of the past, provided for school purposes a collection of instruments and implements, and models of structures employed in forest ecconomy; a collection of forest products, natural and manufactured; a collection of objects connected with the chase, one of agricultural implements, a zoological collection, a mineralogical collection, a botanical collection and garden; a collection of mathematical instruments, and of apparatus illustrative of all departments of natural philosophy; a collection of drawing instruments, a library of works in all departments of forest science, and a chemical laboratory with all requisite apparatus and requirements, and similar work rooms for the study of zoology and other departments of natural history and physical science.

Thus was the Academy equipped when I had occasion to make enquiries on the subject; but there have been changes of which more particular mention will afterwards be made, and I have not at command information in regard to effects which these have had on the equipments which then existed.

In a brochure entitled *The Schools of Forestry in Europe: A Plea for the Creation of a School of Forestry in connection with the Arboretum in Edinburgh,* which I published in 1877, I stated that, preparatory to entering this institution, students were required to have passed through a gymnasium satisfactorily, and, with the sanction of Government, to have passed through a preliminary instruction of eight months, extending from September to May, under a *revier*, or district forester, approved and appointed by Government; to be not above 23 years of age; and to possess means of support during the period required for attendance at the forest school.

The instruction given in the school embraced—(1) Forest Science, or theory of forest administration in all that relates thereto; the physiology of arboreal and arborescent vegetation; forest culture; forest economy and technology, including road making, bridge making, and house building, the preparation of charcoal, potash, turpentine, tar, and lamp-black; the theory underlying forest conservation and forest management in the practical regulations of operations throughout an extensive district.

(2) Physical science, more especially general and economic botany, the latter having special regard to plants of importance to the well-being of the forest and the interests of the country, with practical instruction in gardening; mineralogy, including geognesy and geology, with the use of the blow-pipe; zoology, embracing the natural history of animals interesting to the forester, the huntsman, and the agriculturist, and more especially that of noxious insects and of game; and finally, natural philosophy, including organic, inorganic, and analytic chemistry, in their application to forests and agricultural operations, with experimental analysis of soil, of ashes of plants, of water, of air, and of manures.

(3) Mathematics, including algebra, plane geometry, cubic mensuration, trigonometry, statics, dynamics, optics; mensuration, with practical applications; instruction in preparation of charts, in taking levels, and in estimating the condition and value of forests.

(4) The theory of State management of forests, forest

police, forest legislation, forest administration, and the practical management of forests.

(5) Agriculture, with a special reference to soils, culture, manure, meadow culture, grain culture, and the theory of administration.

(6) A comprehensive theory of the chase: principles and rules for the management of game, *reviern* with deer, boar parks, and pheasantries, and for the utilisation of game—for the hunting or taking of game; and those of the game laws.

Instruction was given by encyclopædic lectures, with illustrations of the practical application of theoretic statements in excursions conducted by the professors, in forests near and distant; and necessary assistance toward meeting the expenses of such excursions was given to the poorer students.

The year of study began fourteen days after Easter, and extended over $2\frac{1}{2}$ years. In addition to this, those who aspired to the higher forest appointments —*e.g.*, those of forest master and upward—after finishing their course at the forest school, were required to prosecute the study of science at one or other of the State Universities at Munich and Wurtzburg; and after this, as at the conclusion of their course at Aschaffenburg, to undergo an examination on the required subjects of study.

Promotion to a higher appointment in the forest service was also dependent on a strict examination, and not more than one opportunity of passing was allowed.

Non-professional students and foreigners might join the forest school, but only on condition that they possessed the necessary qualifications for understanding the instructions given, and that they gave a written declaration that it was not their intention to enter the Bavarian forest service.

For Bavarian subjects the fee was $12\frac{1}{2}$ florins (25s), and for foreigners 25 fls. (50s) per half-year. Besides this, every candidate had to pay a matriculation fee of 4 fls. (8s), and a similar fee for certificate at the close.

Candidates were subject to a rule of discipline, and were

bound to a prescribed college course. Foreigners might obtain from the director a dispensation from particular studies. For the sons of Government officials, and more especially of those who were in the forest service, who were without the means of meeting the expenses, there were. provided five scholarships of 250 fls. (£25), ten of 200 fls (£20), and ten of 150 fls. (£15), and also five scholarships of 250 fls. (£25) for forest candidates of limited means who desired to go to the Universities named to prosecute their studies.

The college staff consisted of a director, who, together with the first professor of forest science, had the rank of a Government and Circuit Forest Councillor, and four other professors with the rank of forest masters, and a *revier* or district forester, who acted as lecturer and as actuary clerk.

The direction and control of the school was vested in the Minister of Finance and the Church and School Department of the Bureau of the Minister of the Interior; and in subordination to them was the director of the school.

To the director pertained the maintenance of order, the superintendence of the course of study and instruction, the granting of certificates, and everything connected with the management of the institution which had not been specially and expressly committed to the director and professors conjointly.

Students on finishing the curriculm at Aschaffenburg either entered on further practical training in the forest or in a forest office, or on attendance at a course of lectures on Political Economy at the University; and they afterwards received appointments to Government employment in the order of the excellence of the testimonials they have obtained.

In general the practitioner was not allowed, without forfeiture of all title to Government employment, to leave the service till he had attained the first or lowest grade of a Government official; but in special cases exemption from conformity to this requirement might be granted by the Government of the *Kreis*, Circuit or District.

The following is a more detailed account of later arrangements derived from the published *Programm und Satzungen für die Candidaten.*

The Institution was under the immediate control of the Minister of Finance and the Minister of the Interior for Religion and Education.

The body of teachers was comprised of a Director, appointed by the Crown, and who was also first Professor of Forest Science; with two or three Ordinary Professors also appointed by the Crown.

(*a*) A Professor of Chemistry and Mineralogy. (*b*) A Professor of Mathematics and Physics. (*c*) A Professor of State Forest Economy and Surveying. And, (*a*) A Lecturer on the Management of Forests. (*b*) A Lecturer on Botany. (*c*) A Lecturer on Zoology. (*d*) A Lecturer on Road-making and the Chase. (*e*) A Lecturer on the Mensuration of Woods and Forests, and (*f*) A Lecturer on Political Economy in its reference to Forest Science and Forest Laws.

Of all candidates for admission to the Institution, there were required—

1. Gymnasium certificate. 2. Certificates of having spent eight months in forest work in the State forest. 3. Certificates of age and of baptism. 4. Certificates of health and of possession of the bodily vigour requisite for the forest service, and of perfect sight and hearing. 5. Declaration of consent of parents or of guardians, when the candidate was not himself of age. 6. Legal guarantee of the possession of means of subsistence while under instruction.

Within eight days after matriculation they must find lodgings and report their address, and subsequently report any change in this, and they must at all times be prepared to produce, on demand, their ticket of residence obtained from the police. Candidates who were foreigners required only to produce evidence of their possessing the education necessary to enable them to understand the instruction given, of their good moral character and of the approval by their parents or legal guardians of their attending the institution.

Aspirants to employment in the forest service of the State, or of the large forest proprietors, and also sons of the latter, who could not produce all the pre-requisites to admission as regular students, but who could produce certificates of good moral character and of possessing the education necessary to their understanding the instruction given, might, as also might foreigners, be received at the Institution as *Hospitanten*.

Regular students were required to attend every class in its order; but to the *Hospitanten*, whether Bavarians or foreigners, it was allowed to choose what classes they should join, and of both of these classes there was required a promise of submission to the laws and bye-laws of the institution, copies of which were shown to them on their entrance.

The curriculum of study at Aschaffenburg embraced three different courses, and extended over two and a half years. The first course began eight days after Easter, and ended on the 31st of July. The second and third began on the 31st October, and ended on the 31st July in the following year—with a vacation of fourteen days at Easter.

In accordance with a resolution of the Minister of State, under date of 24th January, 1865, No 415, slightly modified subsequently as occasions required, the first course consisted of introductory studies.

Three hours weekly were given to the study of botany, the province of which science was explained, with the terminology employed, combined with illustrations in the garden; the requisites of vegetation were shown to be soil, moisture, air, light, and heat; and the distribution of plants was explained and accounted for.

Two hours a week were devoted to zoology, the organisation of animals, and the classification founded on this, and the characteristics of the vertebrata.

Four hours a week were given to chemistry, including exposition of chemical affinity and chemical notation, specific gravity, of combining proportions of elementary substances, and the special study of the non-metallic substances and their compounds, which have a special interest as nutriment of plants, or as constituents of the earth and of different kinds of mountains.

Three hours a week were given to physics, more especially statics and dynamics of solid bodies, with experiments illustrative of the mathematical laws by which these are regulated. Three hours a week were given to mathematics, more especially to plain geometry; and three hours a-week to algebra.

Four hours a week were given to chart and plan drawing, with instruction in the theory of projection; and in the nature of materials used in the construction of instruments employed, and in illustration of the use of them; and two hours a week were given to the study of political ecconomy.

The second course of instruction was carried through two sessions.

In the first, or winter session, of the second course, three hours a week were given to the study of forest management, and the profitable production of wood.

Two hours a week to instruction in the game laws and the chase.

Four hours to botany, embracing the study of embryos and of forms of the elementary organs of plants, and the functions of the several organs, the nourishment and growth of plants, the classification of these, and forest botany, with demonstrations in the garden.

Three hours a week were given to zoology, embracing the natural history of vertebrate animals profitable or injurious in connection with forests, and of forest game, with demonstrations on collections of these belonging to the institution.

Two hours a week were given to inorganic chemistry and the study of the lighter metals, and of their more important compounds, with a special reference to the analytical decomposition of these.

Three hours a week were given to mineralogy—crystallography, physical constitution of minerals, their phenomena under the blow-pipe and in solution, and the determination of different kinds of mineral substances.

Five hours a week were given to physics, embracing the study of atomics, hydrostatics, pneumatics, heat, accoustics, optics, magnetism, electricty, and meteorology and modes of making and recording meteorological observations.

Three hours a week were given to mathematics, trigonometry, and the mensuration of solids, and four hours weekly to plan drawing and the representation of various natural and artifical objects and crops, by the pen.

In the summer session there were devoted to the study of forest management four hours weekly; and two hours to forest protection, in so far as it does not come within the range of forest management, zoology, and meteorology; two hours to matters pertaining to the chase; two hours to botany, with the use of the microscope, in studying the histology of plants; to zoology and the study of the vetebrate two hours; to inorganic chemistry and the study of the heavy metals and their compounds two hours; the chemical anaylsis (qualitative) of soils, of ashes, of plants, of limestone, and of water, &c., two hours, and to mensuration three hours; and to plan drawing of various kinds four hours were given weekly in the course of the session.

The third course of instruction also extended over two sessions.

In the winter session of the third course four hours were given weekly to the study of systematic forest management, including the study of the object to be arrived at in the work, and of the different means by which the attainment of it had been sought, and the historical order of development of forest economy;

three hours weekly to the pecuniary profit of woods, including instruction in regard to the felling of trees, the bringing out of timber, the transport of wood, and the preparation and disposal of other forest products; three hours a week to the study of the management of State forests, embracing the study of the function of forests in nature and in States, and the duty of States in relation to forests belonging to the State, to communes, and to private proprietors; two hours to zoology of insects, profitable or hurtful to forests; two hours a week were given to the study of organic chemistry, in vegetable products; one hour weekly to agricultural chemistry, embracing everything relating to the chemistry of vegetation; one hour weekly was given to the study of soils and everything relating to them, and two hours to geology and mineralogy; three hours to the study of forest engineering, embracing road-making, levelling, bridge building, and dam-making; three hours a week to mensuration in all its departments and details, with two hours a week to the measurement of cubic contents of growing trees, and of wood contents of forests.

In the summer session of the third course—the fifth and last of the curriculum—four hours a week continued to be given to the study of systematic forest management, embracing the practical application of instructions previously given, the description and the estimation of contents of woods, and the whole round of forest operations were more minutely studied in excursions; three hours a week were given to the study of forest laws, three to that of forest administration, three to that of rural ecconomy, soils, tillage, manures, theory of fallows, and of alternations of crops, and the study of cerial and other crops and meadows; two hours a week to the estimation of pecuniary value of forests; and three hours a week to forest engineering, embracing what of hydraulic engineering relates to forests, and all connected therewith—hydrometry, evaporation, mensuration of water-flow in fountains and streams, drainage and irrigation, consolidation of river banks, &c.; erection of houses and other structures required in connection with forestry. Along with these arrangements for the communication of instruction in the class-rooms, corresponding arrangements were made for demonstrations and exercises in the practical application of what is learned in the academy—which was given in the forest, there being very great facilities presented in the immediate vicinity of Aschaffenburg. In the immediate vicinity of the town were public parks, presenting features characterstic of a scientific arboretum; not far off there were facilities for making geological, observations on the western boundary of the Spessart; and in this forest, which is the property of the State, were upwards of a hundred thousand *Tagwerken, or well-nigh a hundred and twenty thousand acres* of oak and beech woods;—while within the forest and around it there were works in which forest products were used; and facilities presented themselves for the study of the chase. At somewhat greater distance in Hesse, might be studied the forest ecconomy of coniferæ; and various forms of forest management might be studied in Odenwald, on the plains of the Rhine to the west of Aschaffenburg, and in the Palatinate. At a greater distance were the beech forests of the mountains of the Rhone and of the Steigerwald, and the pine and fir forests of France, and those of the Black Forest. And the railway intercommunication is such that all of these could be reached with little waste of time.

The arrangements for excursions were the following:— The Director of the Academy, who was also first Professor of Forest Science, in the second course of instruction, illustrated and established his instruction in forest management by practical operations in forests around Aschaffenburg, and availed himself for this purpose of every case of a forest district presenting anything remarkable in its culture or exploitation; and by experimental sowings and plantings of different kinds of seeds, and this with different kinds of implements.

In the third course of instruction he was required to illustrate his instruction in systematic forest management by devoting from fifteen to twenty days at least to practical measurements, calculations of annual increase, estimates of pecuniary value, determinations of vigour of vegetation, and descriptions of trees. And he was required every year to go through, with the students on the ground, the whole system of management to which a forest is subjected, for which the public forests in the vicinity supplied admirable facility; and a complete plan of operations, founded on this, had to be prepared by the students.

The second professor of forest science in his excursions with the students, had mainly to do with the ingathering and utilisation of forest products, the manufacture and disposal of these, the collection of accessary products of woods, such as bark, peat, &c., and the fixation of sand downs, and all that relates to the chase.

The professor of botany and zoology gave his attention to botanical demonstrations and exercises, the determination and classification of plants, according to the Linnean and the natural systems, and to similar entomological demonstrations, for which injured pine trees abounding in some of the public forests in the vicinity of Aschaffenburg, presented a good opportunity.

The professor of mineralogy and rural economy took his students on excursions for illustrations of his instructions in these subjects. And the professor of mathematics exercised the students in all departments of the practical application of these required in the management of forests, in land surveying, levelling, and road projecting—with the preparation of diagrams of the same, and calculations of the cubic contents of earth required, or of earth to be removed, &c.

Besides the excursions which could be accomplished in a single day, to which the Saturdays were as a general rule devoted, there were excursions to the forest districts of the Spessart, to the Odenwald, to the plains of the

Rhine, the Black Forest, the Taunus mountains, and the mountain ranges of the Rhine, which occupied from eight to fourteen days, and which were determined by circumstances, and conducted by the professor of forest science, with the assistance of the professor of geognosy or physical geography. And while these were being carried out, the other professors gave their time to all the students who remained in the Academy.

As these excursions were an integral part of the course of instruction, attendance was obligatory, and with this view provision was made for the expense of the longer journeys, being, in the case of students of limited means supplied to them.

On approval, admission and matriculation, Bavarian students, as has been stated, paid a fee of 12½ florins for the first part of a single session, and of 25 florins a year for each of the other courses. Foreigners paid fees of 25 florins and of 50 florins for these respectively. Besides this every candidate, without exception, paid 4 florins for his ticket of matriculation, and a like amount for his certificate on leaving the institution.

For sons of officers of limited means, in the service of the Crown, and more especially in the forest service, attending the institution, there were set aside annually :—

10 bursaries of	- -	150 florins.
10 Do.	- -	200 ,,
5 Do.	- -	250 ,,

And, besides these, 4 bursaries of 250 florins yearly.

To forest candidates of limited means, who had acquitted themselves well at the institution, and who wished to attend the course of lectures on political economy at the University in Munich or Wurzburg, and to candidates in the first course of a single session a small portion of the aforesaid bursaries might be advanced.

The bursaries might be forfeited by want of diligence in study, or by culpable misconduct; and to remove temptation to submit to undue privations, or culpably to contract debt and injure their parents or creditors, the certificate to be given at the close of the session might, with the sanction of the director, be pledged in anticipation for debts for medical attendance and medicine to the full amount; or for food, clothes, or books, to the amount of 20 florins; for lodgings, goods, shoes, stationery, and washing, to the amount of 10 florins, but not more; and all pawning of possessions was prohibited.

General or trial examinations were held at Easter to enable the professors to judge of the progress being made by the students, and in autumn to determine their admission to the more advanced course of instruction. It was not compulsory on foreigners to submit to these examinations, and it was allowed to them to undergo separate trial examinations, for which special times were appointed by the professors.

Numerical values were attached to the measures of success with which students passed through the different examinations, and, according to the sum of these, was the certificate which was given to the student determined. The certificate related to diligence, to attainments, and to behaviour while in the institution.

In the exercise of discipline, various degrees of censure were sanctioned. The simplest was admonition, and the most severe was censure followed by expulsion. Records were preserved of all censures and punishments inflicted, and by these the terms of the certificate granted to the students on leaving the institution might be modified.

Such was the School of Forestry at Aschaffenburg when I had occasion to make myself acquainted with its arrangements; and as supplying information in regard to such institutions, the report will hold good for all time.

Reference has been made to changes which have taken place since these regulations were issued, and the history of the school is not devoid of interest. The following is a translation of a narration of this to the time at which it was issued:—

THE BAVARIAN FOREST ACADEMY.

In 1807 there came together at Aschaffenburg several professional students, and administrators of forest economy, to arrange a course of study which might advantageously be followed at a forest school with a view to the establishment of one there as a private institute. In this they succeeded, and as such the institute existed for a considerable time. The Prince Primate took a hearty interest in the scheme, and adopted measures to raise it to the position of a State Institute. He granted for it a *locale* in the Schönthal, and a portion of the Spessart for its maintenance and use.

There were political difficulties in the way of the Prince Primate doing all he desired, and the elevation of the institute to the position in question was a gradual work.

In 1814, when the Principality and the City of Aschaffenburg were embodied in the Kingdom of Bavaria, there were seven teachers in the institute, of which one only was appointed to teach forest science, and that relating to the chase. The director was charged with the duties of the Spessart Forstmeister. He, as well as the other teachers of the institute, of which three were professors in other schools in the place, and one a physician, were remunerated by fees; only ten drew a salary from the State, and that amounted only to 150 florins—say £15.

The fees charged foreigners were one Caroline or louis-d'or per session, others paying half that amount; and there was allowed by the State, for experiments in physics and chemistry, 110 florins; for an attendant, 10 florins; and for fuel, 67 florins 20 kreutzer. With this addition the institute was assisted by the State to the extent of 1397 florins 2 kr.—say £140.

Of candidates for admission it was required that they should be able to write legibly, swiftly, and free from mistakes in spelling, be acquainted with the four simple rules of arithmetic, and be able to read fluently.

Lectures in the first course of instruction were given four days a week, from the beginning of November, till the end of May. Friday was reserved for study, and Saturday for chart drawing. The month of May was spent entirely in the Spessart forest. From the first of June till the last of September was occupied with the second course of instruction; and October was spent in practical work in the forest. And thus, in the course of a year, the student completed his study of the forest science of the day.

Aschaffenburg, belonging now to Bavaria, by a Rescript of 22nd September, 1815, it was announced that the institute, having then nine students, should retain the possession theretofore enjoyed; but it was not deemed equal to what was then required of a forest institute, and considerable changes were devised and submitted for consideration by the teachers: one special object being to separate the course of instruction given to candidates for the higher from that given to candidates for the subordinate departments of the forest service of the State, and this to be so effected that in the first section youths to be employed as forest warders or guards might pass through their preparatory studies in six months, and then enter upon their further training in the forest; and that this course of school instruction should prove preparatory for superior students passing into the second section of the institute, in which they might be, in the course of a year, further instructed, so as to be fitted for the administration service; and in a third section, by a course of two years' longer instruction they might be trained for the inspector service.

In view of this the teachers, in 1816, and again in 1817, commended the institute to the favourable consideration of the Government; and, by petition under date of 29th March, 1817, the magistrates of the city, representing the depressed condition to which this had been reduced by effects of war, and by the withdrawal of officials from it as a seat of Government, prayed that it might be assisted to recover a state and condition befitting the See of a Bishop, by the founding of a forest institute there.

Meanwhile, the Bavarian General Forest Administration had expressed an opinion which had an important bearing on such a proposal. On 15th March, 1816, they had under consideration the question, ' In what way for the future can suitable training and instruction be provided for forest officials employed in the different departments of the service?' And a report on the subject, extending over 232 pages, prepared by the Oberforstrath von Olschläger, which was not altogether favourable to the carrying out the proposal which had been made, had been submitted to the King.

In regard to that it is remarked—' An opinion to be of value must proceed on the recognition of the fact that what is required must be contemplated from two different points of view according as it may be desired to have an educational institution for the higher, or one for the subordinate departments of the service. For the latter it is to a great extent sufficient that the official learn in a purely empirical way, under skilled forest officials, the work which is to be done in the forest; though it is the case that the establishment of an institution for the instruction of such has much to be said in its favour. But, on the other hand, while this we admit, we cannot assent to the opinion expressed by the teachers at Aschaffenburg, that they have established the point that there is a necessity for the existence of an institute for the instruction of forest officials of every grade, and this one alike thoroughly equipped for the teaching of theory and practice. The provision for the one must of necessity operate injuriously on the other; and more especially do we affirm it to be impossible to send out young men from the school completely prepared for practical work. The school should only give theoretic or scientific instruction as a preparation fitting both for the superior and the subordinate appointments in the forest service. And for this a University recommends itself on the ground that the lack of practical training there, as is also to some extent the case in forest schools, is more than counterbalanced by the greater advantage of the generally higher scientific education there attainable, while what is awanting may subsequently be acquired in actual work in the forest.' This I may remark, in passing, is an arrangement now strongly recommended.

This professional opinion, published by the General Forest Administration, states moreover, that 'on no account must the fact be overlooked that scientific forest instruction can only produce in such as possess the preliminary instruction requisite for admission to a University, the results which are desired; and that only those who have not attained so complete a preparation should be directed to a special forest institute for instruction in forestry adapted to their attainments and modes of thought, to meet which, the whole method of instruction should be adapted.'

The instruction for the lower departments of forest science, the reported opinion goes on to state, after giving a *resumé* with careful consideration of the grounds on which the opinion is based, 'might be handed over to the forest institute specially organised for this; but the higher branches of forest science should be included in the sphere of University studies.' And this latter measure is advocated specially on the ground that 'only thus can the felt want of scientific and systematically educated forest practitioners, who are required for the higher departments of the forest service, be expected to disappear, and then there might be drawn into the lower departments of the forest service of the districts men of good school education; and the forest schools which were then (1817) indispensable * might be gradually reduced in number, or altogether given up.'

It is stated in the report that the meeting of this necessity for a University scientific instruction might

---

* There were at that time in Bavaria several private Forest Schools at Kempten, Keufreuten, and several other places, give a valuable impulse to the general improvement of the forest economy of the country, and the introduction of the new, securing the combination of this with the old, where this has been tested by experience and proved satisfactory. Care only being required in regard to some matters lying outside the essential, the true worth of which may be readily recognised.

It is laid down that :—

1. Aspirants for employment in the higher departments of the service should go through a three years' course of instruction in the University ; and

2. For the subordinate appointments a two years' course of instruction in a Forest School ; but

3. Instead of this, for aspirants of limited means, three years' instruction in forest labours might be accepted as a valid qualification for the service.

What should be required in regard to 1 and 3 may be easily specified says the report ; but with regard to 2, the selection of a site for a School of Forestry, greater difficulty might be experienced from the small number of places being so situated as to combine all that is desirable in the site of such an institution.

The General Forest Administration specifies the following requirements in the situation of a Forest School :—

'1. It should be situated as nearly as possible in the centre of the country ; and

'2. In a place in which rent and provision are moderate in price.

'3. There should be means of securing life culture at command without temptation to waste time in amusements ; and

'4. It should be in the vicinity of forests, giving an opportunity of learning much of the many-sided methods of exploitation.

'In regard to 1, 2, and 3, Ausbach, Bamberg, and Eichstaed, might be mentioned ; in regard to 4, of these three places, Bamberg offers the greatest advantages, and next to it Eichstaed.

'Against Aschaffenburg it may be objected its general position, and the aridity which prevails there. On the other hand, the means of instruction existing there are not unimportant: there is its proximity to the Spessart, with its forest of broad-leaved trees; its facilities for flottage, and its timber trade; there are existing there the school and its museums; and above all there speaks in its favour its attractions for foreigners; while there is already a school established there. It would be difficult in Bamberg to compete against the attractions of the Forest Schools at Dreissigacker under Bechstein, and at Tharand under Cotta, as well as the newly-founded Forest School at Fulda; and at Bamberg we could only look for foreign students from the Rhine, from Baden, and from Wurtemberg.'

The final proposal was to the effect that for these last reasons the preference should be given to Aschaffenburg; that the school to be established there should be thoroughly equipped; and that students of the country should be allowed to visit those schools in other countries with which they were competing; but that Aschaffenburg should only be considered a school for aspirants for subordinate appointments in the forest service. The National Universities, which alone supplied the best means of skilful scientific general education for all departments of the service of the State, supplying also for the training of the higher forest officials, the most suitable means of instruction in the higher forest science, and the fundamental and auxiliary sciences.

The report treats further of the organisation of the forest institute, and of the instruction to be given in it to aspirants for subordinate appointments in the service, inclusive of that of *revier*, or district forester, so as to secure, in the shortest time practicable, thorough instruction in the fundamental and auxiliary branches required in the profession adapted to the capabilities of such students.

An opportunity will afterwards present itself for a more

full description of the question raised in regard to the most desirable site for a School of Forestry.

Let it suffice to state here that the report, which was in favour of a University training and education being provided for forest officials, shows that the Forest Adminstration of that day (1817) had clear views of the importance of the best and highest possible education being secured for those who should be entrusted with the management of the State forests.

In July the town of Aschaffenburg again addressed the Minister of State with a pressing petition to the Crown Prince Ludwig, praying him to support the prayer of the petition they had addressed to the King some months before, that the forest institution situated in that vicinity might be maintained and extended—the first cost of doing which would be inconsiderable, and the current expense might be met out of the Aschaffenburg students fund.

The District Government, on the other hand, proposed that the education should rather be made more exclusively technical, reducing the number of professors from seven to four, giving up the study there of political economy, and of land and water engineering And the Council of General Forest Adminstration, in a subsequent report, advocated the measure that in Aschaffenburg there should only be a school for the training of ordinary subordinate officials, on the ground that only in a University, or similar educational institution, can the broad and comprehensive training and instruction required in the higher departments be secured.

It seemed to be considered impossible that a School of Forestry so situated could ever become what a School of Forestry might be made. But consideration was given to the circumstance that a School of Forestry already existed there; that aid in the improvement of it was offered from a local fund; and that the town had suffered from its being incorporated in the Kingdom of Bavaria. And in accordance with an urgent renewed application from the town, made under date of 3rd September, 1819, to the King, by Rescript dated 29th September, 1819, the establishment of a new forest school was promised; and in the autumn of 1821 this was opened with provision for instruction both for the higher and the subordinate departments of the forest service. But it was maintained afterwards that this had been done more from a regard to the interests of the town, than from professional advice.

The staff consisted of a director, four professors, a drawing master, an actuary, and a beadle.

Within a year the insufficiency of this school, for accomplishing the purpose of its organisation, it was alleged, began to appear: and in the autumn of 1823, at the instance of the Minister of Finance, a re-organisation of the school was called for. A two years' course of study was required of candidates for subordinate offices in the forest service, for entrance on which a gymnasium certificate was required of the pupils; and a more prolonged course of study was required of others, and of selected pupils to qualify for higher appointments. An increased allowance was made by the State, and the number of professors was increased.

This was effected in the year 1823-24, but in August, 1824, the district government complained of the management of the school, and in 1827 the director resigned, and difficulty was experienced in procuring efficient teachers; and by decree of 19th October, 1832, the forest institute was closed as not having fulfilled the expectations formed of the results to be obtained.

It was thought that something might be accomplished by having a school for the training of subordinates in some other and better situated locality, and by requiring the superior officials to study in a *Hoch-schule* in Munich, and transferring thither two of the professors from Aschaffenburg—a forester and a mathematician.

Nothing having been done to fulfil the first mentioned suggestion, in the Bavarian chamber, in 1840, Dr Müller brought forward a proposal that a special forest school should be organised in which, by a course of study, extending over a year and a-half or two years, candidates might be fitted for the higher departments of the forest service of the country.

In the sitting of the 28th March the Minister of State, Von Adel, replied to the effect that the special forest school at Aschaffenburg had died a natural death; that students of theoretical forest science had now every facility afforded them in the *Hoch-schule* of Munich; that as to the practical instruction students had got little or nothing of this at the special School of Forestry now extinct; and that Government had created bursaries which might be obtained by young foresters travelling for observation or for studying practical operations under *forst meisters* or district foresters; and that Dr Müller's proposal was best.

But the desirableness of a School of Forestry for the training of subordinates was not lost sight of by the Government; and in a memorial submitted to the King on 27th May, 1842, it was stated that for the higher departments of the forest service an appropriate education might be obtained at the University, but that provision for the education and training of subordinates who might not have studied at a gymnasium, or required to do so to fit them for their duties, was still a desideratum. It was submitted that this might be supplied in connection with the so-called *Gewerbeschulen* or Trades Schools of the country; and four towns were proposed as sites for such schools—Nurmberg, Bamberg, Kaiserslautern and Anspach. It was suggested that to the *Gewerbeschulen*, in any place, there might be added two special teachers and an assistant.

It was alleged that this would entail great expense; and Aschaffenburg and Anspach, pleading the saving which might be effected, petitioned the Minister of State that one or other of them might be appointed the site of such a school.

In a note, dated 28th March, 1843, Anspach was declared to be the preferable of the two places named.

On the 13th April a conjoint report as to the necessity for some such institute was made to the King by the Minister of Finance and the Minister of the Interior; and finally, on the 25th August, it was delivered that Aschaffenburg should be the site of the school in question.

I have before me details of the comparative advantages of the two places, but I deem it enough to state the fact. Not a little was done to give prominence to the secondary character of the school, and to the superior education provided at the University; but at the University in the year 1846-47 only seven students of forestry enrolled themselves, and in the following year—1867-68—*none;* and the arrangements came to nought. The Aschaffenburg staff bestired themselves, introduced reforms and improvements; and by ordinances issued under date of 14th September, 1848, and 26th October, 1850, it was declared that Aschaffenburg should be attended by all candidates for the higher appointments in the forest service, there to pursue the special technical or professional studies; but that this should be followed by their going through the University course of study of political economy, with the pre-requisite study at a gymnasium, or a certificate, No. 1, from the School of Forestry, which would absolve them from this last.

In the discussion of this question in the Legislature of Bavaria, the Upper Chamber of *Landesbehörden*, the superior *Forstbehörden*, and the Ministry, spoke strongly for the giving up of the Academy in Aschaffenburg, and of transferring the instruction in forest science and forestry to one of the two National Universities; but the *Ultra-montane* majority of the Chamber spoke out as one man for the maintenance of the Academy, and they voted liberally the money supposed to be necessary for a re-organization of the institution to meet the requirements of the times.

The School of Forestry—the inception of which dates from 1807, dissolved in 1832, but re-organized under the Ministry of Finance in 1874 – was, by decision of the Government of 30th March, 1874, united to the University of Munich. But this was not the last of the changes which have passed upon this institution.

From a statement in the *Centralblatt für das gesammte Forstwesen* of November, 1877, I gather that the Minister of Finance had then addressed to the Bavarian Chamber of delegates a detailed printed memoir (filling 21 pages 4to), in which he expressed his decision that the Forest Academy at Aschaffenberg should be given up, and arrangement be made for instruction in forest science and forestry being given in connection with the University of Munich, stating the motive by which he was led to the decision; and, in doing this, he subjects the historical development of forest institutions in Bavaria to an exhaustive criticism.

The arguments pro and con are stated at great length in the *Denkschrift Betreffend den Forstlichen Unterricht in Bayern* already cited, the result ultimately was the arrangement at present existent—a Forest School at Aschaffenburg, with the theoretic and advanced studies prosecuted in the University, with attendance at the station for experimental researches, in a royal order of 21st August, 1881, is enjoined.

Par. 1. In the Bavarian State forest service there will only be received as candidates for admission such as possess a certificate of having passed through the whole course of study at the forest institute at Aschaffenburg, and the final examination in theoretic forestry in the University of Munich, with the State examination in practical forestry with satisfaction.

Par. 2. The institute of forest instruction at Aschaffenburg has the functon of preparing young men who desire to give themselves to the Bavarian forest service, in the fundamental and accessary sciences, so far as may be necessary to qualify them for pursuing an exhaustive study of forest science in a University, and in the forestal experimental institute in Munich, besides which the forest institute in Aschaffenburg offers an opportunity to students for pursuing the study of forest science with other designs that of entering the forest service of Bavaria.

Par. 3. The forest institute is immediately under the control of the Minister of Finance, and the Minister of Religion and Education.

The staff of teachers comprises:—

Par. 1. The Director, who, as principal of the institution, has to take the direction of the instruction taking part in this according to directions from the Ministers of State entrusted with the charge of the institution.

Par. 2. The Royal Oberforster of the Kleiostheim district, who has his residence in Aschaffenburg, whose subjects of instruction are also determined by the Ministers named.

3. A professor of physics and of mensuration.
4. A professor or tutor for mathematics.
5. A professor of botany.
6. A professor of zoology.
7. A professor of chemistry and mineralogy.
8. An assistant in management, who is also teacher of chart-drawing and librarian. Besides the teaching staff there is a house steward, whose functions are specified in special instructions relative to service.

Par. 9. Students who do not desire to enter the Bavarian forest service may be received as *Hospitanten* into the forest institute. These must bring certificates of good character, and prove that they have such education as will enable them to understand the lectures given. They may obtain certificates of satisfactory attendance on the entire course, or of attendance and proficiency in particular departments; but these certificates are not available for their admittance into the Bavarian forest service.

Par. 11. Aspirants for employment in the Bavarian State forest service, possessing a complete certificate from the Forest Institute at Aschaffenburg, must continue their studies for at least two years at a German University, and must attend one year at least at the practical exercises in the forestal experimental research station at Munich. This attendance may be given during the last year of their attendance at the University.

Par. 14. There shall be held every year in the University of Munich a concluding final examination on theoretic forestry, to which can be admitted only such students as possess a complete certificate from Aschaffenburg, and have met the requirements of par. 11 of this order. The requirements in regard to these examinations will be determined by the Ministers of State for Religion and Education, and for Finance.

Candidates who have passed this examination satisfactorily shall receive a final certificate of their having passed the whole of the professional studies, with a declaration of their competency to enter on the practical work of the State forest service. Candidates who have not been declared fitted for this may present themselves yet again for examination, but only after at the least one year, and at the most two years study at the University, such students may also be required again to attend the forest experiment institute at Munich, and that for at least a complete session. There may be admitted to these examinations students at the University of Munich who do not contemplate aspiring to the State forest service of Bavaria. These will receive a certificate of the result of this examination; but this confers no right to enter the Bavarian forest service.

By *Bekanntmachung*, or proclamation by the Ministers of State, under date of 10th November, 1881, were specified details of the arrangements thus made necessary.

As orignally in the University of Giessen the instruction in forestry were given in connection with the faculty of political economy, a similar arrangement has been adopted in the University of Munich. According to the published *Verzeichnis*, or programme of lectures in the Ludwig-Maximillan's University, for the winter session of 1884-85, five lectures, or more strictly speaking five hours of lectures on sylviculture and forest conservation were given weekly; 4 hours lectures on earth and the chemistry of these; 3 hours on natural laws regulating agriculture and sylviculture, with practical work in the forestal chemistry laboratory; 4 hours on the measurement of wood with practical exercises in the art; 3 hours on Saturday in forest surveying; 4 hours in forestal calculations in connection with forest statistics; 4 hours structure and physiology of plants with microscope demonstrations; 3 hours public practice in use of the microscope, daily private practice in use of the microscope; 5 hours State forest science, and 3 hours history of forestry. And according to the programme of lectures for the summer session of 1885 there were given 5 hours a week to lectures on forest exploitation and forest technology; 1 hour to conservation of forests and woods, with excursions and demonstrations on specified days; 4 hours climatology and meteorology, with introduction to meteorological observations; 3 hours chemistry of plants with regard to forestal and rural economy; 2 hours to forest statistics in rentability or pecuniary returns from forests, with excursions and practice in valuation of trees and all forest produce on certain specified days; 3 hours forest culture plants; 3 hours vegetable pathology with botanical instructions; 5 hours forest adminstration, with practical exercise on specified days; 2 hours road-making and laying out of land, with practical exercises on specified days; land surveying 3 hours, with practical exercise on specified days; 2 hours forestal policy, and means of transport in relation to private and political economy.

The latest information at my command in regard to instruction in forestry in Bavaria is contained in a paper by Dr Tuisko Lorey, Professor of Forest Science in the University of Tubingen, On forestal instruction, and forestal experimental research, in a handbook of Forest Science edited by him. In this it is stated that the latest directions are contained in the *Finance ministerialblatten* of 17th November, 1881, under the heading of royal order relative to forestal instruction 21, VIII. 81 ; and in a proclamation relative to examinations in the University, relative to practical examinations and relative to praxis of 16th November, 1881.

Aspirants to the forest service are educated and instructed in the forest institute at Aschaffenburg, and in the University of Munich, and as has been appointed since 1878 : first two years, or four sessions, being spent in study at Aschaffenburg, and the result of this being shown by an examination. This is followed by two years' study at the University, concluding with an examination in Munich ; of this latter time spent in Munich at least one year must be spent in attendance on practical work in forestal experimental work. The requirements for admission and *Maturitäts Zeugniss*, or exit certificate, from a gymnasium or *real-schule* of the forest order.

In the forest educational institute at Aschaffenburg, which is under the immediate supervision of the division of the Minister of the Interior relative to church and school affairs, and the Minister of Finance, the object, in so far as the royal Bavaria State forest service is concerned, is to impart the preparatory instruction in the foundation and professional sciences requisite to fit for profitable attendance at the University. In view of this the instruction embraces elementary mathematics ; in the higher mathematics, the analytical geometry of plane surfaces, and the elements of differential and integral calculus ; inorganic and organic chemistry, mineralogy, botany, zoology, mensuration, and chart drawing ; in like manner, in regard to forestry, primary instruction in sylviculture and in *extenso* forest protection, the science of the chase and road-making. Of teachers there are in all eight. Along with the director, a second decent of forest science, who is also manager of the attached forest instruction *revier*, or district of Kleiostheim, one for physics and mensuration, one for botany, one for zoology, one for chemistry and mineralogy, one for mathematics, one for chart-drawing. For chemistry there is also an assistant.

In the University of Munich, which is under the immediate supervison of the Minister of the Interior for church and school affairs, the forestal experiment institute connected with the University is under the Minister of Finance. The professional instruction, in so far as this is not completed at Aschaffenburg, is given;* and with this the study of political economy and jurisprudence is attended to. All the branches are treated of every year. Forest science is comprised in the faculty of political economy.

Specially adapted to forestal studies are six regular professorships, four of which are specially forestal, with one for forest botany and one for forest soil, climatology, &c. All the holders of these belong to that faculty. In consequence of excellent railway connections, the excursion district is very extensive and instructive.† The exit examination is held yearly. It is exclusively oral; and it embraces all the branches, the study of which is not completed at Aschaffenburg. The examination commission consists, under the presidency of a high State forest official, of teachers from the University, and occasionally from the technical *Hoch-schule* for particular accessary sciences.

The number of students of forest economy in the summer session of 1885 was 92; and in the winter of 1885-86, 94; of whom respectively 36 and 41 were not Bavarian subjects.

---

* Several of the studies included in the Aschaffenburg programme, such as road-making and mensuration, are also treated of in Munich, but this is done principally in the interest of forest managers who are not Bavarian subjects.

† There is an excellent article by Gayer, on the excursion district of Munich in the *Forstwissenscaftliches Centralblatt*, for 1880, p. 73, and 1881, p. 1.

CHAPTER VII.

ROYAL WURTEMBURG FORESTAL AND AGRICULTURAL ACADEMY AT HOHENHEIM, AND FORESTAL INSTRUCTION IN THE UNIVERSITY OF TUBINGEN.

In the history of the Schools of Forestry at Giessen in Hesse Darmstadt, and Aschaffenburg and Munich in Bavaria, we meet with different phases of the evolution, or development of such institutions, issuing in their incorporation in the National Universities. In the kingdom of Wurtemberg we meet with another different phase of similar transformation.

Until within a few years ago, the study of forest science in Wurtemberg was provided for in the Royal Wurtemburg Academy of Land and Forest Economy at Hohenheim, about 11 *kilometers* distant from Stuttgart, the capital of the kingdom, and near to the Wurtemberg forest.

Hohenheim was formerly a Grand Ducal country residence, with numerous out-buildings attached. It is situated on the high level plateau of Filden, 390 meters above the level of the sea, and 140 meters above the level of the vale of Stuttgart. The inhabitants, inclusive of the students, numbered in 1880 about 300. The number of families was 30.

The palace buildings, with wings and out-buildings, contain about 100 apartments for the accommodation of students.

In 1818 there were founded there two separate Academies: an agricultural one and a forestal one. In June, 1820, these were united; and the combined schools were re-organised September 9th, 1865.

From an official publication entitled *Ubersicht über die Organisation, die Zwecke, den Lehrplan, die Lehrmittel, Aufnahmebedingungen und sonstigen Verhaltnisse der K. Wuerttemb. Land-und Forstwirthschaftlichen Akademie Hohenheim*, it appears that the Royal Wurtemberg Academy of Land and Forest Economy at Hohenheim is a palatial edifice, and is supplied with all the requisites for the study of rural economy, agriculture, and forestry; it is surrounded with grounds of considerable extent, including experimental and botanic gardens; and is supplied with other facilities for the study of practical operations. Instruction was at that time communicated by lectures, exercises, excursions, and experimental work.

The curriculum extended over two years, divided into four sessions, one commencing on October 15th, and closing on 9th March, the other commencing on 1st of April, and closing on 15th of August, and this was followed by a vacation of two months.

There were three distinct departments of study—*Landwirtschaftliche Disciplinen*, embracing what relates to agriculture and rural economy; *Forst-wirthschaftliche Disciplinen*, embracing what relates to the treatment of forests; and *Grund-and Hilfs-wissenchaften*, or fundamental and accessary sciences; and the arrangements were such that students could avail themselves of the provision for instruction in either the one or the other of the two first-mentioned branches of study, or to the full extent of the provision for instruction in one, and to some extent partially of the provision for instruction in the other,—and in many of these cases with or without availing themselves of the provision made for instruction in the fundamental and accessary sciences.

The subjects of study were the following, the order in which they were studied being definitely determined by provision for the convenience of the professors and students.

I. Rural economy.

A History and literature of rural economy.

B Agricultural and rural productions. General doctrine in regards to agricultural productions, and to the reclaiming and drainage of land.

a Agricultural implements and machines. *b* Special doctrine in regard to cereals and similar products. In addition to which, in the concluding session, special lectures were given on the growth and the production of hops and of tobacco; on lime-making; on the culture of fruit trees; and on the culture of culinary vegetables. *c* General doctrine in regard to the rearing of animals, with application of the same to the breeding of sheep and preparation of wool; and in the last session special instruction was given in regard to the breeding of horses, of oxen, and of small cattle, on silk-culture, and on the keeping of bees.

C Rural economy.

a Treatment and disposal of economical products. *b* Valuations, estimates, and exercises in drawing out schemes of operation. *c* Bookkeeping.

D Technology of rural economy.

In connection with these series of lectures there were given appropriate illustrations in the collections of models, of implements and of machines, in the museums of wood and of soils, in the experimental fields, in the nurseries and arboretum and different gardens, in the cattle-folds and in the workshops of the institution, together with practical exercises in making valuations, estimates, and schemes of exploitation, excursions, &c., &c.

II. Forest economy.

A Encyclopædic view of forest economy, with a special reference to the study by students of rural economy of allied subjects in this department.

B History and literature of forest economy.

C Forest products.

a Forest botany. *b* Sylviculture. *c* Forest protection. *d* Technical properties of timber. *e* Uses of forests; and forest technology.

D Forest economy.

a Mensuration of trees and forests. *b* Partition of forests for exploitation. *c* Valuation of forests. *d* Practical management of forests.

E Administration of Crown forests. A special introductory lecture on the subject and exposition of the forest laws of the kingdom of Wurtemburg.

F Encyclopædic view of rural economy for the instruction of foresters.

In connection with these series of lectures there were given, in occasional extensive, and in regular less extensive excursions, &c., similar to those connected with instruction in rural economy, appropriate demonstrations in different forest districts, in the Botanical Garden and Museum of Forest Products, and practical exercises in the calculation of cubic measurement of trees, and cubic contents of woods, and in the laying out of forests for exploitation.

III. Fundamental and accessary sciences.

A Political economy.

B Agriculture.

C Jurisprudence. Legislation in regard to Wurtemberg forest management, legislation in regard to rural economy.

D Mathematics—arithmetic, algebra, plane geometry, geometry of solids, trigonometry, practical application of geometry. In connection with this there was regular practice in land surveying and levelling, and in the mensuration of forests with the theodolite.

E Physical science—experimental natural philosophy; meteorology; experimental chemistry; agricultural chemistry; production of fodder; physical geography; geology; technical mineralogy; botany; anatomy and physiology of plants; diseases of plants: special botany; anatomy and physiology of domestic animals; zoology; special zoology; introduction to the use of the microscope. In connection with these studies there were practice in the chemical laboratory, demonstrations in the botanical museum and garden, and in the experimental fields of the rural economy experimental farm, and regular botanical and geological excursions, &c.

F Veterinary science.

a Materia medica and formulas of recipes. *b* Pathology and therapeutics of domestic animals. *c* Special lectures on epidemics. Veterinary assistance in the birth of animals *d* Theory of shoeing.

G Technical arts—rural architecture, preparation of plans.

Besides these, from time to time lectures were given on general science, and on subjects connected therewith.

The regular course of study of forest economy extended over two years; but every year the lectures were attended by amateur students or others, who were not required to go through the whole course; and the director was always ready, as were also the collective body of instructors, to aid such in determining how long they should remain, and what classes they should attend, with a view to making the most of the time they could spend there.

Of all students applying for admission there were required—

1. Certificates that they were above eighteen years of age; but in rare exceptional cases, by special resolution of the *Senatus Academicus*, youths who had not completed the eighteenth year of their age might be admitted.

2. Certificate in regard to previous course of study. In case of the applicant having previously studied at the University, or other superior educational institution, there was required a regular certificate of disjunction from the officials of the college.

3. In case of the applicant, according to the law of his domicile not being of age, a certificate from his parents or guardians of their consent to his joining the Academy, or otherwise residence of his being independent and free to act for himself.

4. Subscription to obligation to conform to the statutes issued for behaviour of students in the Academy, a printed copy of which was supplied to every student.

Foreigners were further required to produce a passport, or a ticket of legitimation from the proper authorities.

From students of forestry designed for the forest service of the State, in accordance with Royal Ordinance of 20th January, 1868: *In Betreff der Forstdiens-prufung*, and order of the *R. Ministorium des Kirchen, und Schul-wesens* of the 19th June, 1873, in regard to the *Maturitäts-prufung*, there was required, in addition to what has been stated, a certificate of having passed an examination of qualification for entrance on advanced studies.

And from students of forestry who had no view to entering the forest service of the State there was required, as is required of the students of rural economy, satisfactory testimony of their possessing the scholarship and training necessary for profitably availing themselves of the instructions given in the Academy. When they did not already possess a certificate of graduation, or diploma indicative of their attainments, this might be obtained in connection with their attendance at the Academy, which was valid as a qualification for the same.

Others than students, gentlemen whose views were to make themselves acquainted with the discipline and teaching in the Academy or other institutions at Hohenheim, might remain as *Hospitanten*. The admission of such, as a rule, did not take place at the commencement of a session, but some six or more weeks thereafter, and the stay of such as *Hospitanten* was limited to four weeks.

In case of students having to leave the Academy, at least fourteen days notice had to be given of their intention, excepting in admitted cases of necessity.

On regular departure from the Academy, a certificate, in a prescribed form, was given to any student, stating the time he had spent in the Academy, the lectures he had attended, the character of his behaviour, and if he deserved it, the diligence with which he had prosecuted his studies.

Diplomas were granted at the close of their course to students of rural economy, but some attended only a short period. To these, and to students of forest economy, an opportunity was given at the close of each session, by written exercises and *viva voce* examinations, to obtain certificates in regard to their attainments in such of the branches of study as they might desire.

Prizes also were offered as encouragements to study, and the fact of one or more prizes having been taken relieved the student of the necessity to prepare written exercises while under examination for his diploma.

A certificate in regard to his attainments could be obtained by the student only in the form of one or more of the certificates given after examination, at the close of each session: and only in the case of his having submitted to one or more of these examinations. On special application a student might, while pursuing his studies in the Academy, obtain an interim certificate in regard to his diligence and behaviour.

In case of any student being expelled, the fees, &c., paid were not returned. This was also the case if permission to leave in the course of a session were applied for and granted. But in case of sickness, or of a summons to military service, on special application, the fees, &c., in question were re-paid.

For lodging, instruction, and the management of the institution, students of rural economy, if subjects of Wurtemburg, pay 180 marks (£9) per annum; if foreigners, they pay 500 marks (£25) the first year, and 350 marks (£17 10s) the second. Students of forest economy, if subjects of Wurtemburg, paid also 180 marks (£9) per annum; if foreigners, 350 marks (£17 10s) each year; and by paying extra fees these latter might also attend classes connected more immediately with rural economy, which did not come within the range of their prescribed studies.

Hospitanten, who are subjects of Wurtemburg, pay for the use of an apartment one mark a day; but they have to provide their own bed and bedding, and they are free to attend all lectures, and avail themselves of all the means of instruction offered by the Academy. *Hospitan-*

ten who are foreigners have the same liberty, and they are provided with bed and bedding, for which, and the use of the apartment, they are charged two marks a day. Each of the students has a furnished room, and those who are foreigners are supplied with bed, bedding, and towels; these three requisites students, subjects of Wurtemburg, provide for themselves. Arrangements may be made for the occupation of better rooms, or for living outside the Academy: these I need not detail. In regard to food each student may make his own arrangements. He may dine outside, or at the college table. The average expense of board is about two marks a day. Those who board in the Academy lodge with the house steward, and pay 140 marks at the beginning of each session, from which is deducted monthly the amount of their monthly bill.

It is made a special condition of the appointment of the house steward that he, on due remuneration, must provide food for sick students, whether they take their food daily from him or not, and to prepare either such food as they themselves may desire, or such as may be prescribed by their medical attendant, preparing it well, and serving it either in their own room, or in the hospital of the Academy, as occasion may require.

Amongst the numerous provisions for facilitating study at the Academy of Hohenheim, many of which relate more especially to agriculture and rural economy, there is a forest district of about 2,200 hectares or 5,500 acres, partly composed of Crown forests and partly of communal forests, embracing different kinds of soil, different forms of management, and different modes of culture, which were under the direction of one of the two professors of forest economy; and besides this *Forstreiver*, there are others in the vicinity of Hohenheim, to which access was had, and also an arboricultural experimental garden.

There is a botanic garden of $4\frac{1}{2}$ hectares or $12\frac{1}{4}$ acres, with some 2000 species and varieties of plants of importance in forest and in naval economy; and a so-called

ROYAL WURTEMBURG FOREST ACADEMY.

exotic garden of about 8 hectares or 20 acres, laid out with a special view to instruction in forest botany.

There is a collection of models of implements, machines and structures pertaining to forest economy; a museum of forest products, and one of forest manufactures, &c. Some of the models are of full size and in working order, others are in section, or constructed on a reduced scale.

A mineralogical cabinet, with a collection of geological formations and fossils employed in illustration of lectures, coutains about 14,000 specimens.

A botanical museum contains different herbaria, numbering conjointly 10,000 species, with several specimens of many, and a collectiou of numerous microscopic preparations, a collection of vegetable pathological specimens illustrative of diseased malformation, also many models of flowers, fruits, furze, &c., and finally a collection of some 7000 specimens of fruits and seeds. There is a chemical laboratory, with 16 double stations for students, provided with all the necessary appliances for work. A cabinet of natural philosophy containing instruments and apparatus required for instruction of the students in mathematics, mensuration, and natural philosophy. A library containing about 10,000 volumes, open to the use of the students. An experimental forest station, with experimental garden, and a station for making and recording meteorological observations. For the use of the chemical laboratory and chemical agents a charge of eight marks, or eight shillings, per session, is made to the students of practical chemistry.

There is also a reading-room provided with newspapers and periodicals, for the purchase of which a charge of four marks each session is made.

An account of this Academy at Hohenheim is given in detail in a publication relating to the meeting of German agriculturists and foresters at Stuttgardt in 1842, under the title of *Die Konigliche Wurtembergische-Lehranstalt fur Land-und Forstwirthschafttische Akademie, Hohen-*

heim, and in the published account of the semi-centennial celebration of the institution, held 20th November, 1868, under the special title of *Geschichtliches uber die Land-und Forstwirthschaftliche Akademie. Hohenheim, von Professor Dr V. Fleischer*. A concise notice is also given in a pamphlet prepared for the Vienna Exhibition of 1873, *Der Hohere Landwirthschaftliche Unterricht in Wurtemberg*, by Professor Walter Funke.

Professor Mathieu, of Nancy, in describing this institution, in *Revue des Eaux et Forets*, 1874, says : - ' The little kingdom of Wurtemberg, with scarcely two millions of inhabitants, has spared nothing in providing it with whatever could contribute to the success of instruction or to the progress of science. This truly liberal spirit has led to the establishment of magnificent agricultural galleries, where we find collected to the number of sixteen hundred the various tools and machines employed in labours of the field ; elegant rooms filled with forestal collections, implements, woods, and various products ; cabinets in botany, zoology, mineralogy, and geology ; instruments for use in studies of physics and for geodesy ; a station for experiments concerning woods, and another for meteorology. Its library numbers 5,500 volumes, and its reading-room contains numerous periodicals in all languages, of which 49 were scientific, agricultural, or forestal journals, and thirty-five were of the political, literary, or illustrated class.'

It has been reported in a preceding chapter, relating to the Royal Saxon Forest Academy at Tharand, that after existing for a lengthened period as a school exclusively devoted to instruction in forestry, there was introduced into the Academy a School of Agriculture or Rural Economy ; that the two were after a time combined ; but that afterwards the two were dissevered, and the Academy again restored to its primal condition of an exclusively Forest Academy. In Hohenheim the School of Forestry, originally an independent institution, was likewise brought into combination with a School of Agriculture ; and here, too, a severance has been effected. And again, in Wurtemberg, as in Hesse Darmstadt, there existed formerly in the National University of Tubingen provision for the study of forestry. Of this the late Dr Hough of the United States forestry section of the Department of Agriculture has reported :—

'Since 1817 the University of Tubingen has had a Chair of Agriculture and Forestry in its faculty for State economy. It has for its object to furnish students with the knowledge necessary for employment in financial and administrative affairs, and therefore only the more important points of information are presented in the lectures, but they penetrate deeper into the spirit of the different systems of agricultural and forestal economy, with the view of pointing out the motives concerned, and in this manner of rendering their relations to financial matters and to the public interests more fully understood.

'This course of instruction presents little of interest in the practical business of the forester, as compared with the abundant facilities and broad plan of education afforded at the school at Hohenheim. Many of the students of the latter find it, however, to their advantage to attend for some time the lectures of the University for the purpose of gaining a fuller knowledge of the auxiliary sciences.'

Towards the close of 1880 arrangements were under contemplation to combine the School of Forestry with the University as an integral part of the same; and in due time these being completed, the change was made.

Amongst the reasons for this were the following :— Formerly there were two classes of foresters; one of which studied administration and law, besides the usual professional course of study relating to the management of forests; while the other confined their studies to these: mathematics, physical sciences, and forestry. But after a time this second class almost disappeared in consequence of the limited prospect they had for their future, and almost all the young foresters, after having passed their exit examination, went to study at the University.

As there was nowhere a complete curriculum of forestry excepting at the University of Munich, the young Wurtemberg foresters went to Munich, studied there, and only took at Hohenheim their final profesional studies, while the different education of the young agriculturists, and of the majority of the young foresters, also occasioned difficulties. This state of things could not last, and in course of time the study of forestry was transferred to the University at Tubingen, and at Hohenheim was continued the Agricultural Academy. Forstrath Professor Dr Nordlinger wrote to me two years and more after the change had been made:—'We have now more than forty students of forestry, while at Hohenheim we had not more than twenty. Instead of having two professors ordinary we have but one professor extraordinary, which suffices for the accessary and foundation sciences. Our students of sylviculture sit alongside the medical and other students. In a word we constitute an integral part of the University without being an institution apart; our collections, and our exercise ground, and forest arboretum, are the only exception to this.

'Tubingen is exceptionally well situated forestally. We find ourselves on the confines of the most extensive and most interesting forests of the country—the Black Forest, Schoenbuch, the White Forest of Swabia, &c.'

Subsequent experience justified the expectations which had been entertained of good being likely to be the consequence of the change, one result of which is that the number of students has now risen from less than twenty at Hohenheim to upwards of fifty at Tubingen; and the staff of professors of forestry has been increased, from which other benefits have flowed. Unlike what has generally been the case in other countries on the Continent of Europe, in which the whole body of forest officials are educated upon the same principle, though not to the same extent, this being secured by requiring them to be educated at national institutions in Wurtemberg, previous to this change, while the necessity for a higher education in men occupying the higher positions in the service was recognised, there was no national provision for this being given; aspirants were accordingly allowed to procure this where they might or where they choose—it was enough that it was acquired. From this there resulted a risk of want of unity and uniformity in the views and plans of those who had the administration and superior management of the State forests. This was less likely to occur now than previously; and the advantage of a knowledge of what was being done in the forests of other and adjacent countries could be secured by forest excursions.

At the Aacdemy at Hohenheim it was found, as has been intimated, that the preliminary or preparatory studies required in the two departments—forestry and rural economy—did not always accord. To the students of the former mathematics was absolutely necessary; while to the latter, valuable as might be the educational effects of the study of mathematics, these were not requisite as a practical preparation for rural economy, and arrangements required in the interests of the one body of students came occasionally into collision with the arrangement required in the interests of the other: this was now avoided.

Moreover, the advantage of general culture, the importance of which has been more and more recognised of late years, had facilities for this being acquired presented by the University greatly in excess of those offered by Hohenheim—University associations tending to expand the mind; while the general tendency of a special school is understood to be to impair the general development of the intellectual and moral faculties. In the programme of lectures in the University of Tubingen for the winter session of 1885-86 there are specified upwards of two hundred different classes, to any or all of which, in accordance with arrangements in Universities in Germany, the students have access to an extent unknown in our Scottish Universities; and a greater number of classes, upwards of two hundred and twenty, were open to them in the same measure in the summer of 1886.

The studies are arranged as pertaining to one or other of seven faculties: evangelical theology, catholic theology, law, medicine, philosophy, political economy, and physical science. And there are classes for instruction in riding, rifle shooting and fencing, gymnastics, dancing music, and drawing. There are also forty University institutes or educational appliances, inclusive of the University library; the Hoffman library for exercises and discussions in political economy, in the faculty of which forestry is included; forest museum; museum of forestal and rural economy; station for forestal experimental research; workshop of forest technology; technological museum; botanic museum; botanic garden; and museums and laboratories of various kinds, pertaining to the study of different departments of physical science.

In the University forestry pertains to the faculty of political economy, with classes for instruction in matters more immediately or more remotely connected therewith. As pertaining to this faculty there are classes for the study of the following subjects, which are strictly forestal: cyclopædia of forest science; forest botany; sylviculture: forest management applicable to trees of different kinds; forest protection and conservation; forest exploitation; forest valuation and forest statistics; forest economy appropriate to State forests; forest technology; forest road making; structure, physiology, and histology of trees, and in the classes of the faculty of physical science are all the fundamental and accessary sciences generally included in what is considered as complete course of instruction in forestry and forest science.

In regard to forestal instruction in Wurtemberg, Dr Tuisko Lorey, professor of forest science in the University of Tubingen, reports:—'The existing arrangements are determined by order of 30th October, 1882, and order of

7th October, 1885; the instruction is, under the supervision of the Minister of Ecclesiastical and Educational affairs, imparted in the University of Tubingen. All professional subjects, with the exception of road-making and the chase, are subjects of prelection every year, as are also all the foundation and accessary studies, which are treated fully in the University. Forest Science is included in the faculty of political economy. The prerequisities to admission to study are an exit certificate of some Latin gymnasium, or of a Wurtemberger's *real-gymnasium.*'

An appointed period of study for aspirants to the State forest service is as definitely specified as is the place of study. The average of the latest promotions gives a period of from seven to eight sessions. The examinations are twofold :—*A*. An entrance examination held twice a year in Tubingen by professors, in the presence of a commissioner of the government. It embraces mathematics; elementary mathematics, and analytic plane geometry; mensuration and levelling, with drawing of charts; physics chemistry, botany, zoology, and geology. And *B*. First forest service examination, held twice a year in Tubingen, in presence of a commissioner, like as is the case with the entrance or preliminary examination, which embraces forest discipline, national economy, and jurisprudence. To conduct the studies in forest science there are two ordinary and one extraordinary professors. There is no forest *revier* or district appropriated for use in instruction; but the vicinity is rich in forests presenting in this respect great variety and good opportunities for excursions and demonstrations.

An account of the vicinity in respect of forests is given in a paper by Dr Lorey in the *Allgemeine Fort Blatter* for 1882, entitled the Excursion Region of the University of Tubingen.

The number of students in the summer session of 1885 was 16, and in the winter session 1885-86, 26, of whom respectively 2 and 8 were not Wurtembergers.

CHAPTER VIII.

FORESTAL INSTRUCTION IN THE GRAND DUCHY OF BADEN IN THE POLYTECHNICUM IN CARLSRUHE.

In Tharand, Neustadt-Eberswalde, Hanover, and Eisenach, we have what may be characterised as the germ—the forest school—developed into the Forest Academy, Forestal School or School of Forestry. In Giessen, in Bavaria, and Wurtemberg, we have the School of Forestry transformed into a section of the National University. In Baden we meet with yet another phase of development—the School of Forestry taking its place *ab initio* as a section of a Polytechnicum, which has also been the case elsewhere. This educational institution was established in 1832; and in 1834 Dr Klauprecht, who had been associated with Hundeshagen and his successors in giving instruction in forestry in Giessen, was called to take charge of forestal instruction in the Polytechnicum in Carlsruhe. It was established with a view to the development and diffusion of technical science and art; and the instruction given is based on the principle that a thorough preparation for any technical calling must be founded on a *Mathematischer, natur-wissenschaftlicher, wirthschaftswissenschaftlicher, historischer, und künstlicher bildung*, or an education in accordance with mathematics, science, the economical application of these and of art, and a correct acquaintance with history.

It supplies to the engineer, the mechanican, the architect, the chemist, and the forester, opportunities for acquiring education and instruction in general, and in special sciences and arts; while the financier, the pharmaceutist, the land surveyor, the teacher of mathematics, and of natural history, and all who have devoted themselves to other industrial occupations than those named, may find in attendance at it appropriate instruction; and students of pharmacy have the option of attending either the Polytechnicum or the University, as a pre-requisite to examination. The instruction required for different industrial occupations is arranged in accordance with the following divisions:—

1. The School of Mathematics. 2. The School of Engineering. 3. The School of Machinery. 4. The School of Architecture. 5. The School of Chemistry. 6. The School of Forestry. The method of instruction takes the form of lectures, examinations, practice in drawing and in construction, work in the laboratories and workshops, and excursions. Combined with the Polytechnicum are the following collections by which instruction is aided and sustained:—

1. A cabinet of philosophical instruments. 2. A geological and mineral collection. 3. A zoological and botanical collection. 4. A collection of models belonging to the School of Engineering. 5. A collection of models belonging to the School of Machinery. 6. A collection of models belonging to the School of Architecture. 7. A technological collection. 8. A collection of instruments used in land surveying, &c. 9. A collection of models for use in teaching geometry. 10. A collection of plaster casts. 11. A collection of objects connected with forests. 12. A library and reading-room of science connected therewith.

There are also laboratories—(1) a chemical laboratory; (2) a laboratory of natural philosophy; (3) a mineral laboratory; (4) a laboratory of organic chemistry; (5) a laboratory of technological chemistry.

Further:— there is an arboretum, or forest garden;

And finally, workshops:—(1) for making models in clay; (2) for making models in plaster-of-Paris; and (3) for making models in wood.

The Polytechnicum is under the immediate control of the Minister of the Interior, and is governed by a director appointed annually by the Sovereign, on the ground of his election by the professors; a petit council, consisting of the director, his predecessor in office, and three others, elected and appointed annually in the same way; and the grand council, consisting of the collective body of ordinary professors.

The body of instructors, consisting of professors, lecturers, college tutors, and assistants, numbers forty-nine in all.

There are two sessions in the year: the winter session is from the 1st of October to the 15th March; the summer session from the 15th of April to the 31st July; and provision is made for profitably employing the holidays and vacations in excursions or tours of observation, with or without the assistance of professors.

In illustration of the advantages of combining a School of Forestry with other educational arrangements, I may state that there are only two professors of forest science in the Polythechnicum at Carlsruhe. Most of the classes not taught by them attended by students of forestry are classes taught in some of the other schools or faculties of the institution. The exceptions are that the Professor of Economics has a special meeting with the students of forestry one hour a week during the summer session, and the Professor of Rural Economy in the University of Heidelberg has a meeting with them for two hours once a week both summer and winter.

Where it is desirable to minimize as much as possible the staff of teachers, much may be effected by substituting for several separate professorships one of Economic Botany and Forest Economy.

'The requirements for admission are as follows: citizens of the State, who wish to enter the State forestry service, after attending a full course at the gymnasium, are admitted, and must pass through a course of four years, of which the first two are devoted to those fundamental and auxiliary studies which do not relate directly to forest science, but which serve as a preparation for the remaining two which embrace the forest course proper. Foreigners may attend the first two years or not, as they prefer.

The least age of admission is 17 years. At the close of the second year the State students must pass an examination in natural philosophy and mathematics, and if they fail they are allowed one more trial. This examination entitles them to enter upon the last two years of special forest studies in which they are taught agriculture, forest jurisprudence, and the higher mathematics, when they are again examined, and if passed, are qualified for a place in the State service. The examination at the end of the first two years is by the professors of the polytechnic school, and the final one by the forest directors, a person skilled in law, a professor of agriculture, one of forest management, and two professors of mathematics.

'After passing all examinations the candidate is assigned to the general district foresters as an assistant, to enable him to become practically acquainted with his duties, and he receives a tract of forest to manage. After six to ten years, according to the number waiting, he gets a position as general district forester. The number of these districts in Baden is at present 110, and about four of these appointments are made annually. The Forestry Direction has its seat in Carlsruhe, and is composed of six members, who are inspectors.'

The following were the arrangements for study in the School of Forestry during the sessions from 1st October, 1876, to 31st July, 1877 :—

STUDENTS OF THE FIRST YEAR—WINTER SESSION.

Geometry of solids, 3 hours per week ; drawing of plans and diagrams, 2 hours ; botany: morphology, physiology, and cryptogamic plants, 3 hours ; experimental physics, 4 hours ; repetitorum of the same with the assistant, 1 hour ; experimental organic chemistry, 4 hours ; conversational examination on the same, 1 hour ; freehand drawing, 2 hours.

SUMMER SESSION.

Arithmetic, 3 hours per week ; drawing of plans and

diagrams, 2 hours; botany: special natural history of phanerogamic plants, 3 hours; botanical excursions and practice in determining plants, from two to three half days; experimental physics, 4 hours; repetitorum of the same with the assistant, 1 hour; organic experimental chemistry, 4 hours; qualitative chemical analysis, 2 hours; work in chemical laboratory, 5 hours; freehand drawing, 4 hours.

STUDENTS OF THE SECOND YEAR—WINTER SESSION.

Plane and spherical trigonometry, 2 hours per week; analytical geometry of planes, 3 hours; drawing of plans, 2 hours; practice in the handling and use of instruments used in land surveying, &c., 4 hours; mineralogy, 4 hours; practice in mineralogy, 3 hours; vegetable physiology, 3 hours; use of microscope, 2 hours; zoology: general zoology and special natural history of vertebrata, 3 hours; work in chemical laboratory, 5 hours.

SUMMER SESSION.

Drawing of plans, 2 hours; geology, 4 hours; practice in mineralogy, 3 hours; practice in agricultural chemistry and vegetable physiology, 9 hours; geographical distribution of plants, 1 hour; zoology: natural history of invertebrata, 3 hours.

STUDENTS OF THE THIRD YEAR—WINTER SESSION.

Differential and integral calculus, 4 hours; practical geometry, 3 hours; forest improvement and technology, 4 hours; forest protection, 4 hours; forest soils and climatology, 2 hours; forest excursions and practical exercises, Saturdays—encyclopædic study of rural economy, 2 hours; political economy, 4 hours.

SUMMER SESSION.

Elements of mechanics, 5 hours; exercises in practical geometry, afternoons; agricultural chemistry, 2 hours; forest exploitation and history of forest economy, 5 hours; natural history of forest trees, 3 hours; forest excursion, and practical exercises, Saturdays; encyclopædic study of rural economy, 2 hours; financial science, 3 hours history of the German forest police, 1 hour.

STUDENTS OF THE FOURTH YEAR—WINTER SESSION.

Forest policy, 3 hours; taking up of trees, means of growth, and management of forests, 6 hours; excursions in woods and forests, with a view to the establishment and completion of the lectures on the subjects mentioned, Saturdays and free afternoons; forest roads and hydraulic engineering, 3 hours; encyclopædic study of rural economy, 2 hours; popular study of law, 3 hours.

SUMMER SESSION.

Forest engineering and history of forest science, 5 hours; history of the German forest policy, 1 hour; pecuniary valuation of forests, 3 hours; forest police, 2 hours; forest statistics, 2 hours; forest administration and management, 2 hours; encyclopædic study of rural economy, 2 hours; forest and game laws, 2 hours; excursions in woods and forests, with a view to the establishment and completion of the lectures on all the subjects mentioned above, Saturdays and free afternoons.

To students in the forest school there is recommended, moreover, attendance in the following classes:—

WINTER SESSION.

Modern history, more especially of Germany since 1816, 4 hours; modern history of German literature since the death of Schiller, 2 hours; hygiene, or preservation of health; anthropological introduction and domestic hygiene, 2 hours.

SUMMER SESSION.

Roman history, 4 hours; Lessing's Nathan der Weisse. 1 hour; public hygiene, or preservation of health, 2 hours.

The arrangements in regard to admittance, fees, diplomas, holidays, &c., and in regard to hospitanten are similar to those in the Agricultural and Forest College at Hohenheim, though varying in several particulars.

The area of forests in Baden is 510,924 hectares (1,262,493 acres.)

I visited the Polytechnicum at Carlsruhe in going to the International Exhibition held in Vienna in 1877; and I have had no opportunity of revisiting it.

According to the notice of this School of Forestry given by Dr Lorey, it, together with the institution of which it is an integral part, is under the control of the Minister of the Interior. There are still only two professorships of forest science, the holders of which alternately, in different years, occupy the post of President of the School of Forestry. The prescribed course of study extends over three years, during which aspirants to the State forest service may study at a Technical School, a University, or an Academy.

The requisite to admission is an exit certificate of proficiency from a gymnasium or a *Real-schule* of the first rank. The instruction given comprises the special study of prescribed fundamental sciences, and theoretic study of special professional subjects. Proficiency in the first must be determined by the entrance or preliminary examination, which takes place once a year in the Polytechnicum before a commission composed of professional men. Proficiency in the strictly professional studies is tested by the annual principle examination, before a commission composed of some of the members of the commission for the administration of the State domains, and other State officials, and men of learning. Amongst subjects of examination are included rural economy, elementary mechanics, analytic geometry, differential and integral calculus. There is no special forest *Revier* or district appropriated for forest study. The excursion region is the nearest zone of the neighbouring extensive forests of the valley of the Rhine and the Black Forest. The number of students in the summer session of 1885 was 16, and in the winter session 1885-86 26, of whom respectively 2 and 8 were not subjects of the Grand Duchy of Baden.

CHAPTER IX.

REQUIREMENTS FOR ADMISSION INTO THE FOREST SERVICE OF GERMAN STATES, IN WHICH THERE DO NOT EXIST SCHOOLS OF FORESTRY.

IN States of Germany in which there do not exist Schools of Forestry, the lack is met by requiring aspirants for employment in the forest service of the State to study at one of the Schools of Forestry in regard to which information has been supplied, and otherwise to qualify themselves for official appointments. Dr Lorey, Professor of Forest Science in the University of Tubingen, reports the following as the arrangements in the several states named :—

In *Mecklenburg-Schwerin* the requirements for admission to the forest service are determined by Order of the 10th January, 1883. The service is divided into two sections— the service of *Revier*, or district foresters, and that of inspectors of State forests

For admission to the career of a *Revier* forester there are required the qualifications necessary for entering the first class of a gymnasium, or of a *Real schule* of the first order, one years preparatory instruction, attendance throughout a full course of study in a School of Forestry, or at a University in which there are professorships of forestry, and an examination on theoretical forestry. Previous to this examination the aspirant to the service must serve one year as a volunteer in the *Mecklenburg Jäger* battalion. An examination in theoretical forestry is held twice a year by a commision under the presidency of a Minister of the Cabinet conducted by one or it may be two forest inspectors, and two professional men for the examination in mathematics, natural sciences, &c.

For the career of a forest inspector there is required, in addition to what has been mentioned, a full *Maturitäts* certificate from a gymasium or *Real-schule* of the first order, and attendance for at least two sessions at a University in the study of jurisprudence and political economy, and with these the qualifications of an officer of the Reserve.

In *Mecklenburg-Strelitz* for admission to the forest service there is required a *Maturität* certificate from a gymnasium or a *Real-schule* of the first order, one years preparatory instruction, attendance at one of the Prussian Schools of Forestry, and examinations at the same according to the form prescribed for foreigners who are not Prussian subjects, and experience in land-surveying and levelling attested by a geometrician.

In *Oldenburg* the requirements for employment in the forest service of the State is determined by law of 18th April, 1864. There is required a certificate of fitness for entering the first class of a gymnasium, or the equivalent exit certificate of the Upper Burger school in Oldenburg, one year's preparatory instruction, two years' study at a superior School of Forestry, or at a University, and examination by a Commission at the Ministry of Oldenburg.

In *Brunswick* instruction in forestry was given in the Caroline College in Brunswick, for years previous to 1777, but since that time this has been discontinued. The present requirements for admission to the forest service of the State are regulated by an Order of 6th November, 1874. They are a *Maturitäts* certificate from a gymnasium, or a *Real-schule* of the first rank, with unexceptional entry in regard to mathematics, one year's preparatory instruction, attendance of at least two years at a course of study at an Academy, a Polytechnicum, or a University, upon which there follows once a year an entrance examination in Brunswick.

In *Meiningen* the requirements are determined by Order of 8th April, 1871. They consist of fitness to enter the highest class in a gymnasium, or *Real-gymnasium*, one year's forest training, attendance at a School of Forestry, the choice of which is optional, but attendance at the full course of study in which is required, and submission to the forest examination in Meiningen, or instead of this, the production of certificate of having passed the examination of the forest institute in Eisenach.

In *Altenburg* the requirements are determined by Order of 12th November, 1864. They are fitness for entering the first class of the gymnasium, one year's forest training, at least two years' course of study at a School of Forestry, the selection of which is at the choice of the aspirant. Any who study at Tharand, and submit to the final examination required there, need no other testimonials; otherwise they must submit to an examination analogous to that, in the College of Finance. For the higher appointments in the service there are required a complete *Maturität* certificate from a gymnasium, and at least one year's study at a University.

In *Coburg-Gotha* the requirements are determined by law of 24th April, 1860. They are fitness for entering a first class in a *Real-schule*, satisfactory acquaintance with mathematics and skill in arithmetic, one year's preparatory instruction, attendance at the School of Forestry of Eisenach, or other Forest Academy, or alternately at a University, and an exit certificate from this school after passing an exit examination in accordance with arrangement between Weimar and Gotha-Coburg.

In *Anhalt* the requirements determined by Order of 20th October, 1877, are a full maturity certificate, one year's preparatory instruction, a two years' course at least of professional study, the choice of school being left with the aspirant, and attendance of at least a year and a-half at a University for the study of jurisprudence and political economy. In the case of a superior official appointment being desired, besides an examination in the theory of forestry, a *tentamen* in forest science before an examination commission of the Grand-Duchy, or alternatively at a Forest Institute.

Schwarzburg-Sondershausen has the requirements determined by Regulation of 24th March, 1876. They are, fitness for entering a first-class in a gymnasium or *Real-gymnasium;* one year's preparatory instruction, at the least a two years' course of study in an Academy or a University, and examination at Eisenach.

In *Schwartzburg-Rudolstadt* the requirements determined by Regulation of 16th March, 1871, are a maturity certificate from a *Real-schule* of the second rank, or that for the first-class of a gymnasium; and in other particulars such as are required in Schwartzburg-Sondershausen.

In *Waldeck* the requirements are determined by Order of the 12th December, 1883, supplementary to Orders of 12th February, 1856, and 12th June, 1876. They are, a maturity certificate of a gymnasium, or *Real-gymnasium;* one year's preparatory instruction, and, at the least, two years' attendance at a superior forest institute, and submission to a *tentamen.*

Reuss-Gratz has no particular specification, but the younger branch of Reuss requires, according to Orders of 3rd May, 1875, and 6th December, 1882, a maturity certificate from a gymnasium, or *Real-gymnasium* or *Real-schule* of the first rank, at the least six months' preparatory instruction, the study of forest science at any German School of Forestry, with, at the least, a course of five sessions, and a certificate of having passed the whole of the examinations of the same.

Schaumburg-Lippe requires a maturity certificate, preparatory instruction, attendance at a School of Forestry, and a forestal examination.

Lippe-Detmold has the requirements determined by Order of 13th January, 1886, which are a maturity certificate from a Latin gymnasium, or a *Real-gymnasium,* with unexceptional statement in regard to mathematics, and a year and a-half preparatory instruction, military service, with the qualification required of a reserve officer, two years' attendance at a School of Forestry, determined by the Forest Directory, and a general examination at the Academy in accordance with what is required in Prussia.

Alsace-Loraine has the requirements determined in accordance with the law of 30th December, 1870, publication by the Chancellor of the Government of 24th March, 1874, Prescriptions for the examinations of 5th October, 1875, and Order of 13th November, 1883. They are, a maturity certificate of a gymnasium, or *Real-gymnasium*, or *Real-schule* of the first rank, with an exceptional statement in regard to mathematics, at the least seven months' preparatory instruction, two and a-half year's attendance at a Forest Academy or University, and the passing of a preliminary examination, which is held once a-year in Strasburg, by a mixed commission, under the presidency of the Landforstmeister. It is, moreover, determined that Germans who submit to the preliminary examination, and other examinations, are admissable to the practical training, and subsequently to the State examination. Moreover, Germans who do not exceed thirty-one years of age, and have spent at least two years in study at an Academy, and have passed through all the requirements for the superior grades in the forest service of their own country, may be, after a year's perfectly satisfactory employment in the forest service of Alsace-Lothingen, admissible to permanent appointment in the same.

Dr Lorey states that in every case in which no special mention is made of physical qualification, the full fitness for the military service is required; and that this applies also to the before-mentioned States, in which Schools of Forestry have been established.

CONCLUSION.

The Schools of Forestry in Germany are so connected with the general arrangements for primary, secondary, technical, and university education, as to form an integral part of the educational institutions of the country, which affects both the organic constitution of the school and the mode of study, and to some extent, the subject matter of instruction. The School of Forestry in all its phases in Germany is an institution adapted to the school system of the country; but arguments advanced in support of the proposals to transfer the provision for instruction from the special school to classes in the University, or other superior educational institution of the country, may be found applicable in other countries in which the establishment of a School of Forestry may happen to be contemplated as has been shown.

The subject was discussed in documents issued by the Government of Bavaria in connection with the question raised in regard to an *erfkenburshe* maintenance of a special School of Forestry at Aschaffenburg, and the establishment of professorships of forestry in the University of Munich.

After lengthened consideration, in which as an aid to the discovery of arrangements which might most satisfactorily meet the requirements of the service, opinions were solicited from distinguished students of forest science and forest economy known to hold different views upon the subject, which opinions were printed and fully considered, and it was ultimately determined that in all the circumstances of the case it was expedient to maintain a School of

CONCLUSION. 173

Forestry at Aschaffenburg, from which candidates for subordinate appointments in the forest service passing satisfactorily the exit examination, might be received into the service, while students aspiring to appointments to superior offices in the service should proceed to the University of Munich, and if found qualified, prosecute there the study of forest sciences required to fit them for the efficient discharge of the duties pertaining to the offices to which they aspired.

The arguments may be considered as resolving themselves into these two : in a University or Polytechnicum there may be secured at less additional expense superior and more comprehensive professional teaching and instruction than at a special School of Forestry, while the facility with which forests at a short distance, or more remote, may be visited by the students under the guidance of a teacher, or made the field of actual work, compensates any advantage by a special school located in or adjacent to a forest and does so without distracting the attention of the students from their studies. And at a University, or similar institution, there may be secured the general culture becoming a Government official, and advantageous to the individual and to the community in many ways, while the tendency of residence and study at an isolated special school is to cramp and warp the intellectual development and social virtues.

The position in the educational system of the country which is most desirable for a School of Forestry to occupy in the country was more comprehensively discussed in a Congress of German foresters, forest administrators and professors, and students of forestry, held at Freiburg in the autumn of 1874.* The question was submitted in this form : *Forst-Akademie oder Allgemeine Hoch-schule ?* Under this latter designation are comprised the Polytechnicum and the University in con-

---

* In regard to this discussion some additional information is given in a volume entitled *School of Forest Engineers in Spain, indicative of a type for a British National School of Forestry,* pp. 214-217.

tradistinction to which is the *Fach-schule* or training school for some one profession like the *Forest Academy*, which may be considered as differing as completely from the primary, and secondary, and superior common schools, as from the gymnasium, the *Real-schule*, the *Bürger-schule*, the *Gewerbe-schule*, and the *Allegemeine Hoch-schule* if not more so, the difference between the *Fach-schule* and these being this—the *Fach-schule* provides education, instruction, and training for some one special *fach*, trade, or profession; the Polytechnicum does so for several, it may happen to be for many such; while the University, as its designation implies, contemplates provision for the study of everything, or at least of every department of study, and preparation for all, or each of all, the so-called learned professions.

It is in view of this difference mainly that the question *Akademie oder Allegemeine-Hoch-schule?* has been discussed in Germany. This once decided in favour of the *Allegemeine Hoch-schule*; it may have been the case that there may have been in some places local discussions as to the relative advantages of the Polytechnicum and the University; but I have never heard of such, excepting in one case, which will be mentioned immediately. The question seems to have been generally determined by the accidental circumstance of which was at command. Where there was a Polytechnicum but no University the Polytechnicum supplied a home for the School of Forestry. Where there was a University and not a Polytechnicum, there was no room for question; where, as was the case in Munich, there was both a University and Polytechnicum the preference was given in accordance with the guiding principle to the University, in the absence of anything creating a reason why this should not be done.

In regard to all the Schools of Forestry in Germany, of which mention has been made, it is reported by Dr Lorey, that besides the regular demonstrations, forest exercises, and forest excursions, there are more extensive excursions for study and observation undertaken in the same over other States.

The early history of the movement, issuing in the organisation and establishment of Schools of Forestry, shows that it was desired to found forest economy upon a scientific basis; and the arrangements adopted at these stations for forestal experimental research, established at the sites of existing Schools of Forestry, justify the designation Forst-Wissenschaft, or Forest Science, given to the basis upon which the advanced forest economy of the day is based. It is inductive in its method; it has been so from the first organisation of the embrio forest schools of a hundred years ago; and it had been so for a long time before. The schools of Hartig and Cotta were in reality associations of enthusiastic young foresters, acting under the influence of sagacious experienced seniors, by whom they were instructed as to what observations to make while engaged in the execution of their ordinary work; to whom they communicated the results; and with whom conjointly they sought by mathematical calculations and otherwise to evolve the laws regulating the growth and increase and natural reproduction of forests, and of trees of different kinds growing under different conditions. And the importance which is attached to having a true scientific basis, for everything that is done is indicated by the expenditure bestowed upon stations for experimental research, which are established at the sites of several Schools of Forestry.

I have not at command details of the expenditure upon each and all of these. I find it reported in 1863 that the expense of maintaining the stations vary greatly. For the year ending 1882 the expenses of the stations in Prussia amounted to 27,000 marks = £1,356; Bavaria, 44,000 = £2,200; Saxony, 14,000 = £700; Wurtemburg, 7000 = £3,500.

The total amount expended annually for the maintenance of forestal experimental stations in Germany some years ago was about £6000.

The importance attached to the instruction given in

Schools of Forestry in regard to the practical application of forest science as formulated in the past, and as being extended in the present, is indicated by the requirement of attendance at foreign schools by forest officials in States in which there is no national provision for such instruction; and it is further indicated by the amount of expenditure incurred in the organisation and maintenance of such institutions where they have been established.

I have mentioned elsewhere * 'there is some difficulty in stating what may be considered the total expense incurred in the maintenance of almost any of the Schools of Forestry on the Continent,' from this circumstance among others—in the published accounts no mention is made of what might be considered the equivalent of rent for the premises in which the school is located, and of the grounds connected with these—whether a simple arboretum, or an extensive forest, as the case may be. I know not an exception. The premises and grounds, sometimes a mansion, sometimes a palace, with corresponding appointments, is granted by the Government free of reckoning. The rent of such premises, if charged, would add greatly to the actual expenditure.

'On examination I find in the Forest Budget of Spain for 1882, and I have no reason to suppose that that was in any way an exceptional year, the credit asked and granted for the School of Forestry was 33,750 pesetas or francs; but this did not include the salaries drawn by the directors, professors, and assistant professors, as members of advanced grades in the corps of forest engineers, amounting to a much greater sum, probably about 70,000 pesetas; in all, 103,750 pesetas, say £4,600.

'In the French Forest Budget for 1880, and in that of the preceding year, 1879, there was asked and granted for instruction in forestry 208,785 francs, about £8,700, of which sum 98,800 francs were designed for the School of Forestry at Nancy.

---

* *School of Forest Engineers in Spain, indicative of a type for a British National School of Forestry.* Edinburgh: Oliver & Boyd. London: Simpkin, Marshall, & Co. 1886.

'There existed at that time an organisation for imparting what is called secondary instruction in forestry in other schools situated at Villers-Cotterets, Grenoble, and Toulouse, to which forest engineers under forty years of age were admitted without being subjected to an entrance examination. The course of instruction extended over seven months; this was attended by men in active service, and any who passed satisfactorily the final or exit examination were eligible for appointment as *guarde-general adjoint*. But it was found by a sub-committee of the Chamber, to which had been submitted questions relative to the instruction in forestry, that the system followed at these schools failed generally to produce men fitted for the duties which the holders of that office were, by the forest regulations, required to discharge; and the committee recommended that these schools should be given up as not accomplishing the object for which they were organised. The instruction given in these schools represented an annual expense of 22,300 francs.

'The credit granted also included provision for the Ecole Forestierre at Des Barres-Loiret, founded by M. Vilmorin, and so designated by him in contradistinction on the one hand to a nursery, a designation borrowed from domestic life; and in contradistinction on the other hand to a plantation or forest, it being a collection of trees raised from seed obtained from forests or from nurserymen or seedsmen of note, and reared with a view to the study of their habits, their identity, and their differences—an establishment such as an arboretum might be made. Subsequently to the death of the founder it became State property. Since then it has been greatly extended, and there are received into it, after passing satisfactorily an entrance examination, sons of forest overseers, for two years' study, to prepare them for employment as gardeners or as forest warders; instruction being given to them in French, drawing, mathematics, land surveying, sylviculture, and all details of forest service. For this instruction there was allotted 20,610 francs to cover the salaries of a director, of a *garde-general* or warder, and of a brigadier, the wages of the students, and other expenses for materials. The grant for the whole of the schools was, as has been stated, 208,785 francs—say £9280.'

ADDENDA

RELATING TO THE PROJECTED ESTABLISHMENT OF A BRITISH NATIONAL SCHOOL OF FORESTRY.

I.—Suitable Site for a School of Forestry.

WHILE the details given in preceding pages may possess some value as information in regard to an important movement resulting in organisations which have been extending over the length and breadth of Continental Europe, they have been compiled and translated chiefly in view of the possibility of their proving useful in the event of a British National School of Forestry being established at some future time, and in the hope of promoting measures for the accomplishment of such an object.

With regard to a site I may say: With a high sense of the appropriateness of the arrangement adopted in the initiation and early development of Schools of Forestry in Germany, and a high appreciation of what was then effected through work done in connection with forests adjacent to the schools, and appropriated to them as educational appliances, I sympathise entirely with the views now entertained extensively and almost universally in regard to the surpassing importance in the present day attaching to the provision for forestal instruction being combined, if not also incorporated, with universities or similar superior educational establishments.

In visiting Schools of Forestry, and in reading of their origin and existence, it appeared to me, most, if not all, of the old-established institutions were adjacent to forests, while most, if not all, of the later founded schools were not; and that some of these made much more use of forests somewhat remote from them for the practical training of students than did some of the former appear to me to make of like facilities for the work at their own door. It certainly was the case that practical training was not neglected by any; and I never heard a complaint of want of facility for securing this.

The distinction I have drawn between old-established schools, and later founded schools, receives an illustration which may be cited. I have often met with convictions in favour of different forms of ecclesiastical creeds and organisations prevailing on one side, and on another of geographical boundaries; and so have I seen it with these conflicting opinions in regard to these Schools of Forestry.

That the reader may be able to make any allowance which he may think proper for the influence of prejudice or pre-possession, I may here state clearly what I have often indicated or stated elsewhere: my opinion is decidedly in favour of the education and technical instruction being prosecuted in connection with facilities for prosecuting, without interruption, higher studies, with other months spent annually in observing, and, if possible, in practising, forestal operations under properly qualified teachers of practical forestry.

And having made this statement, I feel free to advance, and state that I have never known of a forest official in the south of Germany advocate a return to the old model in so far as it was essentially a school organised in connection with a forest; and I have never known such a location for a School of Forestry advocated in Germany, or out of Germany, by any one known to me to be acquainted with the details of instruction in different existing Schools of Forestry, who had not himself been educated at a School of Forestry so located. I do not call in question the fact that such may have had far better opportunities of forming a satisfactory opinion on the subject from experience than I have from limited personal observation and hearsay; and I mention the fact cited in the full knowledge that it may tell both ways.

In more than one case on visiting a School of Forestry,

I have looked in vain for a forest, or even for an arboretum, such as that in Edinburgh is becoming, and yet may become; and even where a removal of location has been made to the site now occupied by a school adjacent to a forest, it has never been from a university town to an exclusively forest district.

In Denmark, the School of Forestry is connected with the School of Agriculture and Rural Economy in Copenhagen. In Sweden, the principal School of Forestry is in Stockholm, and the practical training is effected at a distance. In Finland, the School of Forestry is at Evois, adjacent to a forest; but the practical training is conducted elsewhere. In Russia, the principal Schools of Forestry are in St Petersburg and Moscow; the practical training is at Lissino. In Saxony, the School of Forestry is at Tharand, adjacent to a forest. In Prussia, the School of Forestry is at Eberswalde, adjacent to a forest. In Hanover, it is at Munden. In Hesse-Darmstadt, the School of Forestry, after mature deliberation, was incorporated with the University of Giessen. In Baden, the School of Forestry is connected with the Polytechnicum of Carlsruhe In Wurtemburg, it was formerly part of the Royal Academy of Rural and Forest Economy at Hohenheim, and is now combined with the University of Tubingen. In Bavaria, the School of Forestry acquired a high reputation at Aschaffenburg, but it has been in part removed to be combined with the University of Munich. In Austria, the School of Forestry has been removed from Mariabrum to Vienna In Italy, the School of Forestry is at Vallambrosa, in the midst of a forest. In Gotha, the School of Forestry is in Eisenach, not far from a forest. In Switzerland, the School of Forestry is combined with the Polytechnicum at Zurich. In France, the School of Forestry is in Nancy, adjacent to a forest. In Spain, the School of Forestry has been removed from Villaviciosa to the Escurial, where an effort is being made to establish an arboretum, but with little prospect of success; and the maintenance of a Crown forest in a distant province, as a special school for practical instruction, has been abandoned; and looking at the experience of Schools of Industry on the Continent, I am satisfied that there is no necessity for the organisation of a School of Forestry in Britain being clogged with the supposition that it must be located in a forest.

II.—Educational Arrangements deemed suitable for a British National School of Forestry.

I was called to give evidence before a Select Committee of the House of Commons, appointed 12th May, 1886, to consider whether by the establishment of a forest school or otherwise our woodlands could be rendered more remunerative. I was asked among other things—

Q. 202. How far do you think a forest school for the use of Great Britain should be formed upon the model of the modern Continental schools? To which I answered—I am acquainted with every School of Forestry upon the Continent, and have visited several. There are many upon the type of which a British school might be formed there is no one to which as a type the British school should be conformed, much less any one which would serve as a model. I was then asked—

Q. 203. Which of their forest schools, upon the whole, do you think would be the one most nearly adapted to our requirements?—If in Edinburgh, I should think the school in Spain.

Other questions followed, which I quote with the answers given.

204. If the school were established in Edinburgh what arrangements do you suggest should be made in regard to it?—It depends very much upon the form that it may take. If it were a private enterprise, managed by the Arboriculture Society, or the Highland Agricultural Society, one form; if it were connected with the Watt Institute, another; if connected with the University, a third; if connected with the Museum of Art and Science under the Committee of Council on Education, a fourth.

205. Which, upon the whole, do you think would be the best?—I have a very strong conviction that, upon the

whole, it is best that it should be connected with the Science and Art Department of the Committee of Council on Education, if it were founded upon some such model as the School of Mines in London, or the School of Science in Dublin.

207. Would you be prepared to give the Committee a rather more definite sketch as to how you would propose to arrange the system?—One great advantage of its being in connection with the Committee of Council on Education is this: it is desirable to have young Scotch foresters thoroughly educated. They are fitted by heredity, and by early training, for giving themselves entirely to forest work; it is, therefore, desirable that they should be specially trained. In connection with the School of Mines in London, and the School of Science in Dublin, there is ample provision made for the support of any of the students who require support, and yet it is not given as a dole, or as an alms, but as the result of competitive examination and merit.

194. Do you consider it would be necessary to have a tract of woodland closely contiguous to such a school?—Not at all.

195. But you would be of opinion, would you not, that it would be necessary to have control of a tract of woodland, although it need not necessarily be immediately on the spot or contiguous?—I may state my opinion, and that is the opinion of the majority of the forest officials, forest administrators, and professors of forest science on the Continent——

196. That the management of this particular tract of forest should be under the control of those who were charged with the instruction in the forest school; is that so?—No; not at all. The question has come up on the Continent in this form: a conference of German foresters, forest administrators, and professors of forest science was held when the question was discussed: Is it desirable to have Schools of Forestry as separate and special institutions, or to have them connected with the higher schools and

universities of the Continent? It was only incidentally that the question of forests came up in that connection. There were only three or four in favour of maintaining the old special schools in connection with the forests; the rest, to a man, were opposed to it.

197. Then you do not think it necessary that the management of the woodlands in which the instruction is given should be under the control of those who give that instruction?—Although it is not necessary that it should be under the control of those communicating the instruction, it is desirable that there should be forests to which the students along with the professor may have access. They may be in the neighbourhood of a school; if in such neighbourhood, so much the better; but they may be 100 miles off, or they may be 200 miles off. It is desirable that they should have forests to which they have access, but it is not necessary that those should be under the control or direction of those communicating the instruction.

210. Have you prepared a detailed curriculum which you would suggest. I assume a three years' course of study?—I have. My suggestions are as follows:—

FIRST YEAR.—In the Winter Session, let instruction be given in the structure and physiology of trees and shrubs, and in the geographical distribution of forests; in the treatment of forests by Sartage, by Jardinage, by *à tire et ai.e*, by *les compartments*, or the *Fachwerke Methode* of Germany; in the application of this to coppice wood, with a view to securing, along with other advantages, a sustained production of wood; and in the application of it to timber forests, according as the object may be to secure from these a maximum size of timber, or a maximum produce of wood, or a maximum pecuniary return, along with natural reproduction, sustained production, and progressive improvement of the woods; and in measures to be employed in the conversion of coppice wood into timber forest, of timber forest into coppice wood, of mixed woods into either, and of either into mixed woods.

With attendance on the classes in the University for the study of natural history, of mathematics, and of engineering; or, with attendance on the classes in the Watt Institution and School of Arts for the study of mechanical philosophy and of mathematics.

SUMMER SESSION.—Attendance on the classes in the University for the study of botany and vegetable histology; and of practical natural history, and of practical engineering; or attendance on classes, if open, in the Watt Institution for the study of botany, and of mechanical and geometrical drawing.

AUTUMN MONTHS.—Tours of observation, with or without the teacher, in woods and forests in Britain, in France, in Germany, or in the north of Europe.

SECOND YEAR: WINTER MONTHS.—Instruction in regard to forest economy, forest legislation, and forest literature in Britain, and in France and Germany, countries in advance of all others in forest science, and in the practical application of it to the management of forests; in Russia, where arrangements are being made to introduce and to carry out extensively the improved forest management practised in Germany and in France; in Finland, where arrangements have been made to manage the forests in accordance with the requirements of forest science; in Sweden, where the latest arrangements suggested by forest science are being carried out with vigour; in British colonies, in America, and in India, where have been introduced many of the suggestions of modern forest science, and the forest economy practised on the Continent of Europe.

With attendance on the classes in the University for the study of theoretic chemistry and practical chemistry, natural philosophy, and the practical application of the same; or with attendance at the classes in the Watt Institution and School of Arts for the study of chemistry and practical chemistry, of engineering, and of geology.

SUMMER AND AUTUMN MONTHS.—Practical experience

in the management of woods, or in the management of nurseries, to be acquired under the direction of approved foresters, or approved nurserymen.

THIRD YEAR: WINTER SESSION ONLY.—Instruction in the chemistry of vegetation and of soils; in the meteorological effects of forests on moisture, on temperature, and on constituents of the atmosphere; in sylviculture, as applied in Belgium, &c., to utilise waste lands; in the lands of France, to arrest and utilise drift sands; in the Alps, the Cévennes, and the Pyrenees, to prevent the disastrous effects and consequences of torrents; on the Karst, in Illyria, to restore fertility to land rendered sterile by the destruction of trees; in the United States of America, to prevent anticipated evils; in India, to secure desiderated good; in Britain, to increase amenity, covert, and shelter;—and instruction in the injurious effects of cattle, insects, and various diseases on trees.

With attendance on the classes in the University for the study of geology, of agriculture, and, if it be desired, any of the following: for the study of political economy, of conveyancing, or of bandaging and surgical appliances; or with attendance on the classes in the Watt Institution for the study of animal physiology, of German, or of French. I may add, that in connection with the above studies I would advise that a course of instruction should be given in forest botany, in forest mycology, or the study of fungi, in forest entomology, in forest ornithology, and in forest masology.

214. *This elaborate course of study that you suggest, I presume, was only for those foresters who are to be employed abroad in public work?*—My view is that the students should be trained as students, and, if necessary, fitted for any appointment in India and the colonies, or at home, by their being thoroughly qualified scientific students of forestry, with the full knowledge of the practical application to be made of the science.

215. What interests proprietors in Scotland more is the kind of smaller education to be given to the foresters to whom we pay, say, from £80 to £100 a-year; have you any plan to suggest which would lay down the principles for the systematic training of such men?—I consider that if such an idea as I have thrown out were followed such students could attend the Watt Institute at comparatively small expense. They might attend one year or more, and arrangements might be made for giving them instruction in the evening, so that they might support themselves by working in the nurseries in the neighbourhood of Edinburgh. If it were considered unadvisable that they should go through a two and a-half years' course, there could be no difficulty in the professor giving a short summary of forest science in its application to practical forestry in 50 lectures, or in 100 lectures; and the attendance upon such lectures, of course, would clearly meet the case of such persons as you have referred to. I have been long desirous that forestry should be introduced into our primary schools. The arrangements made at Kensington are such as would facilitate this being done at very little expense, and thus there would be raised up a body of well-instructed woodmen, forest labourers, and others.

216. Colonel Pearson told us that he thought a sufficiently practical course might be given to foresters of this stamp in three months; do you agree with that?—I do not believe it. Referring to the views that are entertained by foresters, forest administrators who are Government officials, and professors of forest science, their general impression appears to me to be that it is desirable that when students are at college they should be at college, and that when they are in the forest they should be in the forest; that they should be at the school the whole time, except on Saturday afternoon excursions to the forest, and then spend some time, say three months, six months, or whatever time may be allowed them in practical work in the forests.

217. Where would you propose that they should go for their practical work from the Watt Institute?—For practical work there are a number of forests which are conducted in an excellent way, and the foresters there, I have no doubt, would be willing, with the consent of the proprietors, to make arrangements for receiving such students for three months if there be a winter and a summer session, or six months if they have only a winter session. But, apart from that, an idea thrown out by Captain Mackenzie, who has charge of Epping Forest, was that a school should be established in connection with Epping Forest. And he suggested that the students should be engaged in practical work in Epping Forest, and that, after a year there, the students should go on to Windsor Forest for twelve months, or to some other of the Crown forests. I asked him if he would be willing to engage students from Edinburgh, paying them wages and engaging them in the same way as students from the home college, and he said, 'Certainly.'

229. Have you formed any idea as to the probable expense of such an undertaking; how much the Government would be called upon to contribute?—I consider that the cheapest arrangement would be one connected with the Watt Institute, towards which the Government would not be called upon to contribute anything; but then there is the want of prestige, and I refer to the effect of prestige in preventing distinguished teachers getting pupils, and getting employment for the pupils, when once they have passed through the course. The cheapest arrangement, combined with prestige, would be the establishment of a professorship in the University, because then we would have a definite sum, and we could not go beyond it. It would be more expensive, I believe, having a School of Forestry organised in connection with the Committee of Council on Education; but it need not be much more expensive at first. The great expense would be, when once it has been seen, as I have no doubt it will be seen in a year or two years, that it is desirable to go on increasing the training staff.

230. But you have no doubt that a professor in the University of Edinburgh would answer the present purposes?—A great deal would depend upon the professor. You have no security that you would have a professor with the necessary encyclopædic information to succeed the first or the second professor, and there is very great danger of the professorship degenerating into a mere respectable sinecure. There is less risk of that, I consider, in connection with the Council of Education.

231. You would hardly expect, from a practical point of view, a forester who had not had any great training in this way, except practically, to attend classes in Edinburgh over a space of three years?—Hence the advantage of having what I may call an experimental or tentative course of lectures for one year and seeing what could be done, and then entering upon a larger course subsequently if this be found successful.

232. It is your opinion that they could get sufficient information in the course of one year's lectures independently of the practical experience in the forest?—They would get the scientific information with illustrations of its practical application.

233. Then you propose that they should go into the practical work of forestry at a subsequent period of their education?—Yes, and if they would attend the summer course they might keep the autumn free for this. The autumn should certainly be spent in practical work; and if there is not a summer course they should spend the whole summer in practical work. But, as has been mentioned by Colonel Pearson, on the Continent the students go great distances with the professors; they frequently go into other countries, and if they had a professor qualified to take them to any of the countries upon the Continent of Europe, and acquainted with the languages, I have no doubt that this might be satisfactorily arranged. In the last number of *Forestry* it is suggested that they should go even to Canada.

234. Your view would be that these young men should

attend classes at the College, as they attend other classes for the purpose of general education?—Yes; I consider that if in connection with the Museum of Science and Art it is only necessary to have classes in forestry, all the accessary studies can be pursued either at the University or at the Watt Institute according to the means of students. If a student be able to go to the University, and attend the University classes, he can do so; if he have not the means or the disposition to attend the University he can go to the Watt Institute and get a thorough instruction upon the accessary subjects, leaving no necessity for anything more being done but to provide for what are strictly forest professional studies.

235. But you assume that the student would have to give up both time and attention to that particular study while at the University?—That would be exceedingly desirable; but there are many young men who support themselves by teaching while at the University; and if the arrangements of the hours were such, and a forester wished to support himself by engaging in work in the nursery, he might then attend the evening classes of the Watt Institute for all the accessary subjects, mathematics, geology, road-making, and everything of that kind.

236. Then he would pursue his course of instruction during the ordinary curriculum of his University education? —Yes.

211. Hitherto I have asked you questions with regard to the advantages which might be derived from the instruction given to the students; would you suggest that in such a school, if established, there should be any opportunity for research as to the different circumstances affecting forest products?—I consider that it would be exceedingly desirable. There are now established at the seats of several of the Schools of Forestry upon the Continent stations for research; they are not connected with the school, they are supported by the Government, but placed at the seat of the school in order that the students may have the benefit of the professor there; and

in some of the schools I have referred to, as in that in Spain, where they have failed to secure such an experimental station, very great advantage has resulted from the students being encouraged by the professor to engage in research upon a smaller scale.

212. Would you propose that such a school should likewise make any experiments with regard to the suitability of particular soils, exposure, the combination or association of different trees one with another, and other similar problems?—There are no objections to their doing so. These stations for research, to which I have referred, have an international connection; when one is formed they communicate with the others, and state the particular department to which they intend to give their attention, and they leave the rest to the others, so that no two of them shall be occupying the field of research.

III.—SCHOOL OF FOREST ENGINEERS IN SPAIN, CITED AS INDICATIVE OF A TYPE FOR A BRITISH NATIONAL SCHOOL OF FORESTRY.

In 1877 I published a *brochure*, entitled *Schools of Forestry in Europe: a Plea for the Erection of a School of Forestry in connection with the Arboretum in Edinburgh*, in which I stated that with the acquisition of that arboretum, and existing arrangements for study in the University, and in the Watt Institute, there were required only facilities for the study of what is known on the Continent as Forest Science, to enable these institutions conjointly, or either of them, with the help of the other, to take a place amongst the most completely equipped schools of forestry in Europe, and to undertake the training of foresters for the discharge of such duties as are required of them in India, in our Colonies, or at home.

In May, 1886, I gave evidence on the subject before a Committee appointed by the House of Commons to consider whether by the establishment of a Forest School or otherwise, our woodlands could be rendered more productive, and in illustration of a statement made by me in doing so, I subsequently published a volume entitled *School of Forest Engineers in Spain, indicative of a type for a British School of Forestry*. In this I have given information in regard to advantages offered by Edinburgh as an appropriate site for such an institution; information in regard to what might be done by the organisation of a School of Forestry there under the Science and Art Department of the Committee of Council on Education, or by the establishment of a Professorship of Forestry in the University, or a lectureship on that subject in the Watt Institute, or in connection with some public body, with details of the advantages offered by each of these alternative measures, inclusive of the question of expense.

The characteristic type of the Schools of Forestry in Germany is that they are adapted to fit into the other educational arrangements of the country, which are different from what have as yet been introduced into the transitional development of national education in Britain. But the arrangement of the Schools of Forest Engineers in Spain are free from all trammels which might operate prejudicially if imposed on students of forestry in this country. The similarity of the climate and conditions of soil in Spain to what exist in more than one of our colonies, and the encyclopædic character of the education, instruction, and training given under the conditions of of Spain to fit the aspirants for admission into the Corps of Forest Engineers, seemed to me, when questioned on the subject by a Committee of the House of Commons, to indicate a type of the kind of school required in Britain.

I have in common, I presume, with all who know them, an unbounded admiration for students of forest science in Germany engaged in the prosecution of investigations pursued in the stations for forestral experimental research at the sites of several of the Schools of Forestry in Germany and elsewhere, and for the professors and practitioners of forest science and forest economy in that land, and I consider it no disparagement of their attainments or of their work to consider that what meets the requirements of their country would not exactly meet the requirements of ours. Again, my testimony was not of a model but of a type which may be reproduced with divergences which could be inconsistent with conformity to a model,—conformity to a type, leaving the projector free to incorporate in his scheme anything and everything compatible with ideas which he may find anywhere if it can be shown to be desirable for the accomplishment of what is designed; and I have referred to the School of Forest Engineers in Spain only as indicative of the kind of school, which, according to my views, is required to meet our case; and it is all the more so that it

ADDENDA.

admits of the incorporation of an indefinite number of suggestions which may result from the most extensive acquaintance with what is being done in Schools of Forestry anywhere.

It has been gratifying to me to find that my volume the *School of Forest Engineers in Spain* has been approved by competent authorities there; and as the volume may be considered to possess some interest as an account of that School, irrespective of the suggestion that it may supply a type for a British School of Forestry, I cite the following notices of the volume which have appeared in Spanish Reviews :—

Notice in *Revista Contemporanea*, by Senor Don Rafael Alvarez Sereix, Engineer of the First Class in Corps of Forest Engineers, Member of the Spanish Geographical and Statistical Commission, and author of the following works :—

Determinación de la masa leñosa de un monte. por P. Nico (trad. del Italiano).—Madrid, 1880.
Elementos de tasación forestal, por P. Piccoli (trad. del Italiano). —Madrid, 1880.
Cartas de Navarra,—Madrid, 1880.
La desamortización forestal.—Madrid, 1883.
Estudios botánico—forestales (1.ª serie).—Madrid, 1884.
Geografia botánica —Lugo, 1884.
Estudios botánico—forestales (2.ª serie).—Madrid, 1885.
Cuestiones cientificas.—Madrid, 1885.
La opinión de la prensa sobre los montes publicos.—Madrid, 1886.
Discursos pronunciados en la Asociación de Agricultores de España.—Madrid, 1886.
Adiciones y enmiendas á la ultima edición del Diccionaaio de la Academia Española.—Madrid, 1886.

'If we had not known long the distinguished author of this work; if we had not known that he is a naturalist of advanced age, of great erudition and of wondrous activity Professor for some years in Capetown, Cape of Good Hope, and in the University of Aberdeen; if we had not read before now valuable works by him on a multitude of questions, mainly forestal, in which he gives an exposition of modern Forest Economy, describes the Forests of England, of Norway, of Finland, and of Northern Russia, treats of the celebrated French Ordinance of 1669, of the planting of the sandunes of the adjacent Republic, of the works of reboisement in that country, of the hydrology of South Africa, and of the influence of forests on humidity of climate, &c.—even if all these had been unknown to us, the publication of this work, *School of Forest Engineers in Spain*, would have been sufficient to awaken in us interest and to quicken affectionate sympathy. For how can we do other than feel an extraordinary interest in a respected man of science, who, well-nigh an octogenarian in age, undertakes a journey to Spain, establishes himself at the Escurial, examines in detail the School of Forest Engineers there— that school of which many Spaniards are oblivious, and, sad to tell, utterly unknown by not a few — going through its cabinets, examining its rich library, studies with diligence the Spanish language, and, supplied with many of the works which have been published in regard to our forests, liberally presented to him by the authors, returns to his home in Haddington, glances through them full of enthusiasm, reads and re-reads, meditates upon them for hours, and at last composes the work to which we refer?

'In this he first gives an account of the origin of the Corps of Forest Engineers of Spain. In the second and third chapters he occupies himself with the origin and development of the School of Forestry, from its being founded in the village of Villaviciosa de Odon to the present time; details the branches of study taken each year, the extent to which this is carried, and the manner in which the instruction is given. Dr Brown devotes the fourth chapter to an examination of some of the valuable works in the library, and, with a prediliction for those written by the forest engineers, he devotes attention on these. With a view to methodising this work he divides this chapter into seven sections, in which he treats successively of those relating to mathematics, chemistry, meteorology, botany, sylviculture, &c.; and in succeeding chapters he applies what had been seen in Spain to demonstrate the indubitable benefit which would result to the United Kingdom from the organisation of a National School of Forestry, and the abandonment of the system of sending young men who are required for the service of the Government in management of State forests to study in the School at Nancy.

'It is now a good many years since Dr Brown, impressed with the necessity of some such reform to meet the requirements of his country, first directed his energies to demonstrate the benefits to his country which might thence result, and to endeavour to provide for its being effected. Adhering ever since unwaveringly to his conviction on this point, he has been called on to take part in several commissions created in view of this; and besides giving evidence before a Committee of Parliament, in illustration of which evidence this volume has been published, he has supplied trustworthy information on this question in other works which he has published; and now in that country, parsimonious hitherto in what it has done, the idea seems to be making way; and already not a few consider that at least a trial to give effect to it should be made.

'We trust that ere very long this will be done, bringing much good to that powerful nation; and that Dr Brown may live to hail the day as one of the most happy in his long and useful life.

'We who feel ourselves honoured by his devoting a volume to the study of our School of Forestry, pray fervently that that day may come; and meanwhile we send to him in his quiet home, in which he is engaged in the preparation of other works, an expression of our gratitude, and an assurance of our admiration.

(Signed) R. ALVAREZ SEREIX.'

Notice in *Revista de Montes,* by Illustrisimo Senor Don Castel y Clemente, Chief of Second Class in the Corps of Forest Engineers, Deputy to the Cortes, Superior Deputy Chief of the Civil Administration, Chevalier of Isabel, the Catholic, &c., and author of the following works :—

Monografia dasográfica del haya.—Madrid, 1873.
Memoria sobre la influencia de la luna en la vegetación.—Madrid, 1875.
Noticia sobre la fundación y desarollo de la Escuela especial de Ingenieros de Montes.—Madrid, 1877.
Estudios sobre el tanino. (Memoria premiada por la Real Academia de Ciencias).—Madrid, 1879.
Descripción fiscia, geognóstica, agricola y forestal de la provincia de Guadaljara. (Publicada por la Comisión del Mapa geológico de España).—Madrid, 1882.
Memoria sobre las condiciones naturales y produccion agricola y forestal de la Peninsula Escandinava.—Madrid, 1883.
Combustibles vegetales: Teoria y practica de la combustion, carbonizacion y destilacion de la madera.—Madrid, 1885.

'The surprise which undoubtedly will be felt by the greater part of the readers of the *Revista* on the announcement of this work I experienced, and candidly acknowledge that such was the case, on my receipt of the neatly-bound volume, with a most kind dedication, for which I am truly grateful to the distinguished and learned author of it, who has during some years past devoted his great activity to the study and diffusion of Forest Science, and to the advocacy of the establishment of a School of Forestry in Britain. The name of Dr John Croumbie Brown is familiar to all students of that science following the literary movements in connection with it during these late years.

'The *Revista de Modes* — Forest Review — has repeatedly taken occasion to bring under consideration the more important works amongst the publication of this distinguished naturalist; and on more than one occasion, while expressing admiration of the prodigious fecundity, and remarkable persisting perseverance of the author, intimated the satisfaction that a writer of such authority, and one who has such an acquaintance with the organisation of the other Schools of Forestry in Europe, should give his attention, and concede special importance to that of Spain as one indicative of a type deemed suitable to be followed in the organisation of some future School of Forestry in Britain, the creation of which was being advocated by him. To add that Dr Brown, in his last published volume, speaks of things in Spain as one well acquainted with them, detailing facts and citing data which have not previously been published in Spain, will not appear to be an extravagant statement to those who know on the one hand the searching diligence of the forestal chronicler from the other side of the British Channel, and on the other hand the indifference with which is regarded amongst ourselves what relates to the prestige of that which we, having such important interests involved, should take special care to secure that it receives due appreciation in the country.

'The first chapter of the book to which we refer treats of the origin and development of the Corps of Forest Engineers, and of the special school of the Department in our country. He is a faithful chronicler of facts, coinciding in his judgment with the auhor of the *Notitia sobre el origen y desarrollo de la Escuela de Ingenieros de Montes en Espanna*—Notices of the origin and development of the special School of Forest Engineers in Spain. The first part serves as a requisite introduction to the other parts of the volume; and it also serves to show that the necessary reforms have not been impositions practised on the villages, but that in these, and in their evolution or successive developments, they have given a permanent influence to the special character and inherent conditions of the primary impulse at the time of the creation. He describes, in continuation of the School of the Escurial, the studies pursued there by the students, giving in an abbreviated *resumé* the programmes of study in the different branches, and the subjects which constitute the course of instruction required to be given to the engineers. Taking occasion of the examination of this, and in methodic order based on the different departments of science taught to them, the author gives an analysis, with considerable detail in most cases, of all and each of the works written by the Spanish Forest Engineers, and of some which are not so, in reference to the subject matters of this instruction, constituting with regard to this the most complete bibliography which has been prepared and published on this important department of the scientific activity of the forest officials of our country.

'I shall not say a word in commendation of the elevated standard and the careful solicitude with which Dr Brown has prepared this chapter of his work, as the correspondence of our views gives me a personal interest in the matter.

'In the chapter headed Excursions, the respected Ex-Professor from the Cape gives an account of all of the more important excursions made from the founding of the school till now by the professors or students for the study of forest practice; and also those which have been made by professors and forest engineers into foreign lands, either in connection with commissions to visit the International Exhibitions held in London, Vienna, and Philadelphia, or to study particular points connected with instruction, the *reboisement* of dunes, forest industries, &c.

'Dr Brown, who under the snow of age, gallantly sustained by a vigorous constitution, knows what it is to carry a heart always open to recollections and enthusiasm, not depressed by disappointment, but elevated by hope, has made his own the hymn of the first foresters of Spain, transcribing first in Spanish and then in English that hymn with its opening strophe *Al campo marchemos!* Nor less thrilling than the concluding strophe was the effect produced on me by reading in English that anti-strophe or chorus so often sung in our excursions in 1867 to the forests of the Guadarama—

"Cotta the learned! thy children in Spain
Invoke thy name which is now immortal."

'The remaining chapters are devoted to making manifest the conveniences which exist for establishing forestal instruction in Britain, discussing all the questions which present themselves at once relative to the choice of a site for the establishment of a school, the extent and form of instruction required, the expense which provision for this would entail, &c.

'It is nothing new for us to hear well-merited commendations bestowed upon the establishment and organisation of the School of Forestry in Spain. We know the opinions of illustrious foresters in Germany, published some years ago, in accredited reviews of that country, according to which our former school in Villaviciosa, for its programme of study, its regulations, the riches of its museums, and the special stamp which has always characterised it, was presented as a model in that classic land of forest science, which delights to see order, method, and discipline, as the distinctive characters of all its institutions; but it is none the less satisfactory that that judgment should be maintained in the present: and after all, throwing aside all idea of presumption, which would be ridiculous, it is always pleasing and strengthening to conviction to see that there is something deemed deserving of imitation in a country looked upon with such indifference, and that perhaps not altogether unjustified, by its own not unjustifiable neglect.

'The continuous advocacy by Dr Brown during these latter years has been followed with the effect that the opinion is spreading in his country with manifest indications of conviction that the views which he urges in this matter are of grave import to Great Britain, not only in relation to its home territory, but more and more particularly in order to the increase of commerce and production in the vast territories of her colonies. In this matter, if I be not greatly mistaken, it is my belief that at no distant time there will be established a School of Forestry in Edinburgh; and meanwhile, without waiting for that, I invite all my associates, who see in Dr Brown an enthusiast in our science, and a loving friend of the Forest Engineers of Spain, to unite in fraternal salutations to him ; and in conclusion, in the behalf of these foresters, we send to him, with sincere gratitude, these pages of this *Revista*.

'Madrid, 25th October, 1886.

'(Signed)   CARLOS CASTEL.'

IV.—Treatises on Matters pertaining to Modern Forest Science and Forest Economy, Proferred for Publication in the English Language.

Pending the creation of a public opinion in favour of the establishment of a British National School of Forestry, useful information in regard to Forest Economy, based on the advanced forest science of the day may be disseminated through the press; and thereafter the publications embodying this may prove helpful to students desirous of extending their studies beyond the instruction communicated in the classes attended by them.

In the volume entitled *School of Forest Engineers in Spain, indicative of a type for a British National School of Forestry*, I had occasion to state; 'We have an extensive and valuable literature relative to Arboriculture. For this there is, and ever has been, a demand: but with works on Sylviculture, Modern Forest Science, and Modern Forest Economy, it is otherwise. Nor is there yet such a demand for works of this kind as would make it pecuniarly remunerative to any to engage largely in the publication of such works; but as the demand increases so will the supply.

'But a beginning has been made. In so far as I have taken part in this I have done so in anticipation of a future demand, and not in consequence of any manifestation of a felt want. In reference to the rapid supply of works on forestry in the Spanish language of late years, which I have noted, I may remark that this did not occur until after several successive batches of students had entered upon the active duties of their profession. It was then that it became manifest wherein the existing forestal literature of the country was deficient in view of the requirements of the day; and then that the desire for information induced purchase and perusal. And it is noteworthy that even still in connection with the publication of almost all of the Spanish works referred to, including the most expensive and least popular of them, the writers are relieved of the expense of publication. It is not so with us.'

In connection with this statement there are given notices of the contents of several treatises which I have published. I am prepared to proceed with the publication of others; but I am straitened by lack of funds. Silver and gold have I not; but what I have I am prepared to give.

My attention was first given to the Forestry and Hydraulic Engineering of Spain, in consequence of the similarity of the climatic conditions of the Peninsula to those of South Africa, which I had studied with some attention, and of a perception that the remedial measures adopted in Spain were adapted to meet and counteract corresponding evils in South Africa. With both I have long been familiar, but I had occasion to visit Spain in the summer and autumn of 1885, when I had many facilities afforded me of verifying and extending information I had previously procured; and in the end of the year I sent a letter in triplicate to editors of newspapers, published at the Cape of Good Hope, of which the following is a copy:

'Haddington, 16th Decr., 1885.

'Sir,—May I ask of you in the interests of the Colony to give publicity to the following statement?

'During the years 1863-1866 I held at the Cape of Good Hope, along with the Professorship of Botany in the South African College, the office of Colonial Botanist,—an office established in 1858, created with the twofold object—1st, of ascertaining and making generally known the economic resources of the Colony as regards its indigeneous vegetable productions, and its fitness for the growth of valuable exotic trees and other plants; and 2nd, of perfecting a knowledge of the flora of South Africa, and thus contributing to the advance of botanical science.

'Appended to my report as Colonial Botanist for the year 1886 was a list of upwards of 460 names of South African trees, shrubs, and arborescent herbs, upon the natural history, or botanic characters, or economic uses of which a report was forthcoming, if desired ; the list consisting of English, Dutch, Kaffir, Sechuana, Damara, or Hottentot names, by which these are known at the Cape, alphabetically arranged with their botanic synonyms. 2. An abstract of a memoir prepared relative to the forests and forest lands of South Africa. 3. An abstract of a memoir prepared relative to the forest economy of the Colony. 4. An abstract of a memoir prepared relative to arboriculture in the Colony. 5. An abstract of a memoir prepared on the hydrology of South Africa. 6. An abstract of a memoir prepared on irrigation and its application to agricultural operations in South Africa. And, 7. Observations on the agricultural capabilities of the Colony, and requirements for the developments of these.

'Since my return to Europe I have repeatedly, in correspondence with South Africa, made mention of the similarity of the climate and physical conditions of Spain to those of the Colony, and of the appropriateness for adoption in South Africa, of the measures adopted in Spain to secure the conservation and scientific exploitation of forests, and the retention and economic application of the water furnished by the rainfall, as conjointly means of arresting the desiccation, and counteracting the aridity of the country.

'Similar measures I advocated unceasingly during my tenure of office at the Cape, and in a volume which I published in 1875, entitled: ' Hydrology of South Africa, or Details of the Former Hydrographic Conditions of the Cape of Good Hope, and of Causes of its Present Aridity, with Suggestions of Appropriate Remedies for this Aridity,' I endeavoured to show that the appropriate remedies are the erection of dams to prevent the escape of a portion of the rainfall to the sea; the abandonment or restriction of the burning of the Veldt; the conservation and extension of existing forests; and the adoption of measures similar to the reboisement and gazonnement carried out in France, with a view to prevent the formation of torrents, and the destruction of property occasioned by them.

'This year I spent two months in Spain in frequent intercourse with distinguished members of the Corps of Forest Engineers, with some of whom I have had correspondence on such matters for years; and by them I was afforded every facility I could desire for verifying and increasing the information I had previously collected. I have now completed the arranging of the information I thus procured, and incorporating with it the information I had previously obtained; and the whole I have embodied in a series of treatises or reports on the following subjects, viz.: 1. Forestry in Spain; 2. Forestal and Hydraulic Engineering; 3. Forestal and Rural Industries, including, amongst others, the production of cork—the collecting of resin from conifers—the collecting of esparto grass—the treatment of merino sheep—the culture of the olive—the preparation of silk—and the making of wine. 4. The natural history of the phylloxera, and appliances adopted to prevent its ravages. 5. The natural history of the locust, and measures applicable to its destruction.

'It is not my intention to publish these on my own account, or otherwise, than as a contribution towards the development of the agricultural capabilities and rural economy of South Africa, in furtherance of the design of the office of Colonial Botanist which I held at the Cape; and I am prepared to carry through the press, free of all expense, beyond the charge of the printer for paper and work, an edition of 100 copies, or of such other number as may be desired, if provision be made for meeting that expense, leaving me free, if I think proper, to have at my own expense other copies thrown off before the types may be distributed: these extra copies to be at my disposal for distribution by sale or otherwise.

'I take the liberty to offer through you to do this, and to add I shall feel gratified if that offer be accepted.— I am, Sir, respectfully yours, JOHN C. BROWN.'

The offer has lapsed, but I now renew it, and extend the offer to all who may be willing to co-operate with me in the enterprise.

In the communication made in triplicate to newspapers published at the Cape of Good Hope there are mentioned several memoirs or reports which I prepared while holding the office of Colonial Botanist and Government Botanist in that Colony. One of these related to rivers of South Africa, with notices of inundations by which they are characterised, and of irrigation works by which they might be utilised, and of difficulties, physical and other, in the way of works of extensive irrigation being carried out at the Cape, and the means of accomplishing these which are at command. To this I have since added similar notices of the most important rivers of Africa—the Zambesi, the Congo, and the Nile. In regard to that memoir I addressed, under date of 15th September, 1881, a memorial to the Legislative Assembly, stating that, in view of what had been accomplished in Spain, I considered that it would be pecuniarily advantageous to the Colony that the Commissioner of Crown Lands and Public Works, the Members of the Legislature, and others, should have access to the information embodied in it, and offering to carry through the press an edition of it, free of all expense to the Colony, beyond what might be charged by the printer for his work, and for paper and binding.

Others related to forest management at the Cape of Good Hope in times past, latterly, and at present; to the forests and forest lands of South Africa, from the Cape of Good Hope to the Zambesi—to which I have since added similar information in regard to the forests of Central Africa between the Zambesi and the Sahara; and with regard to these the Report on South African trees, arborescent shrubs, and bushes; and the memoir on arboriculture in South Africa, with details of what has been done, and of what may be done, in planting trees at the Cape of Good Hope, with a view thereby to securing ornamentation, moisture, shelter, fuel, or timber. I addressed to the Legislative Assembly, under date of 13th September, 1881, a memorial stating that abstracts of these were appended to the Report of the Colonial Botanist for 1866, which was submitted to Parliament while it was engaged in carrying out sweeping measures of retrenchment; that in the light of the information I had obtained in regard to the advanced forest economy of Continental Europe, and in view of the reported appointment of a Forest Commission in the Colony, I considered it would be pecuniarly advantageous to the Colony that the said Commission, and also the Commissioner of Crown Lands, the Members of the Legislature, and others, should have access to these Memoirs, and offering to carry through the press copies of the original reports, which were still in my possession, and to do so free of all expense to the Colony, beyond what might be charged by the printer for his work, and for paper and binding what copies might be required.

In illustration of the importance of the matters to which these refer, I may mention that Count de Vasselot, now Superintendent of woods and forests in the Colony, reported in 1882 of these, which twenty years before were being recklessly destroyed, and were bringing in to the treasury a clear revenue of but a few hundreds of pounds. 'The first step in enlisting professional knowledge has been taken, allowing us to begin systematic forestry; minor considerations should not be allowed to turn us aside, or impede progress in the path on which we have entered. I may, in conclusion, once more repeat my opinion that the Crown Forests, regularly worked, would produce a revenue of at least £235,000—this being the sum which leaves the country every year to pay for imported wood. Its forests ought to be a mine of gold to the Colony; while the plantations, and re-foresting of mountains will, in conjunction with hydraulic works, turn to the best account the rainfall of the country. Irrigation would then be easier, and agriculture a veritable mine of diamonds.'

In illustration of the importance of what is thus alluded to, and of the subjects treated of in the memoir *On the Rivers of Africa*, I may cite the following statement from the Preface to a volume entitled: *Reboisement in France, or Records of the Replanting of the Alps, the Cevennes, and the Pyrenees, with Trees, Herbage, and Bush, with a view to arresting and preventing the destructive consequences and effects of Torrents*, published in 1876—'I have before me details of destructive effects of torrents which have occurred since I left the Colony in the beginning of 1867. Towards the close of that year there occurred one, the damage occasioned by which to roads and to house property at Port Elizabeth alone was estimated at from £25,000 to £30,000. Within a year thereafter a similar destructive torrent occurred at Natal, in regard to which it was stated that the damage done to public works alone was estimated at £50,000, and the loss to private persons was estimated variously from £50,000 to £100,000. In the following year, 1869, a torrent in the Western Province occasioned the fall of a railway bridge, which issued in loss of life and loss of property, and personal injuries, for one case alone of which the railway proprietors were prosecuted for damages amounting to £5000. In Beaufort West a deluge of rain washed down the dam, and the next year the town was flooded by the waters of the Gamka; and the next year, 1871, Victoria West was visited with a similar disaster. Such are the sums and the damages with which we have to deal in connection with this question, as it affects the case; and these are only the most remarkable torrents of the several years referred to.

'Towards the close of last year, 1874, still more disastrous effects were produced by torrential floods. According to the report given by one of the Colonial newspapers, the damages done could not be estimated at much less than £300,000. According to the report given by another, the damage done to public works alone was estimated at £350,000.'

There are other countries, besides South Africa, in which the information embodied in these treatises might be useful; and I am prepared to carry through the press an edition of any one or more of them on the same terms as those stated in the offer made to the Cape Parliament: That is to say, free of all charges beyond those of the printer for paper and work, provided I be allowed, before the types be distributed, to have extra impressions thrown off, at my own expense, for distribution by me, by sale or otherwise as I may deem expedient.

Some years since, in correspondence with the late Dr Franklin B. Hough, when he was at the head of the Forestry Division of the Department of Agriculture, in the Government of the United States in America, I had occasion to state what aid I could give in the accomplishment of an enterprise in which he was engaged heart and soul, calmly and coolly, but with all the self-denying energy manifested by not a few of his compatriots in endeavours to serve their generation according to the will of God. In connection with this correspondence, I prepared a letter to be addressed to five or six of my correspondents in America, who were like-minded, more than one of whom pre-deceased Dr. Hough, and more than one have followed him to the great gathering—the General Assembly of the First-born in Heaven. It was found preferable to writing out copies to have the letter printed; and this being done extra impressions were ordered, and these were somewhat extensively distributed. Of this letter the following is a copy :—

'Haddington (Scotland), 10th December, 1879.

'My Dear Sir,

'In view of the interest you have manifested in the advancement of Forest Science and Forest Economy, I take the liberty to solicit your kind aid in the matter referred to in the following lines.

'I expect to be able in the course of this winter to bring toward completion a compilation, and, when necessary, translation, of official and other notices of Forestry in the different countries of Europe, a work on which I have been engaged for several years past. I have made such arrangements that these compilations shall, I hope, in no case prove to have been made altogether in vain ; but, by the death within these last few months, of more than one of my near relatives of the same age, by the death, within a period somewhat longer, of more than one of my correspondents in this work, and by a consciousness of my strength being less than it has been, I am reminded that I must not lose time in publishing these compilations if I would have them carried through the press before I die. For reasons, which I shall state immediately, I wish that they could be published in the United States of America ; and I wish much that you would bring the matter under the consideration of some enterprising publisher in America, with such remarks on the subject as you may think fit to offer.

'My attention to the official documents, and other works from which these compilations and translations have been made, was given mainly in consequence of having seen, during a professional engagement at the Cape of Good Hope, the reckless way in which valuable forests were being exploited and destroyed, and my inability, after my return to Europe, to specify any work in the English language in which those who were interested in the conservation, the more economic exploitation, and the extension of these forests, might find detailed information in regard to the treatment of forests in accordance with the advanced forest science of the day ; and having the leisure of old age, I sought to supply the desideratum as I best could. I possessed, perhaps, exceptional opportunities for doing so; of these I availed myself; others presented themselves; they were not allowed to slip past unimproved; and throughout these years I have had correspondence and personal intercourse in their own lands, with many who were engaged in the study, the direction, the administration, or the management of forest operations on the Continent of Europe and elsewhere.

'My desire to have my compilations published in the United States may be in part the result of a life-long intercourse with American friends, whom I have highly esteemed, and of sympathy with the spirit and the principles of American institutions; but it comes more immediately from my knowledge that much is being done to secure the conservation, economic exploitation, and extension of forests in several of the States. It is my persuasion that the information I have to communicate will be more valued, and this by a much greater number of individuals in America, than it will be by the populations of any of our British Dependencies; while in Britain, from the large local supply of coal, and the existing facilities for importing timber of all kinds which may be required, Arboriculture is virtually the one department of forest economy to which attention is chiefly given, while much more is required in the economic treatment of natural forests.

'By the Hon. George P. Marsh, Minister of the United States at the Court of Rome; by General the Hon. C. C. Andrews, who was for many years Minister of the United States at the Court of Stockholm; by Dr John A. Warder, who was the Member of the Scientific Commission of the United States, appointed to observe and report on forest products at the International Exhibition in Vienna, in 1873; by the Hon. Dr B. G. Northrop, Secretary of the Connecticut Board of Education, who was commissioned to visit Schools of Forestry and other technical schools in Europe in 1877; by Dr Franklin B. Hough, writer of the Report upon Forestry, prepared under the direction of the Commissioner of Agriculture, in pursuance of an Act of Congress, published in 1878, and it may be others,* much information in regard to the Forestry of Europe

---

* I may not in silence pass such official documents as that entitled American Forests; their destruction and preservation, by the Rev. Frederick Starr, St. Louis, Missouri, included in the Report of the Commissioner of Agriculture for the year 1865, of which *a hundred and sixty-five thousand* copies were printed by order of Congress—or the

has been published in America; and from the extensive judiciously devised correspondence which Dr Hough, has had, and still has, with the administrators, and managers of state forests on the Continent of Europe, and other countries, there must be in his hands an immense collection of valuable information on all subjects connected with forest economy, over and above what is embodied in the report referred to. But the subject is so comprehensive, and the mine in all its ramifications is so rich, that it is scarcely possible that two independent workers can fail to bring to light important facts and observations to which attention has been given by one, while they may never have happened to come under the cognizance of the other.

'In illustration of the wealth of the mine, I may cite the following statement which I made some years ago in a pamphlet which I published under the title of *The Schools of Forestry in Europe.*

"'I have had sent to me lately *Ofversight af Svenska Skogsliteraturen, Bibliografiska Studieren af Axel Cnattingius,* a list of books and papers on Forest Science, published in Sweden; I have also had sent to me a work by Don Jose Jordana y Morera, Igenero de Montes, under the title of *Apuntes Bibliographico Forestales,* a *Catalogue raissoné* of 1126 printed books, MSS., &c., in Spanish, on subjects connected with Forest Science.

"'I am at present preparing for the press a report on measures adopted in France, Germany, Hungary, and elsewhere, to arrest and utilise drift-sand by planting them with grasses and trees; and in *Der Europäische Flug-sand und Seine Kultur, von Josf Wessely, General Domänen-Inspektor, und Forst-Academie-Direktor,* published in Vienna in 1873, I find a list of upwards of 100 books and papers on that one department of the subject, of which 30, in Hungarian, Latin, and German, were published in Hungary alone.

"'According to the statement of one gentleman, to whom application was made by a representative of the Government

---

Report on the Statistics of Forestry, embodied in the Report of the Minister of Agriculture, for the year 1865—with many other documents, both official and unofficial, which have been sent to me from many of the States in the Union, and from the British Dominion in North America. But these all relate to Forestry in America; those I have cited refer extensively, and some of them exclusively, to Forestry in Europe; and with such alone I have to do at present.

at the Cape for information in regard to what suitable works on Forest Economy could be procured from Germany, "the works on *Forst-Wissenschaft*, Forest Science, and *Fort-Wirthschaft*, Forest Economy, in the German language, may be reckoned by cartloads." From what I know of the abundance of works in German on subjects connected with Forestry, I am not surprised that such a report should have been given. And with the works in German may be reckoned numerous works in French.

"'In Hermann Schmidt's *Fach Katalogue*, published in Prague last year (1876), there are given the titles, &c., of German works in *Forst-und Jagd-Literatur*, published from 1870 to 1875 inclusive, to the 31st of October of the latter year, amounting in all to 650, exclusive of others given in an appendix, containing a selection of the works published prior to 1870. They are classified thus:—General Forest Economy, 93; Forest Botany, 60; Forest History and Statistics, 50; Forest Legislation and Game Laws, 56; Forest Mathematics, 25; Forest Tables and Measurements, &c., 148; Forest Technology, 6; Forest Zoology, 19; Peat and Bog Treatment, 14; Forest Calendars, 6; Forest and Game Periodicals, 27; Forest Union and Year Books, 13; Game, 91; Forest and Game in Bohemian, 44. In all 652 : upwards of a hundred new works published annually. Amongst the works mentioned is a volume entitled *Die Literatur der letzen sieben Jahre* (1862-1872) *aus dem Gesammtgebiete der Land und Forst-wirthschaft mit Einschlusz der landw. Gewerbe u. der Jagd, in deutscher, französischer u. englisher Sprache. Herausg. v. d. Buchhandl. v. Gerold & Co., in Wein*, 1873, which is a valuable catalogue, filling 278 pages in large octavo.

"'Were I to give a like statement in regard to similar lists now before me, it would be much more extensive."

'I enclose a list of compilations, with any one or more of which I am prepared to go to press at once; and to this is subjoined a list of volumes and pamphlets which have already appeared. Applying to the latter a designation suggested by the title of one of the works of Professor Max Müller, I would describe them as chips from the trunk, and boughs and twigs from the tree. From any of these, if known to you, you may gather the character of the others; and should any of these seem to you to promise to supply a desideratum in American literature, I ask of you to bring the matter under the consideration of any publisher who may be likely to further the enterprise.

'I am at present free from all engagements, and am prepared to contract at once for the publication of any one or more of the compilations in question, altogether irrespective of the order in which they appear on the list. I am open to any proposals in regard to terms; but I should like to have a specified number of copies placed at my disposal for presentation to personal friends, to writers cited, and to others who may have aided me in the enterprise, or whose co-operation I may have occasion to solicit, and to public libraries at the Cape of Good Hope, in the interest of which Colony the work was begun and prosecuted; and besides this, I should like to have (1) a royalty on all copies printed, or (2) a percentage on all sales, or (3) a share in any profits which may be realised.

'Should it be thought expedient to print the whole, or a selection of them, as a series of uniform size, for transmission by post, this may be secured by sub-division, or by excision, to any extent necessary; and if it should be desired that the printing should be executed in America, I can get "copy" printed in slips, and corrected in Scotland, at a charge of about 4s 2d per thousand words.

'Soliciting your good services, I am, My Dear Sir, &c.'

APPENDED LIST OF PROJECTED PUBLICATIONS.

I.—*Forest Management and Arboriculture in Great Britain and Ireland.*

In this it is shown in regard to England, that from the earliest times Forest Laws were exclusively Game Laws, and how, in later times, forest economy was subordinated to the chase. Ancient terms and usages are explained; progressive legislation is traced; detailed information is supplied in regard to the several Crown Forests, and in regard to woods and plantations, and the management of these.

With regard to Scotland, there are given abstracts and copies of old forest laws; details in regard to modern extensive plantations; with notices of the forest literature of the country.

With regard to Ireland, there are given notices of extensive forests, and abstracts of the old forest laws of the land.

II.—*The Forestry of France.*

In successive chapters are given—The early history of forest treatment and forest legislation in France—the Forest Ordinance of 1669—the mediæval history of forest economy and legislation in France, including *Defraichment, Jardinage, Sartage*, and forest litigation of the period; notices of the continued destruction of forests, and of the remedies devised for the evil; the *Code Forestiér;* the *Ordonnance Reglementaire*— The recent history of forest economy and legislation in France, including notices of the forest administration; of servitudes, or rights of usage; of Communal woods; of concessions and appropriations given to public works; of thefts of forest products of forest fires; of the exploitation of forests; of the planting of *landes* and dunes; and of the *réboisement* of the mountains; the forests of France; notices of the literature of forest science and forest economy in France, embracing works on vegetation, vegetable anatomy, and vegetable physiology—on subjects connected with forest science—on forest economy, and works on legislation, relative to the treatment of forests; and the School of Forestry at Nancy.

III.—*Development of Modern Forest Science and Instruction communicated in Schools of Forestry in Germany.*

After notices of mediæval forestry in Germany, and of earlier endeavours to improve it, details are given of the development by Hartig and by Cotta of the *Fachwerks-Methode*, known in France as *La Méthode des compartiments*, and of the organisation and development of Forest Schools in different German States, and of Stations for Experimental Researches. And there follow notices of the forest lands and the literature on forestry in Germany.

IV.—*Introduction to the Study of Modern Forest Science and the Forest Economy of Continental Europe, as followed in France.*

In successive chapters information is supplied in regard to forest clearings, effected by *Sartage* and otherwise; the accidental destruction of forests by fire; the reckless destruction of forests for their products; and the prevention of their reproduction by usages incompatible therewith. There is described the exploitation of forests by *Jardinage*, by *La Méthode à tire et aire*, and by *La Méthode des compartiments*. Information follows in regard to planting, with a view to obtaining a supply of timber or firewood; with a view to arresting and utilising sand drifts; with a view to the prevention of the formation of destructive torrents; with a view to securing humidity of soil and climate; and with a view to producing amenity and shelter.

V.—*Sylviculture in France.*

In this is given a *resumé* of the course of instruction in the plantation and culture of woods, followed in the School of Forestry in Nancy, comprising the artificial creation of woods, with information in regard to doing this with seeds, with seedling plants, and with cuttings and layers; the sylviculture to be practised in forests, and the exploitation of timber forests, and of coppice woods; the measures to be adopted in various forms of the conversion of coppice woods into timber forests, and of timber forests into coppice woods; and information in regard to the natural history, seed sowing, subsequent treatment, and exploitation of the more generally cultivated forest trees of Europe.

VI.—*Forest Management in France.*

In this is given a *resumé* of the course of instruction in the management of forests followed in the School of Forestry in Nancy, comprising requirements common to all systems of forest management followed in France; the arrangement of sections of forest for successive exploitation; the ages of the trees at which they are felled; the application to trees of the method of exploitation to be followed in the case of timber forests, of these in an irregular condition, of coppice woods, and of timber forests with an undergrowth of coppice, the object aimed at being, by every operation, to subserve conjointly the amelioration of the forest, its sustained productiveness, and its natural reproduction by self-sown seed.

VII.—*Sylviculture on Sand Wastes and Sand Plains of Belgium, Holland, and Northern Germany.*

Information is supplied in regard to tree planting with

success on the waste lands of Belgium ; in regard to the herbage by which sand dunes have been bound down in Holland, to sand drifts in Prussia, which have been arrested by planting them with trees ; and in regard to the management of forests on the sand plains of Northern Germany.

VIII.—*Sand Drifts.*

In this attention is given to the natural history of sand, what it is, whence and how the constituents of sand have been obtained and brought into the existing condition and places in which we find them ; to the phenomena presented by sand wastes on the shores of the German Ocean, and of the Baltic, and by inland dunes ; to the effects produced by herbage naturally spreading over them, and by trees self-sown or planted upon them ; and to legislation and literature relative to the arrest and utilisation of drifting sand.

IX.—*Danish Peat Bogs and Forests.*

Attention is given to the order in which different kinds of trees have, in a succession which may be naturally accounted for, constituted the forests of Jutland, which, so late as the eleventh century, was characterised as a *silva horrida ;* to the natural history of the peat bogs, in which remains of trees have been preserved from pre-historic times ; to indications of the habits of the early inhabitants, supplied by implements and ornaments there preserved from the so-called stone period, bronze period, and early iron period of these pre-historic times ; to the present condition of the forests or woods of Denmark ; the modern exploitation of these forests or woods, and their products ; and the forest literature of the country.

X.—*Forestry in Norway : with Notices of the Country and its People.*

In successive chapters are given details of forest operations, of the consumption and exportation of wood, of forest scenery, of the distribution of forests, and of different kinds of forest trees ; of forest botany ; of the tenure of land and forest rights ; of agriculture, trade, commerce, and shipping ; of the game and game laws of Norway ; and of the forest literature of the country. These are followed by like details in regard to the physical geography of the country; the early history, mediæval developments, and modern civil and political organisations of its inhabitants; the number, distribution, and occupations of these; and the finances of the country.

XI.—*Sweden: its Forests, Forest Management, the Country, and its People.*

In this are traced the successive measures by which the management of forests has in recent times been brought from what may be described as reckless waste into conformity with the most approved forest economy of the day. Details are given in regard to the forests, their geographical distribution, the home consumption and exportation of their products, the game and game laws, and the agriculture of the country; with information in regard to the general aspect, geology, hydrography, and meteorology of the country; and like information in regard to the history, political constitution, finances, trade, and commerce, and education of the nation.

XII.—*The Finns and Forests of Finland.*

There are described the general appearance of the country and its inhabitants, of its mountains, and of its lakes, which have procured for it the poetic designations of The land of a thousand lakes, and The last born daughter of the sea; its flora, and its forests; its primitive forest treatment, that of *Rhoedens* or *Sartage;* and the successful introduction of the most advanced forest management of Central Europe; its primitive and modern agriculture, its mines, and its minerals; its exports, and its timber trade. And there are added ethnographical notices of the Finns, and the Lapps, and the Letts; notices of the state of education in Finland; and of the legends and literature of the people.

XIII.—*Forests, Forest Lands, and Forest Work in Russia.*

Details are given in regard to forests, forest lands, and forest work in Northern Russia, comprising the Governments of Olonetz and Archangel, the principal seat of the timber trade; in Central Russia, the north agricultural zone, in which are situated many of the mines; in Eastern Russia or Siberia, extending from the Ural Mountains to Kamschatka; in Southern Russia, including the Steppes, the Crimea, and the Caucasus;

and in Western Russia, comprising Poland, Lithuania, and the Baltic provinces of Livonia; the whole supplying illustrations of practical working of *Jardinage*, of *à tire et aire*, of *les compartiments*, and of *reboisement* and sylviculture. There follows a general survey of forestry in Russia, in which are given details in regard to the distribution of forests, and of different kinds of trees, the economic uses to which their products are applied, the relation of the total annual production to the total annual consumption of wood, the Forest Administration, the Forest Code, the Forest Society, and the Schools of Forestry, and the forest literature of the country.

XIV.—*Translation of a Report on the Forests of Greece, and their Products, by Professor Theodore Orphanides, of the University of Athens.*

There are given in this Report information in regard to the extent of forests in Greece; the different kinds of trees of which they are composed; and their economic products. And there is superadded some notices of forests in Turkey.

XV.—*Sylviculture and Forest Management in the Austrian Empire.*

This comprises details of extensive works on the sand-drifts of the Bannat in Hungary, of the natural history of these, of the legislation for which they have given occasion, with notices of Hungarian literature on the subject of sand-drifts; details of observations made in connection with works of hydraulic engineering to effect a rectification of the course of the Danube; details of extensive works of *réboisement* in the Karst, a district on the coast of the Adriatic, undertaken with a view to counteract disastrous desiccation which has followed the destruction of forests; and details of successful forest management, with a glance at the forest lands of Austria, and the arrangements followed in the Royal and Imperial School of Forestry in Vienna.

XVI.—*Forest Administration in Bavaria.*

Trained and instructed administrators and officials being required to carry out forest operations judiciously and efficiently, the Forest administration of Bavaria has been selected as illustrative of the forest administration of Germany, and detailed with annotations suggested by a discussion now in progress in France on the Forest administrations of that country. Details are given in regard to the organisation of the forest service, and the training and instruction of forest officials, with information in regard to the schools of forestry at Aschaffenburg and in Munich; the functions of forest officials in State forests, in forests belonging to communities and corporations, and to private individuals; the forest legislation of the country; matters pertaining to the chase; and matters pertaining to sales of wood, and of other forest produce.

XVII.—*Rèboisement and Forest Management in the Alps.*

Information is supplied in regard to the *rèboisement* of the French Alps by the planting of mountain basins with trees, shrubs, and herbage, as a means of arresting the destructive consequences of torrents, and the formation of new ones; in regard to the management of forests in Switzerland, and the instruction in forestry given in the Polytechnicum at Zurich; and in regard to the evil effects of depasturing forest lands; with notices of forests and forest management in the Austrian Alps.

XVIII.—*Forest Economy, Irrigation, and Sylviculture, in Italy.*

Information is supplied in regard to the forests of Italy; the School of Forestry at Valambrosa; the forest legislation of Italy; extensive irrigation works in the north of Italy; and plantations of the *Eucalptus globulus* in the south.

XIX.—*The Aridity of Spain: its Causes and Remedies.*

The aridity of Spain is attributable primarily and chiefly to the situation and contour of the country, but secondarily greatly to the destruction of forests. Existing forests are described; details are given of a struggle to prevent a threatened extensive destruction of these being carried into effect; of projects, or proposals of extensive replenishing, and of extensive works of irrigation being executed. Information is supplied in regard to the literature of forest science in the country; in regard to the Merino sheep, and the injurious effects of the *mesta;* in regard to sericulture, wine making, fruit, esparto grass, and other vegetable products of Spain; and in regard to the ethnography of the Spanish people.

XX.—*Meteorological Effects of Forests.*

There is detailed the chemistry of vegetation, and it is shown that by this the humidity of the atmosphere may be increased, while by shade evaporation from the soil is prevented, and by roots and stems the superficial flow of water may be arrested, and that the general effect of forests is to produce a more equable distribution of rainfall, both in time and in space. The general and local effects of forests in equalising the temperature is next illustrated, with notices of the correlation of temperature and humidity in their meteorological effects. The effects of vegetation in replacing carbonic acid by oxygen, and of forests in preventing or arresting miasmata are described; and details are given of practical measures which have been adopted in different countries, with a view to secure more extensively for the benefit of man meteorological effects which may be produced by forests.

XXI.—*Application of Advanced Modern Forest Science to the Conservation, Exploitation, and Extension of Forests in India.*

There are given official reports of sylviculture and forest management in the Presidencies of Madras, Bombay, and Bengal; in the North-West Provinces, in Simla, Ajmere, the Punjaub, and Oude; in the Central Provinces, in Berar, Hyderabad, Mysore, Courg, Burmah, Assam, and Ceylon."

Measures which I approved were adopted by Dr. Hough to carry out the suggestions submitted in my letter; but occurences, which it is not necessary to detail, prevented effect being given to his arrangements; and the offer made by me lapsed. But I am equally ready now as then to carry through the press any one or any number of the treatises mentioned on the terms stated; and I shall feel grateful for any assistance which may thus be given me in making available for others the information I have compiled. I have drawn upon the mass of this material for a number of popular works, published in connection with the International Forestry Exhibition, held in Edinburgh in 1884; but the remainder, or any portion of it, is forthcoming if it be desired.

ADDENDA.

The treatises mentioned in the preceding pages were designed to be of a character sufficiently popular to be interesting to any one desirous of information on the subjects to which they severally refer; but I consider something still more popular might be useful in awakening an interest in such studies; and I question whether, if a School of Forestry were established soon, there exists amongst young men so diffused an interest in forestry as would induce many to avail themselves of the provision for study which such an institution would supply.

In view of this contingency, when it was resolved in the spring of 1883 to promote an International Forestry Exhibition in Edinburgh, as a means of promoting a movement for the establishment of a National School of Forestry in Scotland, I submitted to the projectors, through one of their number, for consideration, one measure whereby to some extent young men, such as those to whom I have referred, might have been interested in the matter, and prepared afterwards to judge intelligently whether or no they should take advantages of provision which might be made for imparting systematic instruction in forestry. Another measure, seemingly similar, but essentially different, was ultimately resolved on and carried out. When this was resolved on, I wrote to one of the projectors:—

'I am very glad you have secured lectures from foreign students of Forest Science, but I consider that in order to secure from the Exhibition all the good possible, it is desirable to combine with these such lectures as I suggested.

'I would state my argument thus:—In Denmark there is great interest in Archæology manifested even by the peasantry. This is attributed to Professor Thomsen, M. Worsaac, and others, men of the highest attainments in antiquarian lore, having, on holidays and at other times, joined little groups of country peasants in the Museum, and accompanied them on their rounds, directing their attention to what was interesting, and explaining to them the teachings of different objects. While the second International Exhibition was being held in Paris, there was held an International Congress of Botanists, which I attended. And at specified times members of this Congress from different countries attended the former to give explanations of the articles exhibited from the countries whence they came. Similar arrangements in connection with the British Museum and the Royal Academy have been advocated by the Rev. H. R. Haweis, the Rev. Chas. Kingsley, and others. The measure which I have proposed is a modification of this adapted to our circumstances; and I anticipate it would frequently lead to adjournment to the Exhibition, attracting others who would cluster round to hear what was being said. At Forestry Exhibitions which I have attended in Paris, in Vienna, and in St. Petersburg, again and again I have seen students of Forestry take in at a glance the teaching of some object exhibited; and some one, to whom the subject was new, with catalogue in hand, try laboriously to spell out that teaching; and others simply pass through the compartment as if they felt they ought to see everything, but had no interest in the objects there. I deem it of importance that these should be interested, that the enquirer should be supplied with the information he is desiring, and that the information possessed by the advanced student should be utilised for the instruction of the others; and all this might thus be done. Not only are the panoramas exhibited in the country accompanied by a lecturer, but the menageries have some one to go round and tell the names and the characteristics of the different animals, and the crowd crushing after him, and the pennies with which he is rewarded, tell how much his few words have added to the enjoyment of the visitors.

'Should any such arrangement be made, I think it expedient that each lecture should be printed and sold on the day after delivery, in order that any attending one lecture may be able to purchase copies of any or all of those previously delivered. A half-hour's lecture of 5000 words would fill 16 pages—the printing of which, with a cover, would cost for 1000 copies, 45s. If 500 copies of each were sold this would cover the expense of printing ; and there would be secured the distribution, by sale, of 3000 tracts on forestry a week, to be dispensed over the country, with this beneficial result amongst others. The difficulty, I anticipate, to be encountered in maintaining at first a School of Forestry, is not in getting teachers but in getting students ; and by such a distribution of tracts the subject will come under the notice of a great many more young men, and their parents or guardians, than at present.'

Nothing having come of this proposal, and the Exhibition being closed without provision being made for the continued exhibition of articles made available for the purpose, I addressed, under date of 23rd October, 1883, a letter to the Council of the Scottish Arboricultural Society, of which the following is a copy :—

'GENTLEMEN,

'I am informed that at last meeting of the Society it was resolved, amongst other things, that you should be instructed to take into consideration the expediency of getting prepared and published some simple treatises on subjects pertaining to forestry.

'I am, as you are probably aware, carrying through the press a series of works on forestry for which there is no such demand as would remunerate a publisher, towards which enterprise the Society last year contributed £10. I enclose tables of contents of those volumes which have already been published. I have now in the press one ' On the Forest Lands and Forestry of Northern Russia.' I contemplate following this with others ' On the Schools of Forestry in Germany,' ' On the Modern Forest Economy of France,' the adoption of ' Modern Forest Economy in Sweden,' ' Scientific Sylviculture in Denmark,' the adoption of ' Forest Management in accordance with Modern Forest Science in South Africa, in Australia, and in India,'

&c., &c. The expense of the execution of this enterprise will be far beyond the amount of money I can spend upon the work; and I am prepared to accept from any quarter assistance in the undertaking in any form, and under any conditions which may be agreed upon.

'But irrespective of this, on the assumption of the correctness of the information I have received in regard to the resolution of the Society referred to, I desire to state that I am prepared, if you will meet the expense, to carry through the press, on such arrangements, as may be agreed upon, for distribution next year, monthly, among all members of the Society a series of *brochures* on any twelve subjects which you may select from a list which I send enclosed, each pamphlet to consist of 48 pages, and the issue to commence on the 1st or the 31st of January, as may be found most convenient.

'I believe that an edition of 1000 copies of each, similar in every respect to the volumes I have already published, may be printed for £6, or with a cover for £6 6s; the postage of each copy would be a half-penny; and should the enterprise prove satisfactory, it might, by subsequent arrangement, be continued in succeeding years, till the list be exhausted.—I am, &c.'

The following is a copy of the list of subjects appended to the letter:—

1. Forestry in England in the Nineteenth Century.
2. The Caledonian Forest; and Early Sylviculture in Scotland.
3. Forest Laws of Ireland, and Modern Sylviculture in that Country.
4. Scientific Management of Forests in Australia.
5. Forests in Tasmania, and Economic Management of them.
6. Forestry in New Zealand.
7. Reckless Waste in Exploitation of Forests at the Cape of Good Hope, and the adoption there of the advanced Forest Economy of the day.

ADDENDA.

8. Destruction of Forests by Fire in South Africa; and consequences which have resulted from this.

9. Forests in Natal.

10. Forests in South Africa, between the British Colonies and the Zambesi.

11. Adoption of Advanced Forest Economy in India; and the results.

12. Exploitation of Forests in Honduras and British Guiana.

13. Forests in Nova Scotia and New Brunswick.

14. Forests in Lower Canada.

15. Forests in Upper Canada.

16. Forests in Manitoba.

17. Forestry in the United States of America.

18. Arbor Day in America, and Sylvicultural Operations there.

19. The Training of Forest Officials for Forest Service in India.

20. A School of Forestry for Britain.

21. Ancient Forests of Europe.

22. Remains of successive Forest Trees which have grown in the locality, and been preserved in Peat Bogs in Denmark.

23. Fossil Remains of Pre-Adamic Trees in Northern Europe.

24. Norway and its Forests.

25. Clearing of Forest Land for Agriculture in Finland, with Notices of its Forest Scenery.

26. Forest Exploitation, by *Jardinage,* in Northern Russia.

27. French Forest Ordinance of 1669.

28. Development of Modern Forest Economy in Saxony.

29. Schools of Forestry in Germany.

30. Adoption of Advanced Forest Economy in France.

31. Sylviculture in France in accordance with the Advanced Forest Economy of the day.

32. Scientific Sylviculture in Denmark.

33. Adoption of Modern Forest Economy in Sweden.

34. Forest Operations in the Mining Districts of Eastern Russia.

35. Sylviculture on the Steppes of Southern Russia.

36. Forestry in Poland and Lithuania.

37. Forestry in Hungary, and the Arrest of Drift Sand in the Bannat.

38. Forestry in Austria, and the Replanting of the Karst with Trees, with a view to counteract the desiccation which has followed the destruction of trees there.

39. Switzerland, and the Replanting of Trees on the Alps to prevent the occurrence of torrents and inundations.

40. Italy, and the Planting of its Marsh Lands with the *Eucalyptus*, to counteract malaria.

41. Spain: the Causes or Occasion of its Aridity, and the Remedial Measures which are being adopted, including the Conservation and Extension of Forests.

42. Algiers, and adjacent countries on the Southern Coast of the Mediterranean, and the Extensive Planting Operations which are being carried on there.

43 Former Forests of Palestine.

44. Forestry in Turkey and Greece.

45. Forests and Moisture.

46. Natural History of the *Eucalyptus Globulus*, or Blue Gum, its properties, and effects produced by the cultivation of it.

47. Tree Culture on the Sand Plains of Northern Europe, with Notices of the Composition of Sand.

48. Manufacture of Wood Pulp, and uses to which the product is applied.

This offer, also, I renew, and in doing so extend it to any who may be disposed to co-operate in the execution of such a scheme—publishers or others, including editors or proprietors of periodicals who may see their way clear, in accordance with a practice more prevalent on the Continent than in Britain, to append such *brochures* to the successive issues of their publications, taking this into account in the price charged.

V.—Proferred Gift of Works on Modern Forestry to Free Public Libraries in any of the British Colonies, and in any of the United States of America.

While a British National School of Forestry might be made available for instruction in Modern Forestry to any party who may desire this through the medium of the English language, I know of no insuperable difficulties in the way of such institutions being organised in any of the States of the American Union, or in any of the Colonies of the British Empire, in connection with existing educational arrangements of their own. As a contribution of information, which might be of use to any residents in these, in determining what might be done in the matter, I am prepared to deliver free, to any address in Edinburgh or London, which may be given to me, a copy, in sheets, of any or all of the following works, to be placed in a Free Public Library in any of these States or Colonies, on an application to me certified by the Government of the State or Colony.

1. Origin and History of Schools of Forestry in Germany, with Addenda relating to the Desiderated School of Forestry in Britain—*This volume.*
2. The School of Forest Engineers in Spain, indicative of a type for a British School of Forestry.
3. Introduction to the Study of Modern Forest Economy.
4. French Forest Ordinance of 1669, with historical Sketch of Previous Treatment of Forests in France.
5. The Forests of England, and the Management of them in by-gone times.
6. Forestry of Norway.
7. Finland—its Forests and Forest Management.
8. Forestry and Forest Lands in Northern Russia.

9. Forestry in the Mining Districts of the Ural Mountains in Eastern Russia.
10. Forestry in Poland, Lithuania, and the Baltic Provinces of Russia.
11. Pine Plantations on Sand Wastes in France.
12. Reboisement in France; or Records of the Replanting of the Alps, the Cevennes, and the Pyrenees, with Trees, Herbage, and Bush, with a view to arresting and preventing the destructive consequences of torrents.
13. Hydrology of South Africa; or Details of the former Hydrographic Conditions of Cape of Good Hope, and of Causes of its Present Aridity, with Suggestions of Appropriate Remedies for this Aridity.
14. Water Supply of South Africa, and Facilities for the Storage of it.
15. Forests and Moisture; or Effects of Forests on Humidity of Climate.

The editions of some of the works are nearly exhausted, and I deem it expedient to reserve a limited supply of each for any demand which may arise for them in Britain ; but subject to this limitation, copies of all will be sent to early applicants in the order in which their applications may be received.

In some States or Colonies there may be more than one Free Public Library to which such a grant might be acceptable. To any such certified by the Government, subject to the limitations which have been stated, I am ready to send copies of Nos. 1, 2, and 3, and copies of selections from the others, determined by the greater or less numbers of them which may happen to remain in stock. The expenditure which I have already incurred, is my excuse for not offering to deliver the copies bound ; but arrangements have been made according to which any may be bound here at a uniform charge of sevenpence per volume ; and I shall hold myself bound by this proffer for six months from the date of publication of this volume.

VI.—MATTERS PERTAINING TO SCHOOLS OF FORESTRY, ON WHICH THE AUTHOR IS READY TO SUPPLY INFORMATION TO ANY GOVERNMENT OFFICIAL, PUBLIC ASSOCIATION, OR PRIVATE INDIVIDUAL, DESIROUS OF ESTABLISHING A BRITISH NATIONAL SCHOOL OF FORESTRY:—

1. The need of scientific training in forestry for the administration of indigenous forests in British colonies.
2. The difference between British Forest Economy and what is required for such forests.
3. The advantages of scientific training for British Foresters.
4. The origin and development of Schools of Forestry.
5. The instruction in political economy and jurisprudence given in Schools of Forestry on the Continent.
6. Stations for Experimental Research attached to several Schools of Forestry on the Continent.
7. The extent to which a British School of Forestry should be conformed to the model of such Schools on the Continent of Europe.
8. The expediency of combining with such, facilities for research, and the expediency of including in these carpenters' workshops, &c.
9. Where an eligible site for a British National School of Forestry might be found, irrespective of the contiguity of a forest.
10. What eligible arrangements could be made in Edinburgh if this were made the site of a School of Forestry?
11. The advantages and disadvantages of a School of Forestry founded by private enterprise.
12. The advantages and disadvantages of a Professorship in a University.
13. The advantages and disadvantages of a Class for the Study of Forestry in the Watt Institute in Edinburgh.

14. The special advantages of forming a School of Forestry in the Museum of Science and Art under the Committee of Council on Education, in Edinburgh.

15. The salaries paid to instructors in Schools of Forestry on the Continent.

16. The entire expense of some existing Schools of Forestry.

17. The curriculum of study appropriate for a British School of Forestry.

18. Where qualified Teachers might be found, and salaries which might be offered to such.

19. What has been done of late years, and what previous endeavours have been made to secure the establishment of a School of Forestry in Britain.

20. What has been done to originate some small classes for the study of Forestry.

21. What has been done of late years to introduce the study of Forestry, &c., into Primary Schools.

22. What has been done through the Press to make known Modern Forestry.

23. What has been done to raise money to establish a School of Forestry.

24. The propriety of spending State funds on the establishment of a British National School of Forestry.

THE END.

www.ingramcontent.com/pod-product-compliance
Lightning Source LLC
Chambersburg PA
CBHW021352230426
43666CB00006B/502